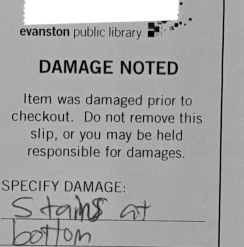

Behind the Smile

Behind the Smile

A STORY OF
Carol Moseley Braun's
HISTORIC SENATE CAMPAIGN

JEANNIE MORRIS

MIDWAY

AN **AGATE** IMPRINT

CHICAGO

Printed in the United States of America.

Library of Congress Cataloging-in-Publication Data

Morris, Jeannie.
 Behind the smile : a story of Carol Moseley Braun's historic senate campaign / Jeannie Morris.
    pages cm
  Summary: "Memoir by a Chicago journalist recounting the 1992 US Senate campaign of Carol Moseley Braun"-- Provided by publisher.
 Includes bibliographical references and index.
 ISBN 978-1-57284-176-5 (hardcover : alkaline paper) -- ISBN 978-1-57284-759-0 (e-book)
1. Moseley-Braun, Carol, 1947- 2. Women legislators--United States--Biography. 3. African American legislators--Biography. 4. Democratic Party (U.S.)--Biography. 5. United States. Congress. Senate--History--20th century. 6. Political campaigns--United States--History--20th century. 7. United States--Politics and government--1989-1993. 8. Illinois--Politics and government--20th century. I. Title.
 E840.8.M67M67 2015
 328.73'092--dc23
 [B]
                        2015014510

10 9 8 7 6 5 4 3 2 1   15 16 17 18

Midway is an imprint of Agate Publishing. Agate books are available in bulk at discount prices. For more information, go to agatepublishing.com.

I know that every person who participated in this unique experience would have her or his version of events, but I offer my view and dedicate this story to all the members of the Moseley Braun primary and general-election campaigns who embodied the word dedication.

And to Carol herself, the magnet that drew them in.

All normal humans are both ignoble and noble, often in close alternation, sometimes simultaneously.

The instability of the emotions is a quality we should wish to keep. It is the essence of the human character, and the source of our creativity. We need to understand ourselves in both evolutionary and psychological terms in order to plan a more rational, catastrophe-proof future. We must learn to behave, but let us never even think of domesticating human nature.

—E. O. Wilson, *The Meaning of Human Existence*

Contents

A Personal Note xi

About this Book xvii

Cast of Characters xix

PART I

Democracy only works when the people we elect to high public office remember that they are the servants—not the masters—of the people.
—CAROL MOSELEY BRAUN
Announcing her run for the US Senate

Chapter 1: *Clarence Thomas Kicks off "The Year of the Woman"* ... 3

Chapter 2: *The Primary Team* 27

Chapter 3: *Matthews Syndrome: Defections* 47

Chapter 4: *Chaos! Shock! Victory!* 63

PART II

Carol Moseley Braun represents the redemption of the American political process.
—SENATOR TOM HARKIN, IOWA

Chapter 5: *Kgosie* 83

Chapter 6: *Black and White and Family* 113

Chapter 7: *Stardom: The Democratic National Convention* 131

Chapter 8: *Race and Religion* 147

Chapter 9: *Campaign Unrest; The Carolvan* 167

Chapter 10: *The Medicaid Bomb* 181

Chapter 11: *Medicaid II* 199

PART III

It's Airplane! *The campaign movie!*
—DAVID AXELROD

CHAPTER 12: *The Debate*.. 217
CHAPTER 13: *An Anonymous Letter Threatens Disaster*........... 235
CHAPTER 14: *Hold On: Less Than Two Weeks to Election Day*... 249

PART IV

What a scene that must have been inside the campaign.
—TOM HARDY
Chicago Tribune, December 20, 1992

CHAPTER 15: *Lawyers Called in on Sexual Harassment* 271
CHAPTER 16: *Off to Africa* 291
CHAPTER 17: *Carol Moseley Braun, United States Senator*........ 305

AFTERWORD: "NOW WHAT DO WE DO?" 315
ONE LAST NOTE 337

ACKNOWLEDGMENTS 339
INDEX 341
ABOUT THE AUTHOR 350

A Personal Note

Chicago. April 1992.

Realizing that there was a good chance history was about to be made in Illinois in November, I scribbled a note to Carol Moseley Braun, currently the Cook County recorder of deeds, suggesting that she allow me to follow her campaign for the US Senate to document it for a book. In '92, Carol, like a record number of women candidates born of the emotional maelstrom that followed the hearings to confirm Clarence Thomas as a Supreme Court justice, had just defeated (the "unbeatable") Democratic senator Alan Dixon in the Illinois primary. Dixon was one of only two Democrats in the Senate who had voted to confirm Judge Thomas.

That was more than two decades ago.

Everything changes.

The past 20 years have seen a technological tsunami; vastly increased globalization; and a couple of recessions, the most recent dubbed "the Great." In addition, there was a Supreme Court decision inappropriately known as "Citizens United," a ruling that became a factor in the increased wealth and insularity of Washington, where inhabitants engage in incestuous rituals of self-perpetuation and where, according to *New York Times* chief national correspondent Mark Leibovich, "cowardice is rewarded every step of the way."

And nothing changes.

Some progress has been made for sure; however, the politics of race and gender that not only inspired the Carol Moseley Braun campaign but also, in the end, came very close to destroying it, are with us still. If anything, when it comes to race especially, we are even more distressed.

But leaving aside the countless other issues that remain to haunt us today, Carol's election to the Senate in 1992 was a significant landmark in the continuum of African American progress marked 50 years earlier, in 1963, by Dr. Martin Luther King Jr. as he stood before the Lincoln Memorial and shared his dreams of what *real* freedom would mean for all Americans. King's passionate plea remained unfulfilled a full 100 years after President Lincoln had signed the Emancipation Proclamation. Following Carol Moseley Braun's election by 16 years—and after serving as an Illinois senator himself—Barack Obama became president of the United States. In Chicago, as a South Side community organizer and as a strong supporter and, importantly, a keen observer of the Moseley Braun campaign, Obama credits Carol with showing the way.

My guess is that Obama admired Carol's inclusive, nonthreatening campaign style, but he was clearly referring to their shared racial heritage. The fact that Carol was African American was also important to me as a citizen who still dreams that one day our political institutions will be representative of *all* the people of the United States. But Carol was also a feminist and a sensible progressive who walked the talk. I listened to her during the primary; I studied her record during her years in the Illinois legislature. She represented me; politically, she *was* me. She was so smart and so candid, and her smile just lit up the world. Like millions in Illinois and, eventually, the nation, I fell in love.

It wasn't fair. We invest too much in our candidates. We project our own hopes and dreams upon them without regard to the political realities they will be facing and without taking into consideration that these people too have needs, priorities, weaknesses, and especially histories that might not match ours. And so for me, that campaign trail in 1992 was a march toward understanding, first of a single, fragile human being; second, it was an immersion experience in our democracy's political process, a process that although it ultimately must address real people with real issues, deliberately obscures reality.

During his 2008 campaign, Obama famously shouted, "We are the ones we've been waiting for!" Well, no, not actually. *You* were supposed to be perfect.

I was to learn that nobody could be more "real" than Carol Moseley Braun: a mother, divorced, smart, insecure, bold, needy, politically courageous, personally vulnerable, accomplished, tired, fun, generous. And black. Carol would become only the second African American since Reconstruction and the first African American woman to be elected to the US Senate. As a white supporter, this was a plus for me for the reason already stated; of course the candidate's color was historically significant, yet for me personally, it was essentially cosmetic. This was a candidate I could believe in, but the woman *within* the candidate taught me how very complicated it was to be Carol Moseley Braun from the South Side of Chicago, how painfully significant cosmetics are in our culture. Although this is an existential truth, when it came to politics, Carol herself identified more with her femaleness than her blackness. In her battle to rise from state representative to US senator, whenever she was dismissed or demeaned, she believed it was more because she was a woman than an African American.

Carol responded almost immediately to my note in April 1992. Why? Because she was a sports fan, and for many years, I had been the only woman covering sports in Chicago. I think my "onlyness" appealed to her feminist instincts. Sports and politics are our city's two favorite games. We bond over them at the bus stop, on the El, in bars where they know how to pour a real drink, and in diners where you get multiple refills by a nice lady who— if you're lucky—calls you "honey." We love to love the players in both games as much as we sometimes love to hate them. Love and hate bind us together, like a family.

So I was thrilled when Carol—who I was to learn had a very powerful sense of her own destiny—called and said, "Yes, you can join the campaign and you can write the book."

I spent the next two years immersed in the Carol Moseley Braun story. I became intimately involved in that 1992 campaign, virtually living with the most dedicated—and integrated—hardworking bunch of true believers imaginable. During, and after, these intense months, I interviewed almost every one of them. My journals reflect the excitement and joy of our days as well as the chaos and controversy. Ultimately, all of us became entangled in a drama that can only be described—in terms of our candidate—as a tragedy.

I would, however, invite you to pay close attention to Carol's positions on issues and her insistence on candid presentation. She never equivocated. She said what she believed. In the primary, she was facing a candidate *everyone* agreed was unbeatable, but she persisted, remained herself, and harnessed the zeitgeist to win.

Carol's consistency on the issues also had a sustaining effect on the entire campaign team. No one, in spite of everything that happened, doubted that Carol could be a very good, even great, senator. Electing her became a personal quest, a life-affirming mission for those who understood what elevating this unique person to the Senate would mean for millions of women and African Americans.

So if you choose to read on, do not expect one of those grand political books where historians have used diaries, letters, newspaper accounts, and opinions filtered through time to shape biographies or even one of those first drafts of history based upon countless interviews with currently involved players who may still have skin in the game. This is the game *as* it is being played.

Yes, Carol Moseley Braun won the election and became a US senator, and I respect her for the real person she is. But I could not publish a story that was not accurate, and in the end, our realities differed. Sex, money, power struggles—these are not strangers to campaigns, and we had them all. As David Axelrod, who joined the campaign in the last two weeks to do commercials when the previous media consultant was fired, described the last days of our effort, "It's *Airplane!* The campaign movie! Everything's falling apart! Question is, do we have enough glide left to land before we crash?"

Thump. We landed. I finished the book. Carol did not want it published because I could not write her story without indicting her campaign manager. And she was still in love with him. Unlike the men whose sexual peccadilloes dot the history of our politics,

Carol's weakness was uniquely female and, given her personal history, understandable. But ultimately, she would not be forgiven.

I did not insist on publishing the book. I wanted Senator Moseley Braun to have every chance of success. Perhaps I made the wrong decision. Maybe if I had forced her to see what this man was doing to her, using her for, she would have dismissed him from her life, and, like Senators Dianne Feinstein, Barbara Boxer, Patty Murray, and many others elected to Congress in 1992's "Year of the Woman," Carol would have served multiple terms in the US Senate.

For me, this is the ultimate tragedy. At this writing, more than 20 years later, there are just *two* (male) African Americans in the Senate—and only 20 women. There should be 50 women. Minimum. And multihued at that.

Because in the end she chose not to move forward on the book, this is not the biography of Carol Moseley Braun I first envisioned, although she provides the inspiration and many insights into her background and political philosophy. Rather, it is an intimate account of a wonderful, crazy, tragic, historic, senatorial campaign, one where issues of race and gender both complicate and glorify the narrative. It is also a cautionary tale that screams "hazard!" where passion and politics intersect.

About this Book

While the candidate supported this effort and was available for brief interviews during the campaign, most of the commentary from Senator Moseley Braun that's presented in italics was recorded after her election, between August 29 and September 2, 1993. Other sources include my personal journals—careful notes made almost daily, sometimes hourly during the campaign as I traveled with the candidate—and hundreds of hours of recorded interviews with key campaign members done during and immediately following the campaign. The book was not published in 1994 when I had completed my first manuscript, and when I approached Carol in 2011 to suggest we return to the project, she rejected the idea unequivocally. What follows is a personal memoir of Carol Moseley Braun's fascinating and historic campaign for the United States Senate, based on a refashioned version of my first manuscript, the vast trove of material I collected at the time, and several follow-up conversations with key people involved in the event.

Cast of Characters

Ethel Alexander—Illinois state senator and a mentor to Carol Moseley Braun when she was an Illinois state representative and 20th Ward committeewoman of Chicago.

Anita Ashton—Chicago police officer. She was assigned to be Carol Moseley Braun's security shadow during the general election.

Gerald (Jerry) Austin—Democratic political/media consultant. Campaign manager for Jesse Jackson's presidential run and Paul Wellstone's Senate victory. He was the most experienced political consultant on Carol Moseley Braun's primary campaign, and he continued to handle media until the last days of the general-election effort.

David Axelrod—Campaign manager for Al Hofeld's Senate primary campaign. Axelrod became an adviser to Carol Moseley Braun late in the general-election campaign. A well-known Democratic media consultant in Chicago, he went on to become chief strategist for the Barack Obama Senate and presidential campaigns.

Sue Bass—Assistant to Carol Moseley Braun at the Cook County Recorder of Deeds Office.

Carolyn Bay—Field organizer who worked with Heather Booth.

Janice Bell—Field organizer for the Carol Moseley Braun general election and longtime Chicago activist.

Dayna Bender—Worked in the issues office for Ira Cohen during the Carol Moseley Braun general election. She frequently traveled with Carol during the last months of the general election.

Marjorie Benton—Prominent Moseley Braun supporter, major donor, and Democratic national committeewoman at the time of the 1992 Democratic National Convention.

Heather Booth—Field director for the Carol Moseley Braun general-election campaign. She had three decades of experience as a progressive political organizer.

Bob Borosage—Washington-based policy analyst at the Institute for Policy Studies. He helped with debate preparations during the Carol Moseley Braun general election.

Matthew Braun—Son of Carol Moseley Braun and Michael Braun. Matt was 13 years old when his mother began her run for Senate in 1991.

Michael Braun—Former husband of Carol Moseley Braun. They met in law school at the University of Chicago, married in 1973, and divorced in 1986. They have one son, Matt Braun, born in 1977.

Steve Brown—A Springfield public relations professional who joined the Carol Moseley Braun press office in the final weeks of the general-election campaign. He worked in the office through the transition period before she was sworn into the US Senate.

Adam Clement—Son of Kay Clement. A committed volunteer, he was one of the people who could sign checks for the Carol Moseley Braun primary campaign.

Kay Clement—Encouraged Carol Moseley Braun to run for the Illinois House of Representatives in 1978. She was the chair of the

Carol Moseley Braun for Senate Steering Committee during the 1992 primary.

Steve Cobble—Political director and fundraising coordinator on the Carol Moseley Braun general-election campaign. He was a former Jesse Jackson aide.

Ira Cohen—Issues director for the Carol Moseley Braun general-election campaign. A computer expert, he also set up the campaign computer system that held all campaign operations information and donor lists.

Ed Coxum—Attorney for the Carol Moseley Braun campaign.

Letitia Dewith-Anderson—Occasional scheduler in the final two months of the Carol Moseley Braun general-election campaign. She was a lobbyist for Illinois Attorney General Roland Burris's office in Springfield.

Alan Dixon—Democratic senator from Illinois, 1981–1993. He was one of two Democrats to vote for the confirmation of Supreme Court Justice Clarence Thomas in 1991. He lost to Carol Moseley Braun in the 1992 Senate primary.

David Eichenbaum—Press secretary for the Carol Moseley Braun general-election campaign. He had worked on the Paul Tsongas presidential campaign in 1992 until Tsongas dropped out.

Don Foley—Political director of the Democratic Senatorial Campaign Committee based in Washington, DC.

Gus Fordham—Esteemed driver for the Carol Moseley Braun campaign.

Julie Gantz—An attorney who worked as an issues assistant for Ira Cohen during the Carol Moseley Braun general election. She cowrote the "anonymous letter" to Carol Moseley Braun telling her that Kgosie Matthews was sexually harassing women on the campaign staff.

Pat Gauen—*St. Louis Post-Dispatch* columnist.

Mandy Gittler—Volunteer for the Carol Moseley Braun general election who helped manage incoming mail to the campaign office. She was from Hyde Park, and her parents were longtime friends of Carol Moseley Braun.

Jan Hensley—Veteran Democratic political fundraiser who worked as the national finance director for the Carol Moseley Braun campaign during the general election.

Albert Hofeld—Wealthy attorney from the Chicago suburbs who challenged Alan Dixon in the Democratic primary for Senate in Illinois in 1992. He lost to Carol Moseley Braun.

Stephanie Holtz—Second national fundraiser for the Carol Moseley Braun general-election campaign, promoted after Jan Hensley left the campaign.

Earl Hopewell—Treasurer for the Carol Moseley Braun campaign during the general election.

Hyde Park—A neighborhood on Chicago's South Side. It is the home of the University of Chicago. Carol Moseley Braun lived in Hyde Park and represented the neighborhood in the Illinois House of Representatives.

Patricia Ireland—President of the National Organization for Women (NOW) at the time of the Carol Moseley Braun campaign.

Jesse Jackson—Candidate for president of the United States in 1988. He met Kgosie Matthews in Europe in 1985 at an anti-apartheid political rally that Matthews helped organize. Matthews worked on Jackson's 1988 campaign for president.

Marlene Johnson—Chief of staff and operations director for the Carol Moseley Braun general election. She was a Chicago native and attended the University of Chicago Law School with Carol. An attorney, Johnson suspended her Washington, DC, practice to join the Moseley Braun campaign.

Jeremy Karpatkin—Communications director for the Carol Moseley Braun general-election campaign. He was "on loan" during the campaign from the Senate office of Paul Simon of Illinois, where he was deputy chief of staff.

Elizabeth Loeb—Attorney who worked as an issues assistant for Ira Cohen during the Carol Moseley Braun general election. She cowrote the "anonymous letter" to Carol Moseley Braun telling her that Kgosie Matthews was sexually harassing women on the campaign staff.

Darlene Mackey—Daughter of Catherine Mackey, one of Edna Moseley's closest friends. A best friend of Marsha Moseley, Carol's younger sister. Darlene grew up with Carol on the South Side of Chicago and was considered family. An ordained minister, during the campaign, she was responsible for ministerial outreach.

Kgosie Matthews—A native of South Africa and mostly raised in Great Britain, he worked on Jesse Jackson's campaign for president in 1988. He met Carol Moseley Braun at a Jesse Jackson event in 1991 in Washington, DC. His father and grandfather lived in exile in London during the apartheid years as leaders of the African National Congress. Kgosie Matthews became the campaign manager for Carol Moseley Braun's successful Senate campaign in 1991.

Alton Miller—Press secretary during the Carol Moseley Braun primary campaign. He had been the press secretary to Chicago Mayor Harold Washington in the 1980s.

Joyce Moran—Attorney brought into the campaign by Carol Moseley Braun to investigate the "anonymous letter" accusing Kgosie Matthews of sexual harassment late in the campaign.

Edna Moseley—Mother of Carol Moseley Braun. She lived in a nursing home at the time of the Carol Moseley Braun campaign.

Joey Moseley—Younger brother of Carol Moseley Braun. A Chicago police detective, he took responsibility for security throughout the campaign.

Johnny Moseley—Carol's closest sibling. He died of a drug overdose in 1983 at the age of 34.

Joseph Moseley—Father of Carol Moseley Braun.

Marsha Moseley—Younger sister of Carol Moseley Braun.

Kathleen Murray—Fundraiser for the Carol Moseley Braun general-election campaign.

Elizabeth Nicholson—Assistant to Kgosie Matthews and Carol Moseley Braun during the general-election campaign. She was one of two women who spoke on the record of being sexually harassed by Kgosie Matthews.

Billie Paige—Springfield lobbyist and founder of the firm Shea, Paige & Rogal, Inc. She was a longtime friend of Carol Moseley Braun.

Sydney Faye-Petrizzi—Managed public relations for Mayor Harold Washington of Chicago in the 1980s. In 1991, she was the Midwest advertising director at *Mirabella* magazine. She left that position to assist Carol as travel and press aide during the primary campaign.

Sue Purrington—A Hyde Park neighbor, Sue Purrington ran Carol Moseley Braun's first campaign for the Illinois House of Representatives in 1978. In 1991, she was the executive director of the Illinois chapter of the National Organization for Women. She was one of the women who encouraged Carol to run for Senate after Senator Alan Dixon voted in favor of confirmation of Clarence Thomas to the United States Supreme Court.

John Rednour—Mayor of Du Quoin, Illinois, during the Carol Moseley Braun campaign. He was a Democratic Party leader in southern Illinois.

Wayne Robinson—Attorney who specialized in labor law, brought into the campaign by Carol Moseley Braun to investigate the "anonymous letter" accusing Kgosie Matthews of sexual harassment during the campaign.

John Rogers Jr.—Chairman of the Carol Moseley Braun finance committee. He is the founder and CEO of Ariel Capital Management. His company, now called Ariel Investments, is the largest minority-owned mutual fund company in the United States.

Barbara Samuels—Hyde Park neighbor of Carol Moseley Braun during her marriage to Michael Braun. Mother of Matt Braun's best friend, Greg. Samuels worked as a buyer for Sears for many years. She joined the campaign as an assistant to Kgosie Matthews.

Larry Shapiro—Called by most the "numbers guy," longtime Moseley Braun supporter Shapiro worked on targeting and analysis in both the primary and general-election campaigns.

Paul Simon—Democratic senator from Illinois, 1985–1997.

Lynnette Stanton—Scheduling assistant on the campaign, Stanton went on the serve Moseley Braun throughout her term of office.

Tina Stoll—Democratic political fundraising consultant based in Washington, DC.

Desiree Tate—Scheduler for the Carol Moseley Braun campaign during the primary and general election. She frequently traveled with Braun throughout the campaign. Tate had been a scheduler for Harold Washington during his second mayoral campaign.

Alice Tregay—Field organizer for the Carol Moseley Braun general election. She was a longtime, highly prized Chicago activist.

Lou Vitullo—Chicago attorney who counseled Carol Moseley Braun on the Medicaid matter during the general election.

Roxanne Volkmann—Assistant to Kgosie Matthews during the Carol Moseley Braun general-election campaign.

Bob Walsh—Issues director, briefly, for the Carol Moseley Braun primary campaign.

Richard Williamson—Republican candidate for US Senate in 1992. He ran against Carol Moseley Braun in the general election and lost.

Velma Wilson—First campaign fundraiser during the Senate primary who continued through the general-election campaign. She had worked previously for Jesse Jackson and Harold Washington.

Jill Zwick—Deputy campaign manager, former republican state representative who frequently worked across the aisle with Carol Moseley Braun during her legislative years. Zwick was in charge of outreach to the heavily Republican "collar counties" surrounding Chicago. She went on to serve the senator throughout her term.

Note: Much of the Carol Moseley Braun political archive resides at the Chicago History Museum Research Center. However, the files that deal with the primary and general-election campaigns of 1992 are sealed until 2068. Thus, this list has been gathered from notes and memories, so for any errors of omission, please accept the author's apology.

PART I

Democracy only works when the people we elect to high public office remember that they are the servants—not the masters—of the people.

—CAROL MOSELEY BRAUN
Announcing her run for the US Senate

CHAPTER 1

Clarence Thomas Kicks off
"The Year of the Woman"

I T WAS OCTOBER 9, 1991. I was dining alone with my television set, my stomach in a grumble as I read the *Chicago Tribune's* coverage of the ongoing hearings that preceded Clarence Thomas's confirmation as a Supreme Court justice. Suddenly, the firm voice of a very angry woman brought my eyes up to the screen. Who was this woman? She was on fire!

> I mean the issue here is one of attitude, the attitudes of Senate members, whether or not they value the whole question of sexual harassment sufficiently to make that an attitude that they will discuss....

Forgetting my pasta and chilled pinot grigio, I jumped up and screamed, "YES!"—sending the pinot sailing across the room. She continued:

> The fact of the matter is that in examining the attitudes and the judgments that this man, Clarence Thomas, has displayed over his years in public life, they not once raised an issue as significant, as substantive, and as fundamental to the whole question of women's equality as sexual harassment!

Of the five panel members appearing with host John Callaway on the PBS show *Chicago Tonight* that evening, this beautiful black woman with her wonderful, expressive face and rich, emotional voice reflected everything I was feeling at that moment about the white male Senate that appeared to be on the verge of betraying at least half its constituency. I was angry and frustrated, but this woman was angry and very clear:

> Most of the women I know, certainly have talked to, since this came up have related some incident of sexual harassment in their lives. The point is, it's an economic issue for women. It has to do with equality in the workplace. It has to do with whether or not just doing your job is enough to keep that job and to move forward and to have opportunities in that job.

Her name came up on the screen:

Carol Moseley Braun
Cook County Recorder of Deeds

The Senate Judiciary Committee had announced that the full Senate vote on the Clarence Thomas nomination to the Supreme Court would be delayed and that the committee would reconvene on October 11 to question Thomas on charges of sexual harassment, charges involving a woman named Anita Hill that had been brought to light by Senate staff and confirmed by an FBI investigation. The Judiciary Committee had chosen not to pursue the charges until the story was broken by National Public Radio's Nina Totenberg and Timothy Phelps of *Newsday*—and switchboards in Senate offices exploded with outrage.

History edits. Memory edits. History records the salient facts, but in a democracy, for better or worse, what grabs people emotionally dictates the politics. So you can look up the transcript or check the videotape, but what so many women across the country *felt* that day is what became politically potent.

These feelings did not magically arise because of what was being broadcast. These feelings erupted from women's lived experience, and we were fired up even before we were presented with this appalling scene. *"You mean there was evidence that this candidate for the Supreme Court had harassed young female employees when he was chairman of the Equal Employment Opportunity Commission? And you arrogant SOBs were going to ignore that?"*

We had put up with boorish, entitled men for too long.

You're walking down Main Street, past a construction site, and a male voice yells out, *"Hey, sweetheart, cute ass. Give us a wiggle, will ya?"* A second voice yells, *"Yeah! I want some of that!"* Followed by a roar of male guffaws.

It's your manager, supervisor, boss:

"Come on, sweetie. Let's go out."

"Hey, you're a nice guy, Mr. Smith, but I don't date married men."

Insistent, gently threatening: *"Just one drink, Sally. Come on."*

"Yes or no?" thinks Sally. *"Promotion or no promotion?"*

We had all been there.

You could have turned the sound off on those October days in 1991 and the televised pictures alone would have told the story that stirred a nation. It was a colorful spectacle in that ornate, high-ceilinged Senate hearing room—packed and alive with tension. Ranged in front, a panel of 14 white men in mostly dark suits: the Judiciary Committee of the US Senate. Before this panel sat law professor Anita Hill, a former assistant to Thomas (first at the Department of Education and then, ironically—as noted—at the Equal Employment Opportunity Commission [EEOC]). Tastefully dressed in a light aqua suit, Hill remained poised and centered despite severe, at times even hostile, questioning. Making appearances before and after Hill's testimony was Judge Clarence Thomas, President George H. W. Bush's controversial appointee to the Supreme Court, who was, for the entire length of the proceedings, majorly pissed.

The judge's strategy was clear: Be angry, condemn the process, say they are ruining your life and trampling your good name, call it racism. Calling it a "high-tech lynching" would be a good phrase. After all, it's "he said, she said." Nothing can be proved.

Of course, it's always "he said, she said," and it's always "nothing can be proved," which is why Professor Hill, a 25-year-old aide to Thomas at the time of the alleged harassment, had kept quiet in favor of her career. And it's why millions of us empathized with Hill and thought (*felt, knew!*) Thomas was lying.

Anita Hill did not ask to be in that room. When first contacted by staffers of Judiciary Committee member Howard Metzenbaum in what could be characterized as a fishing expedition, Hill was left with the impression that there were other women who had similar complaints against Thomas. With the hearings already in progress and after much consternation, Anita Hill wrote a four-page statement for submission to Joseph Biden, the chairman of the Senate Judiciary Committee. She understood the stakes, and though she was afraid her remarks might be misconstrued, she also felt strongly that the man she had known did not belong on the US Supreme Court. Hill's assumption was that Senator Biden would circulate the report, it would be read, and the committee would vote on whether to confirm Thomas and send its recommendation to the full Senate. Anita Hill would have fulfilled her responsibility.

Clarence Thomas *did* want to be in that room—at least for the first round of hearings, now completed, although even his most ardent supporters called his earlier performance "wooden" and evasive ("over-coached" was probably the most telling observation). As for this second round, the enraged man who showed up was, according to several intimates (including his mother), the *real* Clarence Thomas.

Jane Mayer and Jill Abramson, in their 1994 book *Strange Justice*—a detailed exposition of the cynical manipulations leading up to the historic confrontation the Clarence Thomas second-round hearings would become—found people going back decades who had heard Clarence Thomas say he intended to be on the Supreme Court one day. And on July 1, 1991, with President George H. W. Bush, making the announcement from his Kennebunkport, Maine, home, Thomas's declaration came to pass. Unfortunately, Bush called Thomas the "best-qualified" person for the job and added later that Thomas's being black had nothing to do with his choice. Both statements underlay the frantic activities by the administration and outside conservative groups to prepare Thomas, who had spent less than two years on the Court of Appeals, who had never litigated a case before a jury, and whose attitude toward civil rights might best be exemplified by his assertion that the movement's leaders did nothing but "bitch," "moan," and "whine."

In *Strange Justice*, Mayer and Abramson report—citing hundreds of interviews—that the Bush administration and conservative supporters conducted a summer-long and absolutely intriguing *political* campaign using interest-group pressure (on senators), strategic press manipulation (including ghostwritten op-eds), independent organizations like the newly formed Citizens to Confirm Clarence Thomas, and old standbys such as the Family Research Council. The Traditional Values Coalition brilliantly (though covertly) organized a supposedly spontaneous march to Washington by hundreds of black pastors on the opening day of the hearings, September 10, 1991. This had the effect of intimidating a whole passel of senators, not to mention hamstringing those ardent civil rights organizations that knew and opposed Thomas. On the opening day of the hearing, polls showed the nominee with a 65 percent approval rating among blacks.

In fact, the thing we call "race," a force social commentator Michael Rustin called "both an empty category and one of the most destructive and powerful forms of social categorization,"[1] permeated every ounce of breathing space in that Senate hearing room. From the patrician senators who were cowed by Thomas's widely propagated bootstrap progression from abject poverty to this chair before them (Thomas claimed he had never benefited from affirmative action) to the liberals of all hues who had so passionately wished for a qualified legal champion to fill the void left by Thurgood Marshall, race was the spectral presence.

---

1   Rustin is quoted by Toni Morrison, who edited *Race-ing Justice, En-gendering Power,* a 1992 must-read collection of essays stimulated by the hearings and an exposition of the brilliance and diversity of African American thinking.

But outside that room, there was a vast female constituency who was paying less attention to race. For that constituency, the confrontation—and it was that—was all about power and how women, historically and currently, were struggling with inequities in the workplace.

The questioning of Professor Hill took on the tenor of an inquisition. The Republican senators had thoroughly digested her sworn statement—which was as detailed as such documents are required to be in cases of sexual harassment—and were ready to discredit her testimony any way they could. It was high-stakes drama, complete with explicit sexual references, as the senators required Hill to recall each of Thomas's offenses. Who can forget Hill's recounting of how Thomas described the prowess of his self-measured penis, which he admiringly compared with that of the grossly over-blessed equipment of porn star Long Dong Silver?[2] Or the time he walked over to his desk, picked up his drink, then asked Hill, "Who put pubic hair on my Coke?"

Thomas repeatedly asked 25-year-old Hill for dates, which she declined, citing their professional relationship. He talked about pornography in which women with huge breasts had sex with, well, just about everything. And he bragged about the pleasure he could offer with oral sex.

This went on for a significant period, beginning about three months into the time when Hill worked for Thomas at the Department of Education. Then, much to her relief, it stopped. So when Thomas asked Hill to join his team when the Reagan administration, seeking the rare qualified (minority) conservative, appointed him to the top spot at the EEOC, Anita said yes. It was the perfect opportunity to pursue her lifelong interest in civil rights. But after some time in *that* job, the harassment started again. This time, Anita was hospitalized for what was determined to be stress-related problems, and, eventually, she quit. In one of her last meetings with Thomas, she testified that he said, "If you ever tell anybody about this, it will ruin my career."

---

2   Mayer and Abramson gathered ample testimony to Thomas's longtime and unabashed interest in pornography.

The Republicans on the committee, having been deluged with a determined campaign's worth of negative propaganda[3] about Hill, were led to—or preferred to—believe Hill *was* out to ruin Thomas's career. But it was a Democrat, the aging Alabaman Howell Heflin, who came right out and asked Hill directly about the "evil" behaviors being implied by the Republicans' questions:

HEFLIN: Professor Hill, are you a scorned woman?

HILL: No, sir.

HEFLIN: Are you a zealot civil rights believer that progress will be turned back if Clarence Thomas goes on the court?

HILL: I have my opinion but I don't think progress will be turned back. I think civil rights will prevail.

HEFLIN: *Do* you have a martyr complex?

HILL: [*laughing*] No, Senator.

HEFLIN: Do you see that coming out of this, you will be some kind of civil rights hero?

HILL: No!

By this time the entire room—including a few chagrined senators—failed to stifle their laughter. With his pointed sarcasm, Heflin had hit a sweet spot.

Like, as it turned out, millions of others, I was glued to that televised drama. Except when the phone rang. This time, it was Linda Sayers, my old pal from football days. "I just had to talk to someone I knew would be watching and as angry as I am!" she exclaimed. We spoke for a while about the absurdities playing out before us, and then Linda said something that has haunted me.

---

3   Quoting Mayer and Abramson: "She had been portrayed as, among other things, a political zealot, a sexual fantasist, a scorned woman, possibly a closet lesbian, and a pathological liar who had lifted bizarre details from *The Exorcist* in a desperate effort to destroy Thomas. Worse, she, a black woman, was being publicly accused by Thomas of inciting his lynching."

She said her youngest son, Tim, who was not yet school age, had been watching with her, and at one point Tim said to his mother: "I didn't know there were so many smart black people." I pondered that for a long time because little Tim Sayers had plenty of smart black people in his life, notably his mother. But I came to the conclusion it was the way Anita Hill and Clarence Thomas, neither intimidated, presented themselves to this starched white male panel: Anita with poise and intelligence, Clarence with calculated yet measured belligerence. Both were controlled, and both were clearly stars of the proceedings. Young Tim, I think, was impressed not just because these people were smart but also because Hill and Thomas exuded a kind of power he had never witnessed in his young life.

Thankfully, that would not be the case today. While agonizingly intractable *systemic* problems—from poverty to policing—remain, kids now can find role models across the cultural spectrum. A young Tim today can switch the channels from a black woman anchoring an NBA pregame show to a black male president of the United States.

Thomas, despite his manifest rage, maintained his dignity, as did Hill, whose cool demeanor was extraordinary given the *un*dignified way she was treated, especially by the particularly arrogant Senators Orrin Hatch and Alan Simpson (Simpson called it "this sexual harassment crap"). But the most important image in terms of the political tidal wave that flowed from this room was the attitude of the panel of white male senators. They were (or at least pretending to be) squirming along with the rest of us, but the reality was—with a couple of exceptions—these privileged men exhibited no concept even of what sort of behaviors constitute sexual harassment or, more importantly, why it was a problem for women.

Anita Hill was trying to explain to the senators about how Thomas's sexual advances (the pressure to date) and dirty talk affected her decisions, her state of mind, and, ultimately, the direction of her career, and *they weren't hearing*.

But we were.

When we say "we" in American politics, each of us more or less assumes that fellow believers are coming from the same place.[4] But with few exceptions, the white section of cheerleaders in Illinois applauding Carol Moseley Braun's unequivocal opposition to Thomas had not a clue about how brave her stand was when it came to the more complicated African American part of her soon-to-blossom constituency. James Baldwin, a profound interpreter of race in America wrote: "The great force of history comes from the fact that we carry it within us, are unconsciously controlled by it in many ways, and history is literally *present* in all that we do." Thus, when Carol spoke out, she knew she was violating the stand-by-your-man ethos that said our African American men have so much to deal with that we need to keep our mouths shut and subsume our needs, our ideas, and our ambitions to theirs. Clarence Thomas, unquestionably a beneficiary of affirmative action, had advanced his entire career as a minion of the conservative establishment, and virtually every speech during the career of the now nominated Supreme Court justice reflected his *denial* of the African American experience. Then, in these hearings, he had the gall to play the race card, comparing his treatment to a "lynching." This was not only hypocrisy, it was blasphemy, equating the questioning of his character to the unspeakable pain and shame of a crime that remained in the living memory of so many Americans.

Although white women generally saw a simple case of sexual harassment—the older, powerful boss versus his young employee—there was so much more garbage hung out in those few hours to roil the emotions of African Americans who watched. With Thomas leading the way, ancient stereotypes of threatening black male sexual prowess and the female temptress were happily exploited by the (I'll give them a break and say "apparently") ignorant senators. For black feminists, there was a truly vexing problem: they were flat done with men like Thomas, not to mention other abuses that demeaned the sisterhood. But how could they fight back and yet stay loyal to the legions of good black men? It was an emotional earthquake—challenging realities, shaking foundations.

---

4   How often have you heard a politician or pundit say, "The *American people* think ... want ... believe ...?" How arrogant is that?

And yet, polls taken at the time showed that three out of five African Americans supported the nomination of Clarence Thomas, and whether or not Anita Hill's testimony was believed, many thought that she should have declined to testify, that she was wrong to undermine the credibility of a black brother.[5] Thurgood Marshall, the great civil rights lawyer and justice whose seat Thomas would occupy, had set a high standard. Maybe Thomas would change, they thought, as others had done when they absorbed the awesome responsibilities of the Supreme Court. Those supporters were to be sorely disappointed.[6]

As for Thomas, his nomination was approved by a full Senate vote of 52-48, a record negative count for a Supreme Court nominee. But should his values mature, as so many wished, that vote was a validation—should he ever claim it—that one day might allow Clarence Thomas to pronounce *himself* the ultimate beneficiary of affirmative action.

Race, gender, power, and politics had been dumped into the shaker of that hearing room in October 1991, and when the ingredients were tossed on the table, new alliances and new constituencies were born. Between October 9 and October 15, when Carol Moseley Braun again appeared on *Chicago Tonight* to express dismay over Illinois Democratic senator Alan Dixon's vote to confirm Clarence Thomas, Americans sat down together to watch a televised political spectacle that for each individual became quintessentially personal. Black men, white women, black women, white men—each of us brought some very personal experience to this drama and took something else away. In many cases, this was an altered consciousness. Importantly for what was about to happen, individual women became aware that they were not the only ones who had suffered these kinds of indignities. Genes gathered into cells, and cells sought an organism that might have the power to effect real social change.

---

5   One year later, opinions had changed. The District of Columbia's Eleanor Holmes Norton referred to Hill's credibility, saying, "She haunted the public imagination until people conceded they had been wrong."

6   NBC reporter Andrea Mitchell, being debriefed at the close of the hearings by Tom Brokaw on NBC *Nightly News,* was asked, "What have we learned?" And Mitchell, to her credit, responded candidly: "I think we learned that the United States Senate is the last plantation."

In Illinois, Carol Moseley Braun became that organism. Her phone did not stop ringing: run for the Senate; get into the primary now; beat Dixon. "Oh, sure," Carol thought, "he's only the biggest vote-getter in the state."

There was a reason for that. Republicans didn't have a big problem with Dixon. He'd voted against the first Gulf War but had gone along with the George Bush "41" administration on most other issues.

When Dixon heard that Carol was considering challenging him in the primary, he stopped by the Recorder of Deeds Office to see her. "He seemed to be there to defend his vote to confirm Thomas," Carol later told me. "He kept saying Thomas wasn't guilty. 'But Senator,' I said, 'Thomas's guilt or innocence is beside the main point, which is that none of you recognized the seriousness of sexual harassment in the workplace. You trivialized a concern of a major segment of your constituency.'"

Then Carol said she made one other point to Dixon, one that had energized my own anger about the deeply cynical appointment of an unqualified African American to the Supreme Court: "I wanted Dixon to understand that by taking the Republican position and supporting an African American who had done the things Clarence Thomas had done to get ahead in this country, just tap dancing his way to the Supreme Court, Dixon was helping to send the wrong message to young black Americans."

As for Dixon, Carol said, "He didn't seem to have a clue what I was talking about."

"Al the Pal" (that was Dixon's nickname) had been one of only two northern Democrats to vote to confirm Clarence Thomas. Apparently confident because polls showed that his black constituency generally favored confirmation, Dixon arrogantly dismissed the female outrage smoldering statewide. But without exception, political observers, like *Chicago Tribune* reporter Thomas Hardy, didn't even smell the smoke. On October 20, Hardy wrote:

> Hear me now and believe me later: When the foot-stamping and name-calling by Democratic

women's groups over Sen. Alan Dixon's unfortunate vote to confirm Clarence Thomas as a Supreme Court justice subsides, the result will be the same as any other tantrum.

A lot of energy will have been expended, Dixon's eardrums will have been bruised and, acting mildly chastened, the Democrat will still be in office, his conservative, let's-make-a-deal philosophy intact. ...

Cook County Recorder of Deeds Carol Moseley Braun teed off on Dixon last week, but faced with virtual re-election next year to her steppingstone office, she'll prove to be as risk-adverse as any male politician.

"Foot-stamping," "name-calling," and "tantrum"? Rather than discouraging those determined to find a woman to challenge Dixon, Hardy fueled their efforts.

Following the election victories of November 1992, it would be difficult to look back and truly recapture the atmosphere that existed at this time. Clearly, neither the male political establishment nor the fraternity of pundits recognized the depth of feeling the Thomas hearings had stirred. Indeed, exactly 12 months passed before Professor Anita Hill herself put into words what her confrontation with Thomas had ignited. Said Hill, "What the Senate Judiciary Committee did not count on was that their exhibition of abuse of power would become a metaphor for the sexual and gender abuses suffered by women."

This almost indefinable force was what Carol Moseley Braun had going for her. It was *all* she had going for her.

Although Carol was beginning to recognize that her own passions were finding remarkable resonance, she was also a political realist—and the historical realities were formidable. Only three blacks had ever been elected to the United States Senate, none Democrats. Hiram Revels and Blanche K. Bruce were sent to Washington during Reconstruction (1870–1881), and Republican Edward Brooke had represented Massachusetts in the Senate for two terms before being defeated by Paul Tsongas in 1978.

The situation regarding women was nearly as dismaying as that of African Americans. In the history of the United States, there had been 14 female senators, most of whom had inherited their seats from husbands or had been appointed to fill out terms by governors with whom they had some political or personal connection. As the 1992 cycle began, there were two women senators, Barbara Mikulski, a Democrat from Maryland, and Nancy Kassebaum, a Kansas Republican who had been the only winner among the eight women who sought Senate seats in the 1990 elections. The 435-member House of Representatives in its entire existence had only embraced 117 women, and it was 1968 before Shirley Chisholm became the first African American elected to Congress. An accomplished educator and New York state legislator, the gutsy Ms. Chisholm served seven terms in Congress and in 1972, running on the campaign slogan "Unbought and Unbossed," she sought the Democratic presidential nomination. It was a doomed effort, but Chisholm entered the race compelled to highlight her issues: early childhood education, health care, opportunities for inner-city residents. As a pioneer, Chisholm frequently found herself portrayed as "an emasculating matriarch." Like Carol, she felt she was discriminated against more as a woman than because she was black. Chisholm saw this as a power struggle. "The black man must step forward," she said, "but that doesn't mean the black woman must step back."

Now, in 1991, there were 28 women in the House. Interestingly, despite the women's movement of the 1970s, the numbers of female legislators in Washington had only increased by 3 percentage points since 1971.

Washington remained a male bastion self-perpetuated by those twins of political power: money and incumbency. Men were wired into the structure that measures the worth of large political donations by the question, "What can this candidate do for my bottom line?" The conventional wisdom dismissed women as being incapable of raising the kind of cash needed to mount a modern political campaign. But women candidates, like Carol, were about to soar above this conventional wisdom and capture what was blowing in the wind.

On Monday, October 21, the same day Dixon visited Carol in her office to plead his case, *Chicago Sun-Times* political writer Lynn Sweet listed what any woman who chose to run against Dixon would be up against: "Dixon has high name identification, the experience of running four statewide campaigns, and a statewide political network." Also going for him was the fact that the sitting senator, who had not lost an election in 42 years, had $4.6 million (and counting) in the bank, the support of the state party leadership, and the reassuring fact that he'd won his last election by one million votes.

Steve Neal, a *Chicago Sun-Times* political columnist added, "Another factor working for Dixon in the '92 primary is that Illinois doesn't have party registration ... Dixon could attract a substantial Republican crossover vote."

Neal was right about the crossover vote, but it wouldn't go for Dixon.

At this stage, the press could hardly be blamed for reflecting the conventional wisdom, but oblivious in their arrogance, the Democratic establishment kept throwing kindling on the fire. One of Dixon's people said, "These women wouldn't have time to put together an effective campaign and raise enough funds to run against the largest vote-getter in Illinois."

Then, in a statement that was as revealing as it was appalling, Dixon's Senate colleague, Democrat Paul Simon, lit the match: "At some point," Senator Simon told the *Chicago Tribune*, "if Alan or I retire, then that's a point where perhaps we can provide a little more diversity in the Senate."

Ka-BOOM!

Sue Purrington, who had run Carol's original campaign for state representative in 1978 and was currently executive director of the Illinois chapter of the National Organization for Women (NOW), called Carol at the recorder's office regularly. "Our phones are ringing off the hook!" she said. "Do it!"

"From the time Dixon cast his vote until the day it became clear that Carol would run," said Purrington, "we averaged 2,000 calls a week. It was a word-of-mouth thing, phone networks, small meetings. There were a number of names being floated, but the eventual consensus was this: because she knew people around the state, because of her profile in terms of the Democratic party, the answer just kept coming up: 'Carol.'"

During the two years I spent close to Carol and her campaign, I did not find her particularly introspective, something I think is true of many politicians, and she never got around to telling me about her erratic, scary childhood years until after she was elected to the Senate, but there was a moment early on when I asked Carol to reflect on her own self-image.

How do I see myself, really? I guess sometimes I think of that fairy tale about the ugly duckling who became a swan. But the thing about me as a person is that, without any sort of plan, actually, the whole thrust of my life has been to give expression to my own humanity without regard to what might otherwise appear to be limiting factors.

I've done some rather unorthodox things, both on a personal and on a political level, only because I was focused on the possibilities rather than the limitations.

Going to the rather conservative University of Chicago Law School? Hey, it was in the neighborhood. And marrying my husband? Well, then, even now, there is no small amount of curiosity— if not resistance—to interracial marriages. But even though I was aware of that, as far as I was concerned, I was marrying someone I loved—and that was all there was to it.

When I ran for state representative, there were very few women in the legislature. But I didn't run to make a point. I ran because I was interested in government, and I thought I could do the job.

Because I am black and female and independent, all of my political life I have been called a "bridge." I like to think I'm a suspension bridge—strong, yet flexible enough to serve necessary ends without breaking in the inevitable storms. But there are times when I wish I could be like one of those drawbridges we have in Chicago, and I could just fold up my arms and say, "You can't cross me!"

Carol did not allow herself to be dismissed. She listened to the voice inside her that knew she could represent the people of Illinois

better than Alan Dixon had. And then there was her sense of destiny: why had John Callaway called her—the Cook County recorder
of deeds—of all the women he could have chosen to comment on
the Thomas appointment on his widely watched program? What
was going on in the land that caused so many people to react so
passionately to her comments?

One of the best stories about what was going on was told to me
by another deeply rooted Chicagoan, Sydney Faye-Petrizzi, and
the way she got involved is instructive in that Sydney represented
the personal dedication and political zeal the campaign eventually
tapped. Sydney had worked in public relations for the late African American mayor of Chicago, Harold Washington, but she had
left the political world for a more lucrative opportunity. When the
Thomas-Hill show hit the air, Sydney was traveling the country in
her $100,000-a-year job as *Mirabella* magazine's Midwest adver-
tising director. Sydney recalled:

"Everywhere I went, I turned on the television. I was mesmer-
ized by the stupidity of these people, these senators! I remember
Howell Heflin asking Anita Hill about date rape. It was so gra-
tuitous. As a victim of sexual assault myself, I was incensed. 'I'm
aware of something known as date rape,' Heflin says. What? What
could he know? And furthermore, what the hell does this have to
do with what Anita said Clarence did? These men were clueless!
So after the hearings, before the confirmation vote, I'm trying to
call Dixon," Sydney went on, her anger rekindled. "And the phones
in his Senate office were shut off! I went wild. I voted for this man!
He's supposed to represent me!

"I was back home in Chicago by the 14th, in my apartment
all by myself, and when Dixon cast his vote to confirm Clarence
Thomas, I started screaming. I called my parents, my counselors,
who were so bright and wonderful, and I screamed, 'I can't believe
he voted for Clarence, son of a bitch! I can't believe it!'

"So my father, Marty, says, 'You're the schtucker?' which means
'big shot' in Yiddish, 'so what are you gonna do about it, huh? What
are you gonna do?'

"'Watch me,' I said. 'You watch me.'

"I started actively looking for a woman candidate, and when a friend told me Carol Moseley Braun was thinking of running, I called her. I'd met Carol before and thought she was wonderful. I remember exactly the moment I reached her; it was a momentous thing for me, making that commitment.

"I was in Marshall Field's, and I went for a pastry. Now, I learned later that Carol has a fondness for lemon squares, but that's too gentile for me; I have to have something with chocolate. When we traveled together, she and I would never have a problem when we had a sugar thing going on because I would never touch her stuff and she wasn't into my stuff.

"Around the corner from the pastry counter at Field's was a pay phone. With a chocolate pastry in my hand and shoppers swirling around me, I dialed Carol and told her, 'If you are serious about running, I will leave my job at *Mirabella* and I will come and I will help you win this election.'

"She was amazed, not speechless. Carol is never speechless. But she was definitely amazed that I would do that."

Sydney's financial sacrifice probably tops the list, but she was one of the first of thousands to bring a passion beyond purchase to the campaign. Still, at this point, the phenomenon remained in its infancy.

As for Carol, it was time to consult the most important person in her life, her 14-year-old son, Matt, born of her marriage, since dissolved, to Chicago attorney Michael Braun. Matt was reading a book when Carol sat down beside him and blurted out that she was seriously thinking of running for the Senate. Matt grabbed a notebook and pretended to interview his mom.

"Well," Matt asked, "what are your qualifications?"

Figuring she was going to get these questions from others down the line, Carol responded fully and seriously, interestingly going lightly over her years as recorder of deeds and instead emphasizing her 10 years in the legislature representing the racially diverse Hyde Park neighborhood. She talked about coalition building and her record on issues she thought were critical to Matt's future: health care, gun control, minority rights, fiscal responsibility....

Matt interrupted her: "You know, your generation has left this world worse off than you found it!" he accused.

"Wait a minute!" Carol reminded Matt that when she was his age, this was a segregated country, a hot war had just ended, and a cold one was just starting....

"Mom, do realize how hard you are going to have to work?"

"Yes."

"OK. Then you can do it," said Matt, tossing his notebook aside and returning to his reading.

So Mom went off to Washington to see whether she could raise some money.

In DC, the people at the League of Conservation Voters were cordial, but it was clear they thought taking on an incumbent was too risky. Harriett Woods of the National Women's Political Caucus was encouraging but wouldn't make any promises. To Carol, even the women at NOW appeared unconvinced that she could pull it off. (Sue Purrington told me later that, at their request, she'd sent a list of questions to the Washington people, "but they never asked the questions. They just fell in love.")

Then Carol went to see Ellen Malcolm at EMILY's List. ("EMILY" is an acronym for "Early Money Is Like Yeast.") Early money was what Carol needed, and Malcolm was in the process (thank you, Clarence Thomas) of building her organization into a powerful funding mechanism. Malcolm had formed her organization in 1985 to elect pro-choice Democratic women, but the '92 election was about to kick EMILY's List into overdrive. Membership would grow by 600 percent, and Malcolm would raise $10.2 million. But all that was still ahead.

According to Carol, Malcolm told her, "Well, running for the Senate is an important position," and handed Carol a brochure that said, "So You Want to Run for Congress," which had a stick figure of a girl on the front panel.

Laughing, Carol told me it reminded her of a pamphlet she got in high school gym class called "When You Start Your Period"— with its advice like "talk to your family; talk to your doctor"—"and I'm saying to myself: I am right now the second-highest female elected official in the entire state of Illinois. I've been in the leadership of the legislature. I've won five elections. Why is this woman talking to me like this?"

It was a rough start. But just before the March 17 primary, when it looked like Carol might have a chance to win, Malcolm forked over five grand, and by the time Carol was elected to the US Senate had sent her $400,000, EMILY's List becoming the largest contributor to the Carol Moseley Braun campaign.[7]

But that was later. Now, head down and feeling spanked, Carol scurried back to Chicago to see whether she could put together a campaign staff. She called experienced Democratic operatives all over the country, but no one was interested. She got ahold of Democratic Party chairman Ron Brown, who, Carol said, "was polite." She reached Chicago's hottest political consultant, David Axelrod, "who said he didn't think I could raise the money." Very shortly, Axelrod would find a Senate primary candidate who could come up with the money. Lots of it.

Then, at a fundraiser for Roland Burris, who was running for attorney general, Carol ran into a woman named Chris Long, whom she knew had statewide experience. Later, Carol described her first staff.

I knew Chris casually; she'd worked for Dukakis. I simply walked up to her at this party and asked if she'd manage my primary effort. She laughed and said she didn't think her health would allow it—she had a heart problem—but we agreed to talk later.

We felt we should have a woman-run campaign, so, as long as Bill Taylor, who worked for me at the recorder's office, would do the heavy lifting, Chris ultimately decided she could handle the job. Helene Colvin, in spite of the fact that she was suffering from multiple sclerosis, said she'd deal with the press. Barbara Samuels, Matt's best friend's mom and also a friend of mine, had just retired from Sears and said she would join. Kay Clement, who got me started in politics, and her son, Adam, said they'd help.

---

7   By 2015, EMILY's List had more than 3 million members.

And of course, Sydney Faye-Petrizzi—who would soon give up her job at *Mirabella*—was on board. Sydney described an early meeting to me this way:

"It was a great meeting," said Sydney. "It was like that Mickey Rooney and Judy Garland movie, like everybody's a 'gonna be': 'I'm gonna be the campaign manager!' 'My dad will let us use the barn!' 'Aunt June will make the cookies!' 'OK, and I'll be the press secretary!' 'And Sydney will do the national piece!' And we'll have a good time and then we'll all go to the malt shop!"

That settled, it was time to think about announcing this crusade.

The date was set for November 19, 1991. The place: the departure lounge of a private terminal at Midway Airport. Helene Colvin, Chris Long, and Carol would then board a small plane and do a state fly-around. Pulling a number out of her hat, Carol told someone, "Our budget for the primary would be $2.3 million. Also, I said we'd collected about $50,000." Maybe.

On Monday, November 18, the day before Carol was to make her big announcement, Albert Hofeld declared that he, too, would be a Democratic candidate for the Senate. Hofeld, a 55-year-old product liability and personal injury attorney from the wealthy North Shore, let it be known that he was willing to spend from $2 million to $5 million of his own money to unseat Alan Dixon. Hofeld, utterly dismissing her, didn't even mention Carol Moseley Braun. So now Carol had two "Als" to beat. Hofeld's media strategist would be David Axelrod.

On Tuesday, the 19th, announcing her candidacy, Carol Moseley Braun, the cheeky black lady from the South Side with her million-dollar smile and a big bucketful of brains and guts, set out to seriously disturb the political comfort zones of a couple of very rich Als. She said:

> My name is Carol Moseley Braun and I am a candidate for the Democratic nomination to the United States Senate.
> I am running against the Big Lie....

> Democracy only works when the people we elect to high public office remember that they are the servants—not the masters—of the people....
>
> I am running for the Democratic nomination to the United States Senate because I—along with everyone else—saw my Senator stand on the floor of the Senate and say that it didn't matter to him what I thought.
>
> I watched him side with the people who have ruled us so badly, as he has again, and again, and again.
>
> And I was ashamed.
>
> I am ashamed because my senator makes the Big Lie possible.

Carol went on to accuse Dixon of faking left and going right, 72 percent of his votes favoring Republican positions, and saying that "after 42 years in elective office, our senator has become so secure in his job that he has forgotten that he is not a free agent, that he has to work for the team."

"I am ready to work for Illinois," Carol concluded.

By mid-December, the struggling campaign had an office across the street from the county building, which allowed the candidate to spend some time on her real job. "During this period, I was being scheduled both by my assistant in the recorder's office, Sue Bass, and by, well, somebody at the campaign. I was never quite sure who," Carol later confessed. At this point, campaign manager Chris Long had informed the candidate that she had to have heart valve surgery, so Bill Taylor was running the show, although he would shortly leave to be slated for a judgeship.

On this fateful December day that Carol was later to think of as her campaign "renaissance," she (or someone) had scheduled Carol to make an announcement to the press about a plan for national health insurance, and press secretary Helene Colvin had brought in a group of health care providers to discuss their concerns. Back at the recorder's office, in Sue's book, this was the day Carol was to host the state's recorders of deeds. And Bill Taylor, not to be left out of this circus, had set up a third ring down at 93rd and

Commercial where Carol was supposed to be talking to a bunch of steelworkers.

All of these events were scheduled at 10:30 a.m. Carol was frantic.

Then Helene's MS flared up, and she had to be hospitalized. Chris, of course, was already gone. Sydney couldn't be there because this was the day she was officially quitting Mirabella, *and her boss was in from New York to meet with her and accept her resignation.* (Had Sydney and her wonderful sense of humor been around, she might have said, "Screw it. Let's all just go to the malt shop.")

Then a friend who was on a stopover in Chicago on his way to South Africa called and asked me to lunch. I really wanted to see this guy, so I told him where the press conference was and said, "Just go there. Sit. Wait for me. If I survive, we'll eat."

That friend was Kgosie (pronounced *Hoe*-see) Matthews, who, it turns out, had been casually advising Carol by telephone ever since they had spoken at a Jesse Jackson event during that unsuccessful trip to Washington, DC, a few weeks earlier. The handsome 34-year-old South African had given Carol his card and offered to help. He had worked on the Jackson presidential campaign in 1988.

Carol told me later that she once mentioned Matthews to a mutual friend, Betty Magnus, and that friend responded, "That's the African prince I told you about!"

"African prince?" Carol continued. "How could I have failed to register that?" And then she went on to describe—again referring to serendipity and destiny—the rest of that fateful afternoon.

So now Kgosie was on his way back to South Africa to spend Christmas with his family. He'd been at a conference in California and planned this stopover in Chicago in order to leave some materials with me that he thought would be helpful in the campaign.

What campaign? We were in the dining room at Marshall Field's munching sandwiches. It was mid-afternoon, and I told Kgosie I was throwing in the towel. "I have no money, no campaign structure. I'm done."

Kgosie said, "You can't quit. This is too important," and he went on about the history, the possibilities, and how much women and minorities would benefit should I win.

I said, "Well, that's all wonderful in theory, but unless you want to come in and manage this campaign, I'm outta here!"

"Excuse me," he said, pushed his chair back, and left the table. He called his mother in South Africa and told her he wouldn't be home for Christmas after all.

And that was the real beginning of my campaign for the US Senate. The Kgosie Matthews campaign.

CHAPTER 2

The Primary Team

W HEN CAROL SAID TO KGOSIE, "Unless you come run the campaign...." she was flirting with a purpose—as I suspect they both had been doing in their communications over the previous weeks.

When Kgosie got up from that table at Marshall Field's, it was clear he had the invitation he'd come for. Win or lose, he now had a job. Matthews surely thought he knew all he needed to know about Carol. But there was so much more.

I am a city person. Other senators may say they are from New York or Los Angeles or Cleveland or Detroit, but how many of them grew up tangled among the roots of these cities? Very few, and those who did found it easy, as white males, to melt upward into the higher echelons of business, law, academia, politics. But I will never escape the city. Nor do I wish to. It is just another way that I am different.

Edna and Joseph Moseley were living at 201 East 41st Street when Carol was born on August 16, 1947. It was an all-black South Side neighborhood, mixed economically. Because Chicago was so strictly segregated, everyone from doctors to domestics lived on the block; one of the reasons inner-city neighborhoods were more stable back then was that the middle class was still there. Carol's parents owned the three-story row house that was big enough to accommodate two tenant families. Carol does not remember "even a moment of peace and solitude." During those early years, Joseph was a Chicago police officer. Edna worked as a medical technician at Central Community Hospital.

When Carol was 18 months old, her brother Johnny was born. To this day, she remembers Johnny as her very best friend. Sister Marsha joined the family seven years later and, in three more years, baby Joey.

Marsha graduated *cum laude* from Yale and earned her law degree at Harvard. Little Joey became a Chicago homicide detective. But it is Johnny whom Carol remembers being close to.

Johnny and I were inseparable. Everyone called us Bunny and Brother. We were so close, like twins. He was my reliable sidekick, my partner in a never-ending series of schemes and adventures. Brother was as quiet as I was voluble and as easygoing as I was high-strung. He never, ever disagreed with my pronouncements and demands, even though, as I was to discover as time went on, Johnny was the smartest of the two of us.

Brother had a way with people that made everybody like to have him around, grown-ups and children alike. I had then, as now, a tendency to attract controversy. People either loved me or hated me. One time, when the tough kids at the end of the block decided to beat me up, Johnny came to my rescue, talking my enemies out of what I had become convinced was certain death. Ugly duckling that I was, I truly needed Brother. I didn't feel right with my peers, so Johnny was my social life, my protector—he was everything. It was a very special relationship.

Johnny Moseley died of a drug overdose in 1983 at the age of 34.

Carol's mom, Edna, like her daughter, had a wonderful anecdotal memory.

"We had tile on the children's bedroom floor because it was easier to keep clean, and I told Bunny and Brother to stay on the bed while I was waxing the floor. So, 'tickle, tickle, tickle,' they're rompin' and gigglin' on the bed, and all of a sudden—boom. Carol hits the floor. And Carol says, 'Brother, you see me hit that damn floor?' Now, they're four and five years old and clear as can be, she said, 'damn!'

"So I get after her for swearing, and she says, 'No, Mama. I said *damp.*' And she purses up those little lips and makes 'p' sounds: 'puh, puh, puh, dam-PUH,' because I'd been teaching them to read by phonetics.

"Clear as a bell, that little child said 'damn,' but that's how quick Bunny was."[8]

The Moseleys lived on 41st Street until Carol was seven years old. This home occupies a romantic corner of Carol's memory. Except for her beloved brother Johnny, there were no younger siblings yet. Joe was employed, going to school at night, and still hopeful of getting his law degree. Edna, matriarch of her own home with its extended family, was happy. Her close friends, the sisters Otha Hysmith and Catherine Mackey, despite their own large families, were surrogate mothers to Carol and Johnny. "201," as Carol characterizes this early period of her life, was an exciting place, a nurturing place, a protected place.

Darlene Mackey, who eventually joined the campaign staff, grew up with Carol. But by the time Darlene remembers being a part of the extended Moseley family, Joe's frustrations had caught up with him. "I didn't know a lot about Carol's father, but I didn't like him. He frightened me. Most of the time he wasn't there, but when Mr. Joe walked in, everything changed, just froze up."

"Joe just couldn't find himself," remembered Edna. "He had a fine mind, he was well educated, he played beautiful music, and he could be sweet as a doll sometimes. But if things didn't go his way, he'd want to fight. And he could be very abusive at times.

8   When I first asked Carol if I could interview her mother, she said, "Sure," and directed me to the long-term care Barr Pavilion on Chicago's Near North Side. "But you should know," she added, "my mom's a liar."

"He had a short fuse, and he'd beat up on the children, too. He took a rope one time and was hitting Carol across the back with it. Then he took a swing at John, and John ran, knocking down chairs in his path so Joe couldn't catch him. Joe had a terrible temper. We were all afraid of it."

What happens to a dream deferred? Does it dry up like a raisin in the sun? My father just saw his dreams smashed over the years. He was a police officer, and maybe that was a fallback position from the law degree he so badly wanted. But Joe didn't last long on the force, and I think—from what I heard my folks talk about—that it was a brutality issue. He quit before he got in trouble. He was in real estate, insurance, worked in a store, and finally, he got a job with the department of corrections. I'm sure he had a problem with authority. He was a "You don't like it? Kiss my ass!" kinda guy.

My parents had a tumultuous marriage. It was awful, just awful, particularly in the years before they separated when I was 11, 12, 13. There was violence—fists, knives, even guns. They threatened each other; he threatened us. It was bizarre. I know lots of families go through this, but I remember, as a kid, standing in horror, watching my parents battling.

I think that violent atmosphere had something to do with why I am such a laid-back person now. I don't handle violence well. I'm willing to be confrontational when I must, but I don't relish it.

As an adult, in hindsight, I think my parents were into a Who's Afraid of Virginia Woolf *kind of thing. You know, if you're with a man whom you know is violent, then when you see it coming, you shut up, leave the room, go shopping or something. Edna wouldn't. She would push and push right up to that explosion.*

The divorce, in 1964, was traumatic, but in a very real sense, it was a relief.

Carol talked about her father's violent streak, but there was a more insidious form of abuse that she seemed to feel.

Edna was very focused and persistent. I think her controlling nature came out in the way she was always so helpful and supportive to others. Such a sweet lady, people thought, beloved by all. Yet with me, she was strangely withholding of affection. In place of warmth, she communicated expectations: she expected that I would succeed in school, she expected that I would take care of the younger children, she expected that I would work as hard as she did. Mama expected that I would do my duty in all ways. She did not expect so much from Brother—and that may have contributed to his downfall. It is said that black mothers rear their sons and raise their daughters. It was certainly the case in our family. If Johnny failed to do his chores, I was expected to do them. In an ironic way, this unfairness redounded to my benefit. I learned to do what I had to do. Nevertheless, I think I developed a deep resentment regarding the caretaker role my mother created for me. As I grew older and she increased her expectations, our relationship was frequently stormy.

As a very small child, my mama used to tell me that my soul was like a glass of milk and that every bad thing I did was a speck in my milk. And so I would imagine that whenever I used a cuss word or took more than my share of Brother's candy, my glass of milk would get more and more polluted. Mama never said whether good deeds would erase the specks.

Still, I tried very hard to do my duty, trying to eliminate the secret specks that I knew were there.

Edna herself was the epitome of a dutiful wife and mother. She gave more than human effort in order to provide for us, sometimes working two and a half jobs to make ends meet. Mama did what had to be done to care for her family. Not long ago, I met a man who said he'd sold insurance with my father, that he and Joe had been "running buddies." He knew Joe had died some years back, but when I told him Edna had passed away in December of 1993, he said he was sorry not to have seen her before she died. Then this man said, "She was such a sweet lady. She never got angry, did she?" If only he had known.

Mama was as volatile in her own way as my father. In fact, I now suspect the violence that later became the defining secret of our home was as much her initiation as his. I remember trying to learn my multiplication tables. We sat on the bed in the room I shared with my brother, Mama with a strap in her hand. This was years before I discovered I had a learning disability that caused a problem with numbers (in my twenties, I discovered I was mildly dyslexic), *and I simply could not remember the tables by rote. When I made a mistake, Mama would hit my legs with the strap. After countless mistakes and hits, my legs were beet red and Edna, in exhaustion and disgust, would give up. I was an adult before I finally got those numbers right.*

Yet, if you talk to people who worked with my mother over the years, to her friends, they will tell you she was a giver. I can remember my mother and father arguing over the fact that every time he came home, the kitchen was full of women, sitting and having coffee. She was always nurturing somebody.

While Carol remembers a warm, cheerful kitchen, often including her mother's two best friends, Auntie Otha Hysmith and Auntie Catherine Mackey, who between them had nine children (to this day, Carol calls them all "Cousin"), she had few blood relatives. The one she remembers most is her mother's sister, Auntie Darrel Davie.

Auntie Darrel was like Auntie Mame: you never knew what outrageous thing she was going to do, except that it would be dependably flamboyant and often exciting. She would choose a favorite niece or nephew, then take us to the opera, museums, the movies. She would just pop into our lives with all that good stuff.

Actually, it wasn't always so good. I remember once I needed a dress for grade-school graduation and Auntie Darrel took me to Saks on Michigan Avenue. Blacks had finally been permitted to shop in the stores along Chicago's Magnificent Mile, but it was still not common, and a pretty intimidating situation for a 12-year-old. I was, as I still tend to describe myself, a "chubbette," but my Auntie was a gorgeous woman, very thin, about 5'9"—she looked like Diahann Carroll, only prettier.

A saleswoman, with what I will generously call "an attitude," was helping us, and we took several dresses into a fitting room. I tried on three or four and nothing fit. Finally, this woman with her phony airs said to me, "Well, you should be thin like your mama." I was angry and so hurt—and that was the end of my shopping. My mother had to make my graduation dress. It's strange how I remember that so vividly.

Strange? Really? Even without the racial implications, no 12-year-old girl on the planet would forget such an incident. She might suppress it, she might redirect her ambitions from beauty queen to politician, but she would not forget.

When Kgosie Matthews took over Carol's primary campaign in December 1991, she did not know him well. There had been a couple of brief encounters and those several phone calls—hardly a sustained relationship. Carol was both impressed and intrigued by the young South African, but, even over time, Matthews would prove a hard man to know.

If not precisely an "African prince," as Carol's friend Betty Magnus had described him, Kgosie Matthews was heir to an impressive political lineage. His grandfather, Zachariah Keodirelang (called "Z.K.") Matthews, a writer, lawyer, and prominent South African educator, was an influential leader of the African National Congress (ANC). During the family's years of exile in London, Kgosie's father, Joseph, edited the ANC magazine *Sechaba*. Joseph Matthews had returned to South Africa in 1990 and was now a top adviser to Chief Mangosuthu Gatsha Buthelezi, president of the Inkatha Freedom Party. Kgosie's father and grandfather had both spent time in jail as political prisoners.

Although Kgosie's grandfather, who died in Washington, DC, in 1968, is credited with helping to create the Freedom Charter, a historical South African document that set a course for all races to share power in his beleaguered country, grandson Kgosie was now destined to lead a historic American political campaign.

In 1985, Matthews was an organizer of what was to become the first large antiapartheid rally in Europe. A guest speaker from the United States was the Reverend Jesse Jackson. As a result of their meeting, Jackson invited Matthews to come to the United States and join his Rainbow Coalition.

Kgosie Matthews got his American political baptism when he signed on as a special assistant to Jackson during the 1988 presidential campaign. He played several roles for candidate Jackson, including traveling aide and advance man. Linguistically talented (Matthews speaks four languages in addition to his precise and charmingly accented English), Matthews is also very fashionable, favoring Armani suits and Italian footwear. By the time the worldly 34-year-old met Carol Moseley Braun, Kgosie Matthews, according to his official résumé, had earned two degrees, including one from Harvard's Kennedy School, and, in addition to his experience with Jackson, had held positions with the Greater London Council, Hill & Knowlton, and American Express.

Matthews was between jobs, having just left his post at American Express, when he met Carol for lunch on December 19, 1991. Contrary to campaign legend, the young South African did not ride into Marshall Field's that day on a white horse. It just felt that way to Carol. A bright but inscrutable man, Matthews could be meticulously mannered and erudite—or rude and contemptuous. In any event, during the 11 months he worked to elect Carol to the Senate, no one was overheard describing the campaign manager as "warm." As Carol became fond of saying, "Kgosie could never win a Mr. Congeniality contest."

As for Carol, frantically seeking leadership for two months now, the slender bachelor, whose style and intelligence were abundantly evident this December afternoon, seemed an answer to her prayers, a guiding star in the sense of destiny that had so frequently overcome her during her still infant endeavor to become a US senator.

Even the chaos of the day had played to this moment: the three meetings scheduled at one time, the untimely illness of her aide, and the botched press conference. It had been a day from hell.

When Kgosie Matthews pushed back his chair and elegantly excused himself to make a phone call, the clouds parted above Carol's head and the sun came out. The man's decisiveness alone gave her comfort. Kgosie Matthews would bring to the campaign what it clearly lacked—direction—and would bring to Carol a man to fill a role for which she felt a deeply rooted need: a protector.

You might think the small, struggling group of dedicated people— bright, progressive, male and female, black and white—who were at the core of Carol's young campaign would resent the stranger from South Africa who was introduced to them that afternoon as their new boss. Not so. The need for leadership was unanimously recognized, and Carol's obvious confidence in Kgosie was enough to ensure his welcome.

Thus, as the December holidays approached, Carol became reenergized. Winning the Illinois primary the following March remained a formidable long shot. Yet, there was something in the nature of the enthusiasm Carol met wherever she went, something "out there" that was more felt than quantifiable. Carol called it "the light." "I saw a light," she said, "and I followed it."

Still, the deep inspiration felt by Carol and the sense of need at large in much of the electorate must be joined, and the democratic device for doing this is called a campaign. A successful election campaign is about nothing if not detail, and managing detail means organization. It was time to get organized.

A top agenda item was to find an assistant for Kgosie, and Carol thought Barbara Samuels would be perfect. Barbara was already in the fold, working on the "volunteer problem."

Barbara Samuels had been a buyer for Sears for a couple of decades when she decided to retire and start her own fashion consulting business. Shortly after announcing her candidacy in November, Carol, knowing her friend was in transition, asked Barbara to join the campaign. The telephone conversation went something like this:

> CAROL: Help! Barbara, I need someone to organize these volunteers!
>
> BARBARA: I have no idea how to do that!
>
> CAROL: Barbara, you have what Harold Washington called "transferable skills," that is, you are a person who is smart, adaptable, and flexible enough to learn a new area of expertise. Please? Please?

Barbara and Carol had been brought together 12 years earlier by their sons, Greg and Matt, who remained best friends. "I'd met Carol briefly when she first ran for the Illinois House, and I'd been so taken with her. She seemed pure, like a young teenager, very sweet, sincere, without guile. At the time, I felt a powerful kinship with her. I knew we'd meet again."

When Barbara moved into a townhouse complex years later and it turned out that the Brauns—Michael, Carol, and Matt—lived next door, the women reconnected. Barbara recalled, "I was traveling all over the world for Sears, and Carol was back and forth to Springfield. Our sons would move freely between our two homes. Carol and I had the kind of friendship where she'd call and say, 'Turn on channel five!' and I'd look at the clock and it would be 1 a.m. We'd talk for hours about everything that girls talk about. Carol learned to trust my intuition—because it rarely failed me."

It's easy to understand why Barbara and Carol would be attracted to one another. Barbara is bright and funny, and while Carol values Barbara's intuition, Barbara praises Carol's savvy—and loyalty. She said, "I'm telling you, single-handed Carol got me through the most horrendous financially and psychologically debilitating divorce....

"My husband left me so far in debt I didn't think I'd ever get out. The creditors were coming in like missiles; every time the phone rang, it was another hit. But Carol got me off the hook. She just took my hand and said, 'Let's get this thing straightened out.' She nailed my ex-husband, got him to sign certain agreements, called me all the time from Springfield to see how things were going, offered to loan me money.

"One day, we went to this bank in the southwest suburbs regarding a loan. We walked in, and we were the only blacks in the building—I daresay, in the whole town. So this woman, this bank officer, was very cool. 'What can I do for you?' she asked. I introduced myself. The woman said, 'You were supposed to bring your attorney.' Now, Carol had this head wrap on—every now and then she gets into exotica—and was looking very unlawyerly. But when Carol handed the woman her card and started talking, well, that was the beginning of the process. It took her a week of phone calls and arm-twisting, but Carol turned herself inside out because a friend was in trouble. And I'll never forget that."

Every now and then, Barbara has what she calls "psychic flashes." "I used to suppress them," she said, "but then I decided life's too short. I need to explore this."

A powerful one of those flashes had to do with Carol Moseley Braun. Barbara recalled, "It was a few years ago. Carol was already recorder of deeds, and she called me one day and told me she was thinking of running for lieutenant governor. I said to her—it came on me that suddenly—'NO! This will not work. Don't bother with it. The recorder job is just a way station. I see your picture everywhere, even on magazine covers. You're going to Washington.'"[9]

Now Barbara had a chance to help fulfill her own prophecy by sending Carol to the US Senate. Heeding her friend's call for help, Barbara went downtown to the campaign office, an overheated warren of tiny rooms in a recently remodeled old building in the heart of Chicago's Loop at Randolph and Dearborn. Barbara didn't have any trouble finding the volunteer file; it consisted of "a stack of about 1,300 names, addresses, and phone numbers written on cocktail napkins, church programs, paper towels, business cards. It was a nightmare," Barbara recounted. "And that list swelled to 6,000, 14,000. I think we peaked at 18,000 volunteers. In the primary!"

Connecting 18,000 volunteers to a viable campaign would take real money, and there was precious little of that. There was, however, genuine camaraderie in the early group of people drawn to Carol. "We had no money, so when we ran out of stuff—coffee, toilet tissue, paper towels—we'd bring it from home," recalled Barbara. "Carol was very accessible, although she was in her office at the county building most of the time. She was very conscious of her need to do the job the people had elected her to do. Besides, it was hard to stir up invitations for her to speak. There is no question that the campaign had a credibility problem."

Matthews got right to business, mining his contacts from the '88 Jackson campaign, and Carol added her years of Illinois expertise to create a viable team. In addition to the women who were the earliest members of the campaign, Kgosie inherited Bob Walsh, a policy buff with Washington experience, and Alton Miller, a "good get" as far as the struggling Braun campaign was concerned because Miller, as former mayor Harold Washington's press

---

9   Carol's attempt to be slated for lieutenant governor in 1985 ran afoul of city and state Democratic power brokers. She credited her failure to a "fatal combination of ambition and naïveté." The same might be said for state senator Barack Obama in 2000 when he tackled community icon Bobby Rush for Congress and lost by some 31 points. In his book *The Audacity of Hope,* Obama wrote (prophetically) of his humiliation, "In politics, there may be second acts but there is no second place."

secretary, was well acquainted with the local media. Matthews's most experienced recruit was nationally recognized Democratic political consultant Gerald Austin.

As 1991 drew to a close, Carol's campaign, which she had only weeks before characterized as "a little band of neophytes and stringers," was beginning to resemble the real thing.

As nobody in the GOP wanted to be fodder for "shoo-in" incumbent Alan Dixon, it took Illinois Republicans until shortly before the mid-December filing deadline to come up with a candidate. His name was Richard Williamson. Currently with the blue-chip law firm of Mayer, Brown and Platt, Williamson had been a White House adviser to Presidents Reagan and Bush. The wealthy lawyer lived in the posh North Shore suburb of Kenilworth with his wife and two children. Williamson was a perfect Republican.

But the announcement of Williamson's candidacy was pretty much the last anybody heard of the Republican, who was to run uncontested. The Democratic primary battle promised to be much more interesting.

Consider the numbers the *Chicago Tribune* came up with in its six-county poll at the outset of the campaign: 51 percent of Republicans and 46 percent of Democrats said they approved of the job Democrat Alan Dixon had done in Washington. On the negative side, only 21 percent of Republicans and 28 percent of Democrats disapproved of the senator's performance.

Even in downstate Illinois, where the conventional wisdom said Dixon had his strength, voters who thought they would vote for Dixon were not particularly enthusiastic; they could be swayed. In political parlance, Dixon's primary numbers were "soft."

By mid-January 1992, Illinois began to recognize that there was an election coming up on March 17. Carol had been quietly working her base in the African American community and among women, meeting with the rare political ally who chose to defy the organization or the still rarer Democrat who would write a substantial check. Now it was time to heat up the effort.

Three factors go into the slick political campaigns to which Americans have become accustomed, and the first of these is *money*. But after that, most candidates are backed by solid organizations, as Alan Dixon was in this campaign. And, finally, these

organizations have media, visibility, and field strategies planned
well in advance, all fortified by polling and led by professionals.
It's important to remember that this was BBD (before big data),
before computing was sophisticated enough to influence, much
less guide, these processes. For perspective, today's super-stat-
istician Nate Silver turned 14 in January 1992. In 2012, Silver
correctly predicted the presidential vote in all 50 states plus DC,
besting by just one state his 2008 record. Kinda takes the fun out
of it!

Carol had no lead time, no money, and few professionals on her
team. Her decision to run was spontaneous. Yet that spontaneity
clearly had resonance throughout the state. Braun's primary campaign, despite its wobbly legs, proved that down where it is rooted,
the prairie grass remains healthy.

And there was another factor in her favor: Carol was a magical
candidate, and Illinois, struggling along with the rest of the country with recession and frustrated by gridlock in Washington, was
ready for magic; nothing else seemed to be working. The political
aura was not unlike that surrounding another Chicago South Sider
who became president of the United States 16 years later: "the rich
white guys are screwing things up; let's try something different."

Sue Purrington, Carol's pal from the old neighborhood who
was currently executive director of Illinois NOW, knew exactly
what to do to get Carol elected. Sue *did* have an organization, and
nobody from NOW waited for a call from the campaign office.
NOW printed its own signs and T-shirts and organized statewide
meetings, rallies, and fundraisers. Sue understood the magic. She
knew Carol could win. She'd always known.

"The first time I met Carol," remembered Sue, "was in Hyde
Park in 1978. Kay Clement brought her to our legislative district search committee meeting and suggested that Carol be
considered to run for the seat being vacated by Bob Mann. Bob
was a very honest and independent guy whom we all dread-
ed having to replace. Carol came in and she just lit up the place.
She was young—Matt was just a baby. She'd been in the US attorney's office, but she was very open and honest about her lack

of experience. She brought a flash of electricity to the room I'll never forget.

"Everyone who was in the room that night left enthralled, swept away. Politically, I fell in love—which is a very dangerous thing to do."

(Indeed. I heard that phrase used to describe first meetings with Carol so often that I actually thought about what *"falling* in love" really meant. What causes a fall? Usually a trip. You go down fast and by accident—and very often you are hurt).

"What makes Carol unique is the fact that she's natural; she's real," said longtime supporter Larry Shapiro at the outset of the Senate campaign. "Politicians spend years developing layers of artificiality. Carol can't be remanufactured. She's Carol Moseley Braun, not 'the Candidate.' She understands 'high touch'; she looks people in the eye and communicates."

Sue and Larry knew that Carol would have the same effect on voters in 1992 she'd had on them in 1978. It was just a matter of getting her out there.

Velma Wilson, an experienced campaigner who'd worked for Jesse Jackson and Harold Washington, set about raising the money to do just that. Sorting through the napkins, business cards, and other scraps of paper out of which Barbara Samuels was assembling a volunteer file, she targeted people who might hold fundraisers in their homes.

"Everybody I reached was fascinated, interested, anxious to help. People just wanted to do something, and in the beginning, it was mostly white women. Sometimes Carol would make three parties in one evening," Velma said. At an average of $35 a pop, the money started coming in.

And the money came from some surprising places. DuPage County, just west of Chicago, was a white suburban conservative enclave. Purrington's women from NOW were the literal "movers" at a memorable rally held in a Unitarian church that drew 500 wildly enthusiastic supporters.

"The women wanted to do a rap for Carol," Velma remembers, laughing. "The words were fine, but these ladies had no rhythm at all. I was clapping, trying to help them keep the beat. I just fell out laughing. It was fantastic."

Campaign finance laws at the time allowed individual contributors to donate up to $1,000. "We had a list of the big Democratic
money people and made cold calls," said Velma. "Sometimes we'd
get through. Often people said they'd call back but didn't. In the end,
we raised almost $400,000 with only a handful of $1,000 checks—
and those were from people who'd supported Carol throughout her
political career."

The most veteran campaigner in the Braun primary was Gerald Austin, and he was connected mostly by telephone. "Kgosie
would call me maybe 10 times a day," said Austin.

The two men became friends in 1988 when Austin, who has a
political consulting firm in Columbus, Ohio, was campaign manager for Jesse Jackson's presidential run. Austin and Jackson eventually had differences, and Austin left the Jackson campaign in July
1988, but he and Matthews remained in contact.

With 102 clients, all involved in 1992 elections, Austin was
a busy man and a man who, as a former college basketball player, liked to keep score. His final stats for '92: "12 of 13 winners of
congressional seats, including 8 of the 12 freshmen; two of three
statewide offices, and in other races—state reps, county commis-
sioners, and the like—35 of 39. And one senator."

In the case of the Braun campaign, which didn't have the funds
to hire him during the primary, Austin was willing to "bet on the
come," not because he thought Carol would win necessarily but
because she was his kind of candidate.

"I was a child of the sixties; my parents were children of the
thirties, very active in the labor movement. Growing up in a liberal
New York Jewish household, we were always protesting things. In
1963, when Martin Luther King made his 'I Have a Dream' speech
in front of the Lincoln Memorial, I was there.

"But eventually I saw that protests weren't enough and, also,
that so many people around me sort of got off on protesting: 'Oh,
another march, we gotta try out some songs!' Marches and songs,
marches and songs. So finally I just looked at it and said, 'If politics
is a game that you want to win, how do you win this game?' Finding
answers to that question was what led me into political consulting."

While Jerry Austin and Kgosie Matthews were trying to figure how to win the game without putting any money on the table,

Carol's opponents began tossing chips like the millionaires they both were. By the end of January, Al Hofeld, whose get-go chore it was to simply introduce himself, had four television ads on the statewide tube, and Alan Dixon had two.

Dixon's problem was that, although his name recognition was high, as a back room kind of Washington guy, people weren't clear on what their senator really stood for. Uniquely, for a 64-year-old politician who had never lost an election, Dixon felt the need to define himself.

One Dixon TV ad had him schmoozing in a health care facility while the voiceover (not his) talked about the senator's sponsorship of a national health insurance bill. Unfortunately for Dixon, he had been a latecomer on this very hot issue, signing on to the bill six months after it was introduced and, coincidentally, three weeks after Harris Wofford won his special Senate election in Pennsylvania on this issue and just days after Dixon found he was to have real live opponents in the Illinois primary. These qualifiers were eminently exploitable.

The theme of Dixon's second television ad was free trade. The visual had him earnestly discussing job problems with Illinois factory workers. There were no women in the picture.

When challenged on this point, Dixon responded, "I don't make the commercials. I am only the poor actor up on the stage."

"Al the Pal" remained clueless.

Rookie politician Al Hofeld, on the other hand, was in remarkably good hands. Media consultant David Axelrod designed a set of commercials that showcased Hofeld's anchorman good looks and trustworthiness. Hofeld was very adept with a script and a camera as he spoke directly to the people of Illinois and told them what he was all about. He did this during what seemed like every commercial break on television for two and a half months.

Chicago Sun-Times columnist Ray Coffey probably best expressed the feeling the Hofeld ads inspired in the electorate:

> Nice looking guy, this Al Hofeld who's on the TV every time I turn it on. Seems pleasant. Makes a good appearance. Gray hair. Dignified. Well-spoken. Fresh shirt. Sharp tie.

But every time I see him on TV I am reminded
of Ronald Reagan's big line (later the title of his auto-
biography) in that old movie "King's Row": 'Where's
the rest of me?'

The fact was that the Republican's successes in 1988 with slick
commercial, sound bite, photo op, message-a-day, control-the-
press campaigning was still the model during the 1992 primary
season. The country had not yet been exposed to the huge political
power of talk that would be first demonstrated by the Ross Perot/
Larry King alliance; would later metastasize to Fox, MSNBC, and a
proliferation of radio jabber-heads; and would, finally, today, move
to social networks and a vast chorus of tweets.

In part because campaign coffers were anemic, Carol was
forced to give the people what they *really* wanted. She traveled the
state, hugged folks, looked into their eyes, smiled, and told them
where she came from and what she believed in. To meet Carol was
to immediately become comfortable with her candidacy. And Jerry
Austin wrote Carol a couple of radio commercials that by February, she could afford to air.

NARRATOR: [*male voice*] Carol Moseley Braun, candidate for the United States Senate....

BRAUN: Nobody ever said that law school would be
easy, especially at the University of Chicago. And
you don't get extra points on the bar exam for being
a woman.

NARRATOR: Carol Moseley Braun was a prosecutor
in the US attorney's office for four years. She earned
her reputation as tough—and smart.

BRAUN: Being a legislator in Springfield was really
a great learning experience—meeting with farmers,
nurses, executives, really every level of life in Illinois.
I think a senator needs that experience.

NARRATOR: She was named best legislator every
year of 10 years by the IVI [Independent Voters of
Illinois]. She won her election to county office with

a million votes. And now she's a candidate for the United States Senate.

BRAUN: I'm a candidate for the Senate because I'm convinced: we can do better.

NARRATOR: Paid for by Carol Moseley Braun for Senate.

This ad said "smart" (University of Chicago Law School), "tough" (prosecutor), "experienced" (legislature), and "accomplished" (Independent Voters of Illinois endorsement). It assured the electorate that Carol Moseley Braun was a viable candidate.

While the first ad might be titled "Where Carol Went," the second could be called, "Where Carol Came From." And the order here is important: First you establish the candidate's credentials, then you can allow her to be sensitive.

BRAUN: You know, even if this recession ends soon....

NARRATOR: *[a deep, soft male voice]* Carol Moseley Braun speaks about families

BRAUN: Most middle-class families will still be caught short. I guess when I think about the United States Senate and the difference I want to make, I think about all those families like mine. That Washington, DC, just forgot about.

NARRATOR: Carol Moseley Braun thinks it's time the United States Senate got a dose of reality.

BRAUN: I mean, I'm a working mother—that paycheck's always bought necessities. And I see all these people on the bus after work and I think, how are they going to make it?

NARRATOR: Carol Moseley Braun will push for family-oriented economic policies for a change, instead of the usual handouts to millionaires and big corporations.

BRAUN: Frankly, I'm running because we can do better. We can do a lot better.

NARRATOR: Carol Moseley Braun for United States Senate. We can do better.

According to the creator of these ads, Jerry Austin, he has a problem that actually works in his favor, considering his occupation. "It's called 'ADD,' attention deficiency disorder. You think I'm kidding, I know," said Austin, "but what it means is that my mind wanders. So the 30-, the 60-second ad is perfect for me. I think that way." (Austin's rival consultant Axelrod has confessed to the same "disorder," now commonly referred to as ADHD or attention deficit hyperactivity disorder).

Austin added, "We had $39,000 for TV. I wrote our one and only ad, produced it, and it was in the can on December 26. But we didn't have the money to air it until March 13—the Friday before the election. It was simple: 'This guy thinks he owns the seat, this guy wants to buy the seat, I want to earn the seat.' I mean, that was it!"

And that's what Carol said, everywhere in Illinois, for two months before the ad hit television on the final weekend before the election: "I have one opponent who thinks he owns the seat, one who wants to buy the seat. I intend to earn a seat in the United States Senate."

The beauty of it was: it was true.

CHAPTER 3

Matthews Syndrome: Defections

F OR A BRIEF PERIOD AFTER JOE LEFT, Carol remembers that Edna was "paralyzed" and that "it must have been something like post-traumatic stress syndrome." But eventually, Edna got back to work and so did Carol, as a checker in a Kroger supermarket. In school, she performed well enough to be chosen for a program geared to exceptional students, then held at South Shore High School, a virtually all-white school in an all-white neighborhood.

One day after class, Carol stopped into a coffee shop near school. She sat at the counter—and was ignored. Carol stayed there, unmoving, for an hour. Finally, patience worn thin, the waitress asked her what she wanted. When Carol was finally served her coffee, she put a quarter down on the counter and walked out.

Carol says today that she doesn't "allow negativity" to be a factor in her thinking—or feeling.

I think it started then, when I was about 15. Life had fallen apart in terms of everything I considered stable. I can remember days and days going over to the rocks by the lake and just sitting there and looking out at Lake Michigan and thinking about why things were the way they were.

I think it was a time during which I kind of freed my own spirit, decided to continue plugging along, doing what was expected of me, but staying open—looking.

And eventually, something did happen that was critical, not only in terms of my attitude about race relations but, even more, in determining the way I would meet challenges.

As my own neighborhood became when we lived on Prairie Avenue, many South Side neighborhoods in the '60s sat side by side—one all white, one all black—with absolute lines of demarcation. Such were the neighborhoods of Englewood and Gage Park. In Englewood, the median education level was 11th grade; in Gage Park, ninth grade. But the average income level in Gage Park was more than double the median income of Englewood. Englewood was black. Gage Park was white.

Dr. Martin Luther King decided that Chicago would be his northern challenge. And one of the places he chose to stage a march was Gage Park.

My mother didn't want me to go, but then, she didn't want me to wear an Afro either, while my father had always told me black was beautiful. I made a decision for my absent father—and Dr. King.

We gathered—it was very well organized—and I was so awed by Dr. King. I marched beside a man whose face I can still see. He was white, about six feet tall, and kind of balding. He told me he was a veteran of these marches. He'd marched in the South. And as we started out, he explained what we should do if—when, he actually said—the crowd started throwing things.

I'll never forget: there was a group of nuns marching in front of us. And when I heard people yell, "Are you sleeping with those niggers? Which nigger are you going to bed with, Sister?" I was shocked and overwhelmed. I'd gone to Catholic school; these women were the Virgin Mary incarnate! But my companion kept saying, "Don't let them rattle you. Just keep on going."

Then, as we walked into the park, the rocks and glass started flying. We followed the instructions we'd been given before we set out: form a circle with the veterans on the outside, the less experienced men next, then the women and children. And close to the center, Dr. King.

Martin Luther King was within touching distance of me, really physically close, when the rocks and bottles began to come in thick and fast. We got down on our knees and laced our hands over our heads as we'd been instructed—and that's when Dr. King got hit by a rock.

There was a good deal of chaos and concern—"Dr. King is hit!" I remember being so angry, wanting to throw something back. But then, as I crouched there on the pavement, I grew to understand that our strength came in the fact that we were not retaliating, that it was precisely our nonviolent resistance that gave us authority. We were right. Our cause was correct; our behavior was civilized. We were a force for good.

And that was our protection. For me, it was a life lesson, not only in terms of civil rights issues but for other situations as well. It was a matter of intent, not simple good intentions, to think good thoughts and be a good person, but I realized then and believe now that there is in all of us a duty to reach out and make good things happen.

This was an epiphany for me. In a way that I didn't fully understand at the time, my course was set. That was in 1966. In 1992, the people of Gage Park helped elect me to the United States Senate. Dr. King was dead, but he had shown us the way.[10]

Remember Carol's campaign declaration: "I have one opponent who thinks he owns the seat, one who wants to buy the seat. I intend to earn a seat in the United States Senate."

To earn means to work hard for something and/or to deserve it on a record of achievement—in this case, achievement in the public interest. Given the choice, Carol would have preferred to have Hofeld dismissed (because he had virtually no record), to match Dixon's legislative record with hers on the things the electorate cared about in this election year—the economy, health care, women's issues, education—and, presto! She wins.

---

10 Carol, like many others who participated in the Chicago marches, may have misremembered the name of the park in which this incident took place. It was Marquette Park, not Gage Park.

Unfortunately, to earn her shot at a seat in the US Senate, Carol had to campaign. But the Carol Moseley Braun paradox is this: while she is a wonderfully effective campaigner, she hates the process. This conflict, internalized, set up an exhausting, and sometimes debilitating, tension in the candidate, not to mention among other members of the primary and general-election campaigns.

Yet, as much as she was uncomfortable with the process of selling herself, Carol fully intended to work, to earn the Senate seat by campaigning hard. Without money, this had to be a labor-intensive effort, and she knew it. Kay Clement, who'd been Carol's first sponsor for elective office and was now chair of the Carol Moseley Braun campaign steering committee, said Carol declared once during the primary, "See, Kay? Haven't I changed? Remember how we used to fight?"

Indeed, Kay did remember. "That winter of 1978 [when Carol made her first run for the legislature] was very cold, and some mornings, Carol just couldn't get out of bed. I'd call her, and I'd say, 'Carol, you've got to get out! Currie [one of her opponents, Barbara Flynn Currie] is everywhere! At the El stops, the bus stops, everywhere!' And she'd just resist. Oh, we had big fights. She was mean to me, and I was mean to her."

Sue Purrington was also intimately involved with Carol's early campaigns, as well as those of many other women. One of the big differences between male and female candidates, Purrington has observed, is that while men are accustomed to having services performed for them, women are used to having a hand in everything—writing, scheduling, personnel decisions. They also want to walk the child to school and cook Sunday dinner.

Sue observed, "Carol has always been that way, and the higher you climb on the political ladder, the bigger that problem becomes for those surrounding the candidate. Getting up in the morning and following a relentless schedule that someone else has designed, reading words that someone else has written is dehumanizing. But that's model campaigning. Carol's nature rebels against that model, yet that rebellion is part of her likability—her charisma."

Women are also likely to make an emotional investment that can be exhausting. "I used to look at Ronald Reagan," said Sue, "and ask myself how can a person as vacuous as this reach the highest office of the land? But then I realized that's exactly the kind of person who can go the distance."

Virtually anyone who's ever led a political campaign has lamented that he or she could run an ideal operation—if only they didn't have to deal with the candidate. Reagan, the actor, with a lifetime of setting aside both intellect and personal emotion and responding to direction, was perfect.

In the world of political candidates, Carol Moseley Braun inhabited the opposite pole from Ronald Reagan. She brought emotional and intellectual richness—and a fair portion of accompanying turbulence—to the campaign process.

Months later, the national press would invent a term to describe a characteristic of another somewhat chaotic campaign: "Clinton Standard Time." Bill Clinton, like Carol, a "high-touch" candidate, was also chronically late. There are many reasons for habitual lateness, and one is that it is a control factor. Lateness can generate anger, but it can also raise levels of anticipation and, if not overdone, will heighten the resultant response.

In the course of Carol's primary and general-election campaigns, she earned the ire of a number of people by being late or canceling engagements, even though neither practice is unusual in campaigns. This had the positive effect of allowing her to miss hearing countless boring business announcements and eating a lot of bad chicken. But Carol's background would suggest that while some tardiness is calculated, there is also an engine of anger smoldering inside her that may manifest itself in the passive-aggressive reaction that lateness represents: Carol Moseley Braun will not march to another's beat, even if she must pay a price all out of proportion to the offense.

And she *would* pay a political price, one that had resonance in part because it played into a stereotype: Carol Moseley Braun, it was said by some, was "lazy."

Even though Sydney Faye-Petrizzi would eventually have a falling-out with her political idol, it was well after Carol had been elected to the US Senate that the woman who had been virtually joined to the canidate's hip during the primary campaign bridled at any suggestion that Carol might have been less than diligent.

Said Sydney, "Carol Moseley Braun is *not lazy*. We had a grueling schedule, constantly changing because there was no time to plan for anything, and we had to grab every opportunity. The stress was tremendous, but the minute she was in front of an audience, she'd light up and wow 'em. Then everybody would want to talk to her, touch her—and she wouldn't leave! Then we'd be late to the next thing."

"Other problems were so mundane," Sydney continued, "but they stemmed from inexperience with the scope and demands of the situation in which we found ourselves. For example, it took forever for Carol to get an answering machine. Her number was listed, and she'd answer the phone and have a conversation. Also, unlike some women, Carol is not handy with herself, yet at the same time, she is meticulous about her grooming. So it would be, you know, the bath, the phone, the curling iron, the phone, the makeup, [so] we often got a late start. Carol should have had more help at home, but she didn't want that."

Because the schedule, not to mention the press secretaries (Helene Colvin followed by Sydney, Alton Miller, Celia Daniels, Sydney), kept changing during the primary, television and print reporters who had schedules to make and deadlines to meet would call Carol's faithful road manager, even during the periods when she wasn't doubling as press flack: "Sydney, are you sure she's going to be there?"

So while Carol reassured her supporters and the press that the campaign was in great shape, there is no denying that chaos prevailed. Carol Moseley Braun's primary campaign, nontraditional from its inception, remained, by definition, disorganized. How could it be otherwise? The campaign had no money, no advance planning, an inexperienced campaign manager who had had little exposure to Illinois, and a candidate who had only competed in a neighborhood (state representative) and a county (recorder of deeds). And though there were thousands upon thousands of voters, mostly women, nestled throughout the state who wanted to help, there was no statewide network with which to reach them.

Instinctively, people seemed to understand and forgive— even members of the press. Months later, in the midst of the general-election campaign, a reporter said of those primary months: "We were much too easy on her. She charmed us."

Nevertheless, no matter what they might believe ideologically, reporters must print the news. And when the campaign's (ordinarily) high-visibility press secretary Alton Miller disappeared in February, it was news.

"It was a weekend," remembered Sydney. "Velma Wilson had organized a big fundraiser, a fashion show, and there was supposed to be a press conference, as well—but nobody could find Alton. Carol and I must have tried to call him 15 times. And the next thing we know, he's blabbing to the *Chicago Tribune* about how he left the campaign!"

"I was appalled," continued Sydney, a woman who never fails to speak her mind. "The thing was, Alton couldn't get along with Kgosie—and neither could I, for that matter. But you don't screw the candidate over it! You have enough balls to say, 'Your campaign manager is a son of a bitch. I told him he's a son of a bitch. I'm telling you he's a son of a bitch. And I'm outta here!' Then at least you're a mensch!"

Both Carol and Sydney liked Alton and had welcomed him aboard when he joined the campaign in December. Miller, who had recently completed a book on the Harold Washington mayoral administration, was now teaching at Columbia College in Chicago, and Carol felt lucky to find a press secretary with Alton's unique experience in the city and the state.

Miller, a slim, active man with a slightly disheveled appearance, always had a pair of sunglasses perched on top of his head—indoors and out—a trademark that drew constant comment, even in print. According to Harold Washington biographer Gary Rivlin, when the mayor himself asked about the sunglasses, Miller replied that now that the press had made a big deal of it, he wasn't about to remove his sunglasses. "That was an explanation Washington could understand," wrote Rivlin. "With a smile, [Mayor Washington] said, 'They're the chip on your shoulder. I got no problem with that.'"

As Harold Washington's trusted adviser, Miller had enjoyed clear and consistent access to the mayor. This was, however, not to be the case with Carol. Kgosie Matthews insisted that all communication with the candidate go through him. Carol was comfortable with this arrangement. Kgosie would insulate her; he would be her firewall.

"I think Alton Miller did a great job while he was there," Carol later admitted.

For example, one day, he heard that Gloria Steinem was going to be in town to sign her book Revolution from Within *at a North Side feminist bookstore called* Women and Children First. *Alton said we should drop by, and I should introduce myself to Gloria and ask for her help. I did that. And she was wonderful!*

Then, late in the campaign, when I thought we'd never make it, when we were down to, I remember, $332. Gloria called and said she was out West and on her way back, she would stop by Chicago for a day and we'd campaign.

We didn't have much lead time, but we threw together a press conference that was packed. And Gloria wrote us a check for $1,000 herself. I was thrilled. It was snowing, and she didn't even have a warm coat, but it was her idea to get out in the street and shake some hands. We hiked over to Illinois Center, where there were lots of people, and it was terrific. What Gloria Steinem did for me not only gave me a tremendous emotional lift when I was truly despairing but with the press attention we got and the wonderful pitch she made at the news conference, money started coming in, and I knew we'd have enough to get us through Election Day.

I don't know any other way I could have enlisted someone like Steinem, as obscure and discounted as my candidacy was, except to have done what Alton suggested— just go right up to her and ask.

It was also Alton who urged me to show up at Dixon's health care forum and confront the senator on that issue. Alton knew how to be proactive with the media, and he had good relationships with members of the Chicago press, so when we did these things, we got coverage.

But Alton wanted to have more of a policy-making role than Kgosie was prepared to give him. As he had done with Harold, Alton wanted to get together every morning and work out the entire day's strategy. My view was that to be a press person meant I would interact with him as regarded positioning with the press. But in terms

*of where I go and what I do overall, I was not prepared to give that
to Alton.*

*In hindsight, I never really articulated that, and I suppose that I
just didn't want to deal with the confrontation. So Alton and Kgosie
ended up in these constant pissing matches.*

Miller was frustrated. A few days after he quit, he told Florence
Hamlish Levinsohn of the *Chicago Reader,* "Every campaign is either a tragedy or a comedy," (Alton had a significant background
in theater), "but Carol's campaign is surreal. She's by far the best
choice among the three candidates, but it's going to take a miracle
for her to win."

Miller blamed Matthews entirely, saying that he had no people skills and, further, that he had no real campaign experience.
In a published remark that would infuriate the campaign manager, Miller added that Kgosie's job with the Jackson campaign had
been to serve as "Jesse's valet." Six months later, on the day Carol
Moseley Braun was elected to the US Senate, Matthews was seen
sporting a lapel button that read, "I survived Alton Miller."

Carol told Levinsohn, with some accuracy: "In a campaign,
you don't have time to iron out differences."

But Miller wasn't the only defection. Bob Walsh, a man who
not only believed in everything Carol represented but also personally adored her, left as well, although with a little less drama.

Bob Walsh's title was issues director. Chris Long, the first campaign manager, knowing Walsh's policy interests and appreciating
his computer skills and passion for politics, had urged him from
the outset to join the Carol crusade. Walsh demurred at first. His
ambition was to get back to Washington, DC, and he didn't think
Carol was going to be making that trip. Then, at Chris's urging,
Walsh attended Carol's announcement event at Midway. Walsh
recalled, "I just loved it. Ate it up. Carol kicked butt. And I thought:
I can do this! She can do this!"

Not wanting to harm Carol's chances by quitting the campaign
and, unlike Miller, still believing she could win the primary, Walsh
refused to air his grievances publicly, saying only that he left because of differences with the campaign manager.

But like many people drawn to Carol, Walsh had found the answer to deeply held beliefs in her campaign, and he did not leave without emotional turmoil. Writing Carol a four-page letter, he fulfilled what he felt was a last responsibility to himself, to Carol, and to the fundamental values that he believed they shared. His letter read, in part:

> I came to work for you because I believed that you were a person who could and should leave a strong, pioneering mark on Illinois and American political history. Your integrity, intelligence and exuberance gave me much hope that my fine-tuned political cynicism was soon to be dispelled ... I had been trying to do many of the same things that you had been trying to do ... making government more personal, accountable, honest, more focused on improving the quality of most individuals' lives than that of those already privileged.
>
> Since seven weeks have passed since Kgosie started, it is no longer possible to hang one's hat on the "campaign's false start" hook. By affirming and retaining him, you
> - have endorsed his claim to having sole and complete control over your every move;
> - have continued to rely on a person with few personal or administrative skills, crippling an already weak organization (which still has no plan, direction or coherence);
> - have allowed him to publically bully and belittle you to build his own importance;
> - have watched while he humiliated and ostracized Alton, the only person who can get the message to the world of what you are about, frequently in front of the staff;
> - have given him free reign to make numerous and constant judgment errors, and to turn your staff into a bitter, contentious group of exhausted persons.

In closing, Walsh said:

I must seem horribly presumptuous to say this as I resign, but even though I have only known you for a few months, it greatly concerns me to see you so trusting and influenceable. You owe no one but yourself, in the long run, for your many successes, past and future. You deserve the very best, and you have not always gotten it. I can only hope that the situation changes for you, and soon.

Said Carol, "Walsh wrote me this four-page, really heartfelt letter, but basically he said, 'Either Kgosie goes or I go.' For me, it was a no-brainer. Adios, Bob."

Adios, Bob, Alton—and who would be next? It was around this time that those closest to Carol realized that she was in love with her African prince. Love, especially a love emanating from deep emotional need, is incompatible with good judgment, as would be proven again and again in the coming months.

Setting a pattern that he would follow throughout the primary and the general elections, Matthews refused to face the press, to put the matter to rest by offering some rationale for losing those particular individuals. Therefore, allegations of unrest and dissension continued to be repeated, and even though there were no complaints about the candidate, she was forced to confront questions about the actions of her elusive campaign manager right up to primary Election Day—and beyond.

Carol Moseley Braun, in addition to everything else she had to deal with, became Kgosie Matthews's protector. It was an irony that she willfully refused to recognize.

When asked who Carol's first scheduler was, Sydney Faye-Petrizzi replied: "Schedule? Scheduler? We were just a little group of people who decided we wanted to be represented in the United States Senate!"

The nightmare of every campaign is scheduling. The decisions involved focus issues and determine priorities. The scheduler is the wrangler who rides herd on the candidate. And when you have a candidate who is not fond of campaigning, the scheduler also doubles as a lightning rod.

Desiree Tate wasn't looking for a job when Velma Wilson called her one Saturday afternoon in December: "Des, you need to come down here to Carol Moseley Braun's headquarters. Carol has a new campaign manager, and he wants to see you—now."

Desiree had helped Velma with Harold Washington's scheduling during his second campaign, so Des had some experience—but little desire to get reinvolved in politics. Yet a scant two hours after that phone call, Desiree Tate became the campaign scheduler.

Desiree has qualities that helped her absorb and sometimes deflect the heat that scheduling inevitably generated. She's smart and willing to work long hours—despite the fact that she is a single mother—and her infectious laugh came easily.[11] Des had an ability to diffuse short-term anger and frustration into a long-term philosophy regarding politics and life that would stand her in good stead from the time she walked into Matthews's office until the day she left Carol's employ one year later.

"The primary was much less chaotic than the general [election] because Carol was not in great demand at that time," Desiree recalled, "but the crux of the problem all along was that Carol fought you every step of the way. She just hated it, hated campaigning. With Harold, I mean, he would literally call me and say, 'Why do I have this 30 minutes at 12:30?'

"'Well, you know,' I'd tell him, 'that's your lunch.'

"'I can eat in the car!'

"Harold Washington, like most politicians, was energized by crowds; they kept him motivated," Desiree continued. "Not Carol. It was almost as if they drained her. She'd work herself up, then the life would get pulled out of her; three or four speeches a day, and she was exhausted.

"Kgosie took the input we gave him in terms of ideas, invitations, and so on, but he made all the decisions. The final cut regarding scheduling was his. I was literally an appointment secretary with virtually no control. The problem for me was that I hadn't any access to Carol, so I couldn't ask her, 'Do you want to do this or that?' And I was never sure how I was being represented to her

---

11   Desiree's daughter, Ashley Tate-Gilmore, would become travel director for the Obama White House.

because what came back to me was that everything that got on Carol's schedule was something I, personally, wanted her to do."

Desiree and others credit Kgosie Matthews with what structure the campaign did have. She explained, "He tried. I mean, when we did start getting paid, Kgosie saw that we never missed a paycheck—and you do miss paychecks in some campaigns. He would order food for everybody and pay it out of his pocket. But," Des hesitated, sighing painfully, "it was like he wanted to manage by confusion. For example, he told me Sydney was telling Carol things were my fault, and I'm sure now, in retrospect, that Sydney was told I was undermining her.

"It was like an evil was in there, almost like something you couldn't control, and nobody knew what it was. It was frightening, and it still is. I get chills sometimes when I think about it. I feel bad that we couldn't get above and beyond that, but it was out of our control and we just couldn't."

Said another woman of Matthews when she first met him: "I felt nothing. Just this scary—void."

Something was at work deep inside the campaign that clearly did not feel right to those who were laboring hardest to elect Carol. But where it would count on Election Day, out where the votes were, people were ready for what Carol was calling "a healthy dose of democracy."

So important to the outcome of the election was the fact that throughout Illinois there were people who "just did it." Some individuals and organizations, like NOW, even printed their own materials. Velma Wilson remembers a man in Lake County: "He asked me to come by and pick up some checks, and he took me down to his basement. 'This is Carol Moseley Braun's Lake County headquarters,' he told me. 'This is where the volunteers work.' The room was all decorated with Carol stuff. It was great."

The fashion show in February, the day Alton Miller disappeared, was an eye-opener, especially for Carol, who many people thought never really expected to win.

It was a Saturday. "Why are we doing a fashion show?" asked the candidate. Carol hated fashion shows—perhaps dating back to age 12 when she was so thoroughly dismissed by a snotty saleswoman—but Velma was creating anything she could to raise money.

Velma's friend, boutique owner Cari Davis, volunteered to put the clothes together. Velma crossed her fingers, held her breath, and hired the grand ballroom of the Chicago Hilton. Everyone on her rapidly growing list of volunteers was asked to sell a table of 10 at $35 a seat. NOW sent out the call to its membership.

"Carol was a little late getting to the hotel, and I was in the lobby to meet her," Velma recalled. "I said, 'OK, we're going through this....' She was talking to somebody, so she was a little distracted, and when she walked into the room, she was shocked. More than a thousand people, mostly women, stood up and chanted, 'Carol, Carol, Carol.' It was the first time she'd seen a crowd that even approached these numbers—or that level of enthusiasm.'"

Carol Moseley Braun had a huge subliminal connect with the women of Illinois. They didn't see her on television; they rarely heard her on the radio. She didn't get around the state as much as she might have either. But women understood this. Carol wasn't wealthy and powerful like the two feuding male candidates.

But maybe there was something more at work. Perhaps Carol was benefiting from a kind of transference from Anita Hill. Fresh in the memories of countless women was the image of Professor Hill—so poised, so intelligent, so outwardly unflappable—as she battled the tide of disrespect ("Are you a scorned woman?") flowing from that panel of arrogant white men.

Now, here in Illinois, before them was another smart, eminently qualified African American woman challenging the establishment. Women seemed to be saying, "We failed against that panel of clueless senators, but we sure as hell have the power to knock off chief culprit Dixon and while we're at it, stick it to that other empty suit as well!"

On television, Dixon and Hofeld were rapidly becoming overexposed. As for newspapers, the coverage was slim. But for Carol, what did appear in print was almost universally positive, perhaps because she was not considered dangerous enough to attack. Typical was the Peoria *Journal Star,* which endorsed Alan Dixon but said of Braun:

> [She] is not as impotent as her quiet campaign makes her appear. She was an outstanding state

legislator during a decade in Springfield and gets high marks for shaping up the recorder's office since her 1988 election.

Braun is a liberal and a clear thinker whose stances are not always predictable. While she supports Canadian-style health care and is a strong voice on minority and women's issues, she's the only candidate to oppose a middle-income tax cut (she rightly calls it a deficit damaging ploy). She supports a capital gains tax cut with the stipulation that those who benefit must invest the proceeds in research, development, training or job creation. Interesting.

Wise, too. Carol did not harp on the Thomas/Hill event; she believed her presence was testimony enough on that score. Even where there might have been subconscious race or gender doubts, people were refreshed by Carol's clarity on the issues. In an early February column praising her record of achievement, Steve Neal of the *Chicago Sun-Times* said: "Braun has something that her opponents both lack: a well-defined philosophy."

The two Als were on television, spending serious money but not effectively communicating. At every opportunity, Carol was clearly stating her fundamental beliefs and political goals. And from time to time—as journalistic fairness required—the press was passing that information on.

Back in '92, you couldn't beat free ink.

CHAPTER 4

Chaos! Shock! Victory!

*A*LTHOUGH I NEVER NOTICED IT AS A CHILD, *I now find it interesting that there was a complete absence of discussion about race in our home. Debates would rage about the nature of existence, the relative merits of capitalism and socialism, about whether Dexter Gordon's music took inspiration from Gene Ammons, yet there seemed to be a total avoidance of talk about racial matters. Reflecting on this later in life, I thought perhaps it was because of the multiracial nature of our visitors (Auntie Darrel even had a Japanese boyfriend) or that my parents' views on race were so different that they'd just decided not to inject this conflict into our household. But neither of these explanations seemed sufficient.*

I now believe my father was so determined to make race irrelevant in his own life that he made a conscious decision not to dignify the subject by making it a part of his intellectual existence. He was so secure in his "Africanness" that I think Joe concluded being black would occupy no more important space in his universe than would the ethnicity of a Pole or an Italian.

My mother, on the other hand, was intimidated by the issue of race. Having spent a good deal of her childhood in the Deep South, she both feared and revered white people. I can remember hearing her talk "proper" in the presence of whites, changing her voice. She would affect a nasal intonation that was a dead giveaway for her discomfort. Yet somehow, despite this primal reservation, she made real friends with the mix of folks who came into our home. In truth, Mama was the more genuinely social of my two parents. In a way, Edna and Joe were like the old joke about Democrats and Republicans: he loved the people; she loved people.

Carol was her father's daughter when it came to race and her mother's when it came to people—all people. She simply connected.

Because Chicago's population was close to 30 percent African American[12] and because suburban women were showing a great interest in Carol's candidacy, many political experts might have urged Carol to use her very limited resources to cultivate her base in and around the city. Kgosie Matthews, however, understood his candidate's universal appeal, and it was Matthews who insisted that Carol spend a good deal of time campaigning in the mid- and downstate counties.

Carol made all the usual stops: churches, forums sponsored by professional groups, shopping malls, radio call-in shows. Then there were the more aggressive, Alton Miller–inspired appearances, like the time she showed up at a Senate hearing and confronted Dixon on his Al-come-lately conversion to a national health care policy.

Nor was that the only party she crashed. When the state AFL-CIO endorsed Alan Dixon, Carol, knowing that many rank-and-file members were unhappy with the senator's positions on family leave, occupational safety regulations, and striker replacement legislation, showed up outside the endorsement session wearing a sticker featuring her lifetime labor ratings, which were significantly higher than Dixon's. She got a great deal of positive attention from a hard-ass, mostly male constituency, which the experts were not eager to concede.

Although she understood the AFL-CIO decision, privately, Carol was pissed that the state's largest labor organization didn't have the guts to endorse the candidate who had best represented their interests. From that time forward, between themselves,

---

12   Chicago is now (2010 census) 36.8 percent African American.

Sydney and Carol called the AFL-CIO "the e-i-e-i-o." (With an "oink, oink here and an oink, oink there....")

On the road in the backseat of driver Gus Fordham's town car, littered with newspapers and makeup paraphernalia, never sure where their ever-changing schedule was going to take them, Sydney and Carol found ways to keep laughing. Gus, quiet, white-haired, wise, and grandfatherly, was a man both women held in high esteem, and with Gus smiling indulgently in the front seat, the women had some rollicking good times. "Carol loves to enjoy life," said Sydney. "She has the gift of fun, a wonderful sense of humor. We both knew old Marx Brothers routines. We could throw lines with the best of them. She's so quick."

As lifelong Chicagoans, Carol and Sydney often drew from shared cultural experiences. Generations of Chicago's children knew WGN's noontime television show, *Bozo's Circus*, cohosted by Bozo the Clown and his ringmaster, Uncle Ned. For many years, the program was broadcast live. Then came the legendary event that caused WGN executives to rethink that policy.

The centerpiece of the hour is called the Grand Prize Game. A child is chosen from the audience and stands at the end of a line of buckets; the idea is to get a ping-pong ball into each bucket, and if you make the last one, you win the Grand Prize. Bozo and Uncle Ned would lead the audience in dramatic cheers and groans, according to the performance of the child.

One day, a six-year-old boy got all the way to the fourth bucket—then missed the fifth. Bozo groaned mightily. The kid looked up at the clown and said, "Fuck you, Bozo."

"Now, son!" protested the shocked ringmaster.

"You, too, Uncle Ned," said the child, stomping off the set.

And that became Carol and Sydney's code. Every time some ignorant male did or said something stupid or sexist, one of them would smile sweetly to the other and say, "You, too, Uncle Ned." It was such a pleasant way for a lady to say, "Fuck you, bozo."

On March 8, with the election nine days off, Senator Alan Dixon met his opponents, Al Hofeld and Carol Moseley Braun, for their one and only televised debate. Carol recalled:

I was terrified—terrified. A recorder of deeds, I was going to be up against a millionaire trial lawyer and a United States senator. I know I've been doing speeches for years, I know people say I'm good at it. But I get crazed, my stomach tied in knots. Just because you go ahead and do it doesn't mean you're not terrified!

Under stress, I'd always felt that I was talking faster than my brain was working, so my words would get ahead of where I wanted to be, and I'd be disjointed. That's been a problem. And I worried about it.

Then about two weeks before the debate was to take place, I got this call, it just sort of happened, from a woman named Jessica Woods. She said she was a speech coach and she wanted to help me. I thought: Why not?

But the first time Jessica and I sat down together, I wondered what I was getting into because she didn't talk about speaking at all; she talked about attitudes. She wanted to know how I saw myself. She spoke of the lingering aspect of what being female is all about: the lack of self-confidence. You may know the subject thoroughly, but you aren't altogether comfortable in communicating it.

I'll never forget how Jessica talked about being grounded: put your hands flat on the table, uncross you legs, keep your body aligned—and unplug the negatives. Are you nervous? Yes, I'm nervous. Why are you nervous? Because people will laugh at me; they won't take me seriously; I won't be able to articulate what I have to say.

And she told me, for every negative thought, there is a positive truth, and the one I remember most is: I do have something to say. I have something important to say.

So I went through this whole mind game that Jessica gave me, and it did make a difference. I was nervous; there were no pencils, no paper, no props—just me, the two guys, the lights and cameras. I knew that what I had to say made more sense than anything they would have to say. I put my hands flat on that table, my feet flat on the floor, I stayed grounded, I stayed calm—and I did it.

While ad battles up until this time had the two men slashing at one another, in the debate, Braun and Dixon appeared to gang up on Hofeld.

Hofeld had earlier been forced to admit that he had failed to vote in previous Democratic primaries and had volunteered that, should Dixon be the party's choice, he would not support the senator in the general election. Still feeling that Hofeld was the more serious threat, Dixon invited Carol to explain to the political neophyte why party unity was important. The pleasure was all hers.

Flashing her dazzling smile, Carol said, "Senator Dixon, I think the problem is that he is clueless about how government works, and that's the problem. He's a product of his media handlers." She talked about understanding the responsibilities of government, then said to Dixon, "I've criticized you on your record, Senator, but at least you have a record."

Carol also managed to repeat the theme that she had found very effective in her limited forays around Illinois, that "the Senate has been a locked institution, serving the interests of only the very few for too long," and that it cried out for a voice that would speak for average people, working people.

Clearly, neither the multimillionaire lawyer nor the smug senator flanking Carol Moseley Braun fit that bill. It was, as we say in the television business, "a sound bite with a perfect visual."

Indeed, Dixon's main aim seemed to be to appear "senatorial." He took no shots at Carol, leaving that to Hofeld. Hofeld accused the recorder of deeds of shady ethics in recommending that a multimillion dollar computer contract go to Arthur Andersen & Company because a minority subcontractor in the deal was a friend and contributor to Carol's campaign. Carol called the charge ridiculous and disputed it in detail in the press conference that followed the debate. Reporters who covered the event dropped the matter.

At that same press conference, Dixon was asked how he thought the debate went. The senator chuckled: "I felt pretty good about it. It's terrible how those two people beat up on one another."

A confident Dixon, still not understanding what was alive in the land, failed himself by playing "Al the Pal" for the entire hour, rather than taking this live opportunity to show the people that there was a real man behind the poor actor in his commercials. Instead, he passed the baton to Carol—and she was more than ready to run with it. Hell, this was free TV! Even if she'd had $1 million, she couldn't have bought such an opportunity.

Right from the top, Carol dispensed with what she called "the perception of incompetence." Then, because there was time and opportunity for eyeball-to-eyeball disputation, she was able to score points on each of her opponents. Beyond that—and most important—Carol Moseley Braun from Chicago's South Side got into countless homes where she never would have been invited. And people liked her. Furthermore, it made them *feel good* to like her.

Months later, accompanying Carol to an event in the southern Illinois city of Carbondale, an elderly gentleman told me *his* primary election story: "Our kids were all at the house for dinner on election night, five of 'em, all votin' age, and my wife asks me, 'Well, Henry, who did you finally vote for?'

"And I kinda hesitated, then I told 'em, 'I just went and voted for that black lady from Chicago.'

"And every one of those kids, all at once, said: 'So did I!'"

The debate was on the evening of March 8, a little more than a week before the election. A poll, taken March 3–5 by the *Chicago Sun-Times* and Fox News and released on March 9, had Dixon at 44 percent, Hofeld at 23 percent, and Braun at 22 percent. A poll by the same organization taken after the debate, March 11–12, found Dixon at 41 percent, Braun up to 29 percent, and Hofeld at 22 percent.

Another poll, this one with a small sampling and done for WEEK Television in Peoria, had 37 percent for Dixon, 35 percent for Hofeld, and 18 percent for Braun.

Carol's ad went on television statewide the Friday night before the election—at least it went as wide as $39,000 would send it. Actually, a complete TV buy in the state of Illinois at the time would have cost at least $300,000. Carol sent out her single televised message: "I have one opponent who thinks he owns the Senate seat, one who wants to buy it. I intend to earn my place in the United States Senate."

Interestingly, on this last weekend—even as they were predicting that she would lose—political writers across the state consistently boosted Carol Moseley Braun. Matt Krasnowski of the *State*

Journal-Register in Springfield was typical. After repeating the charges about Kgosie Matthews driving away top campaign staffers, Krasnowski went on to say:

> Whether it be inadequate staffing or funding, Braun was unable to disseminate her message statewide.
>
> In a state campaign one must have credibility, a message and a way of getting that message across. Braun is a highly credible candidate and an impressive speaker. However, the media normally will not follow unless someone leads.
>
> Fortunately for Braun, she received new life at the end of the campaign—when it matters—from the first and only debate between the three candidates. By most accounts she won that encounter by her sharp wit and candor. That has helped fire up her supporters and earn her more headlines.
>
> But is it too little, too late? Probably. But if there is any justice in politics, Braun—one of the brightest policy people in Illinois government—will have another shot at high office.
>
> The likely winner Tuesday will be Dixon.

Said Senator Dixon on Election Day: "I am confident about the results and delighted to see this matter come to an end so that we can go on to the general-election campaign." And when asked about the Republican he would face? "I'm embarrassed to say this [but] I don't know much about Rich Williamson. To my knowledge, I've never had the pleasure of meeting him."

Meeting Richard Williamson was a pleasure that would never be required of Alan Dixon.

By primary Election Day, March 17, 1992, I had yet to meet Carol Moseley Braun. But like many in Illinois, I'd found her candidacy as compelling as it was—I thought—futile.

While I figured victory for Carol was unlikely, a late afternoon call from a television producer friend had sparked my interest. She said exit polls indicated that Carol was showing surprising strength: "If she gets 38 percent of the vote, she could win." Then my friend described an incident that, although isolated, was even more telling in this strange election season. She said, "I couldn't believe the numbers that were coming in, so I stood up on a desk in the newsroom and yelled for quiet and then asked: 'How many people in here voted for Carol Moseley Braun?' Virtually everybody in the room raised their hands."

"The men, too?" I asked.

"The men, too," she said, her voice betraying disbelief.

As the evening hours crawled by, Carol's numbers kept going up. It was fun to watch Chicago's incredulous commentators. No one had predicted this.

Then, around 10 p.m., with the cameras trained on a raised platform at Braun headquarters, Carol appeared—beautiful in a purple dress, her arms raised high, moving with the music, her smile warming the world, surrounded by family and friends, a sea of happy, happy faces.

"No, Carol. Not yet! Go back. Don't embarrass yourself!" I screamed at the television. It was a reflection not only of my own lack of confidence in the candidate—not to mention the electorate—but also my reliance on the station I was watching at the time, which, apparently unable to believe the numbers, had not yet declared Carol the winner. I'd forgotten an old lesson: TV anchors might talk like God—after all, the aura of authority is a job requirement—but all they really can convey is whatever is set before them or whispered into their earpieces.

Thus, what neither the guy with the microphone nor I knew was that someone more important had recognized reality. Alan Dixon, after 40 years of elections, knew a dead candidacy when he saw it. Moments before she appeared, Senator Dixon had called Carol and conceded.

Later, Carol told me that March 17, 1992, was the most exciting, tension-filled day she'd lived through to date. It was so excruciating, the candidate hid from it at her favorite beauty salon.

I couldn't afford to do the state fly-around that was later available to me, so after breakfast at Lou Mitchell's with Rev. Addie Wyatt, the pastor of my church, the Vernon Park Church of God, and Kay Clement, I just visited a few polling places and a couple of ward offices. I went to see Senator Ethel Alexander, my mentor during the Springfield years and the 20th Ward committeeman. At the time, Ethel and Dorothy Tillman were the only female ward committeemen in the city. Ethel just gave me a hug and said, "Baby girl, everything will be just fine." That's Ethel's name for me, "Baby girl."

Then I went to my salon, Van Cleef. I basically locked myself up with the hairdresser, the manicurist, a masseuse, a stereo that played nothing but soothing classical music, and people who talked about hairstyles and fashion, not politics. I was at Van Cleef from one o'clock in the afternoon until about six. Then, along with Sydney [Faye-Petrizzi] and Gus [Fordham], I drove home to change. Nobody was there; the house was dark. I was getting ready for whatever was going to happen. It was like the quiet before the storm.

Carol, like many women, viewed the beauty shop as a sanctuary. It's a place where girls can be girls, much like boys are boys in a locker room. Although Carol never discussed this, others affirm that the beauty salon takes on an added social dimension in the African American community, serving as a hot spot for community activism and information. Like locker rooms, beauty salons are also culturally dictated gender reinforcements: He gets strong; she gets beautiful. Politically, Carol was a feminist, and she would cheer the fact that women now are choosing the gym and the athletic field as well, yet in every traditional way, Carol nurtured her femininity.

March 17, 1992, found the Carol Moseley Braun campaign underfunded, understaffed, and overwhelmed. "Chaos" was the first word that popped into the minds of those describing what would become a historic day. Kgosie Matthews, who had never before prepared an election headquarters for whatever might come to pass, relied heavily on scheduler Desiree Tate and fundraiser Velma Wilson.

Headquarters was at the McCormick Center Hotel, just west of sprawling McCormick Place, the huge convention complex that squats beside Lake Michigan. As Chicago hotels go, the McCormick was tacky and ill suited for large crowds (and since demolished, by the way). If you were writing the movie, however, this hotel, roughly as disheveled as the Braun campaign, would be the perfect location for the finale—or "nightmare," as Desiree Tate described March 17. Fortunately, this was to be one of those nightmares where the dreamer spends most of the time falling off the cliff but ultimately lands in a pile of life-sustaining feathers (or the arms of her lover, as most staffers would have guessed on this night of nights).

What Desiree remembers, however, is the falling-off-the-cliff part.

Fundamental to the problem was that virtually everyone close to the campaign, as hard as they'd worked—and even though each and every one of them had felt "maybe-we-can-do-it" flashes—really believed Alan Dixon was unbeatable. Thus, there was little preparation for the momentous event election night was to become.

"I guess we started to realize at about two o'clock in the afternoon that the vote was maybe going to be close," Desiree recalled.

"We didn't have any money, so Des and I went over to the hotel to decorate the party room ourselves," Velma Wilson added. The two women were partnered for most of what would be an astonishing 24 hours.

"Then, at about two," Desiree recalled, "CNN phoned. I said to Velma, 'These people don't ever call us. What's going on?'"("What's going on?" would become a litany for Braun supporters during this long day).

Velma continued: "Then, at about three, someone said, 'Ted Kennedy is on the phone.' Ted Kennedy? Then Paul Simon. I said, 'Des, something's going on. Why are these guys calling? They get those exit polls. Des, this girl's gonna win this thing! She's gonna win!' Des said: 'Don't jinx her.'"

"Then *Good Morning America* called!" remembered Desiree.

Naturally, each major local media outlet had assigned a reporter to cover Braun headquarters, so some influx of press was expected at around 3 p.m., in time for TV to prepare for early newscasts. But with the sudden perception that history might be in the making, by four o'clock in the afternoon, the media influx had turned to a flood tide. Peoria said hello to London—and the next question was, "Where do we set up?"

"Reporters were calling; people were beginning to arrive," Velma recalled. "And at that point, the woman who was currently our press secretary just freaked out. She was frightened and overwhelmed. I can't even remember her name."

"Her name was Celia," offered Desiree. "She joined the campaign maybe a month and a half out to be Alton Miller's assistant. Celia was there not more than three days when Alton just left."

Kgosie, Des, and Velma went to visit the young press secretary where she was holed up in her hotel room.

"Celia literally broke down. There was this sea of people coming in; she said she couldn't set up interviews. It was not something she'd ever dealt with. She stomped. She screamed. She threw things. She wouldn't come out of her room," Des remembered, shaking her head.

If there is ever a key individual in a campaign, it's the person assigned to connect the candidate to the press. However, because Kgosie was not comfortable with a proactive press secretary, Celia had been required to do little beyond handling sporadic calls and occasionally accompanying the candidate. Certainly she was not prepared to coordinate coverage of a breaking national story; but then, nobody was.

An important part of a press secretary's job is to know each and every reporter and producer on the beat, understand his or her needs, and provide for them. Beyond that, in a case like this when national media suddenly becomes involved, an experienced press secretary would still be prepared because he or she would be intimately familiar with the news organizations present and understand their priorities. National media people expect to be "handled," (then, of course, they complain about being handled).

On the night of March 17, press people were desperately searching for handlers.

Velma, remembering the media's needs for Harold Washington's election night, hastily set up a workroom for the print people and a separate one for television interviews.

"Kgosie and I started working with the press," said Des. "But there wasn't much we could do, so we just kind of went with the flow and made a lot of people mad. They were like, 'I can't believe you all don't have a press secretary! *Who's in charge here?*'"

No one was worried about Carol. Sydney, virtually alone in her confidence about the outcome of the election, had shepherded the candidate from place to place, ending with those comforting hours at the beauty salon. Carol had said she didn't want to know about the progress of the vote. Still, at about 4 p.m., Carol called Sue Purrington, who was following events statewide from the Loop office of NOW.

Sue couldn't quite believe it herself, but the evidence was mounting that she was about to be a part of a signal achievement in a distinguished career devoted to promoting the interests of women. She remembered, "I'd had a call at about 1:30 from a friend with a government agency. She said, 'You didn't hear this from me, but you wouldn't believe what the numbers are.' I said, 'Yeah, but that's got to be Cook County.' 'No,' she said. 'It's all over the state!'"

Still, when Carol phoned that afternoon, Sue opted for caution. She knew how flaky early numbers could be, and she didn't want to foster false hope in the candidate.

"Can you tell me what's happening?" Carol asked the woman she'd trusted in all of her campaigns.

"I told her what we'd said all along: that the campaign was fluid, that it could go either way, but that we were very optimistic. Then I hung up the phone and said, 'I'm not sure what's going on out there!'"

Carol arrived at the McCormick Center Hotel at 8 p.m. "I saw her coming down the hall," said close friend Barbara Samuels. "And it was one of those things where you don't say anything but speak volumes. I walked toward her, and we just looked; then we grabbed each other and started crying. We really didn't know for sure yet what was going to happen. I went downstairs with my eyes all puffed up and someone said, 'What happened to you?' And I said, 'I just saw Carol,' and they said, 'Oh, God!'"

The tension was almost unbearable.

The campaign hadn't had enough money to rent the penthouse, so Carol and her family and close friends were gathered in one of the hotel's smaller suites. Carol recalled:

Larry Shapiro was in charge of the numbers. And he's very good. But this was his first statewide race, and he was nervous. He wanted hard numbers, and we just didn't have the capacity to know the downstate numbers right off the bat. But I knew Dixon would have up-to-date information. So when he called, that was it for me. And everyone went crazy, KA-RAAZY! Matt was so happy, so happy! It was phenomenal. And I can remember feeling this catharsis, like this great weight had been lifted from me.

Carol set down the telephone after speaking to the cool but courteous Alan Dixon. As she turned, her smile lit up the room. Joy and adrenaline fairly burst from the eyes of the small group of "true believers," as she called them, who surrounded her. Then the new US Democratic senator-elect raised her chin ever so slightly, pointed to the door, and said to her happy band, "Let's go."

Barbara Samuels saw Carol once again, this time on the way to deliver her acceptance speech. "She was surrounded by these guys, [her brother] Joey's friends who were off-duty police officers working as bodyguards. She was such a little thing, looking almost waiflike because she was so scared, so keyed up, and I knew she was nervous about her speech. We gave each other the thumbs-up. I said, 'Don't worry. It'll be OK.' She said, 'Oh, God. I hope so.'"

The arrangements Velma Wilson had made to keep the burgeoning crowd back from the platform did not work. The ropes and stanchions were trampled the minute the new Democratic nominee for the US Senate appeared in the room. Someone managed to lift Edna Moseley's wheelchair up on the stage so that she could be near her daughter, but Carol's son, Matthew, was crowded off the platform, and so was Barbara Samuels. Surrounded by her family, old friends, and more than a few very new friends, Carol, her eyes shining, reached the microphone and said, "Praise the Lord!" Then she delivered her acceptance speech:

> This is not just a victory for me; it is a victory for all the people of Illinois and of this nation who want to believe that the system works, that the American Dream can be realized, and that amidst the

> controversy and the scandal, the great promise of
> democracy still remains in the hearts of men and
> women everywhere....
>
> I am grateful to every citizen of Illinois for the
> opportunity—the gift that has been given to me—
> the chance to contest for a seat in the United States
> Senate; and to that small handful of people who
> believed from the very beginning that you can still
> dream the American Dream.

Hiring a band for the occasion had been out of the question, but someone put on a recording of "That's What Friends Are For." Everyone clasped hands and sang, and tears flowed freely from "that handful of people" who, truth be told, had never been sure that this particular American Dream could ever really come true, certainly not in their lifetimes.

Barbara Samuels was happy to be in the audience. "I wanted to see her. The look on her face was just like she was ready to jump out of her skin. She was so excited. I was standing there, and she looked at me. And that smile—it was so great, so intimate, so personal. Just a wonderful, wonderful moment."

No one who worked on the Carol Moseley Braun primary campaign is quite sure when the "night of" ended and the "morning after" began. At 3 a.m., Desiree and Velma drove back to the darkened Randolph Street headquarters to put together the next day's schedule "because Kgosie had all this stuff he wanted her to do. And the first thing was an El stop—at 6:15 a.m."

Larry Shapiro heard Kgosie's plan at around midnight. He said, "I had to laugh. Carol hates early mornings. I can't tell you the campaigns I'd scheduled her—not this one, but in previous campaigns—for El stops, and they would either be x-ed out or she'd get there as the last commuter was getting on the train. So we were partying, and there was no way anyone was going to bed for another two or three hours, and I was saying, 'Oh, yeah, Braun, sure. You're gonna get up and do a 6 a.m. El stop, sure.'

"But she did it. It was a great idea and got wonderful coverage, front pages all over the country, and all those morning

shows—pictures of Carol laughing and hugging crowds of delighted people. I was back at the McCormick arranging a press conference for later that morning when the reporters started straggling
in, the ones who had been with her earlier. They said they'd never
seen anything like it, like the affection and spontaneity from the
people Carol met everywhere she went."

Sue Purrington had collapsed in a room off the official suite at
about 3 a.m.: "I was too tired to drive home. But the phone in the
room was ringing all night: somebody from DC to congratulate
Carol, somebody who'd just arrived home from Europe and wanted to talk to her. Finally, about 6:30 in the morning, I turned on
the television—and there was Carol, so fresh, looking very girlish,
laughing happily in that infectious way she has. Twenty minutes
later, she walked back into the room."

"Now we had a few quiet moments together," Sue recalled,
"just the two of us. We talked about when we first met and where
we were now and that this was the right spot to be in at the right
time. Then Carol said, 'Now that we're alone, did you really think
we could do it?'

"I said, 'Carol, quite frankly, I didn't think we could pull this off.'
"And Carol said: 'Neither did I.'"

The Chicago Tribune, March 25, 1992
"Carol Moseley Braun ran a multimillion-dollar race.
It just wasn't her money, it was ours."
                    —David Axelrod, media consultant for Al Hofeld

When the final numbers were in, Carol got 38 percent of the
vote to Dixon's 35 percent and Hofeld's 27 percent. Carol spent
a little over $400,000 and Hofeld, $4.5 million, mostly his own
money. The strategy dictated by necessity—letting the two guys
beat up on each other while Carol remained, as Axelrod put it,
"under the fray"—worked.

Conventional wisdom, which the press bought into right up
until the moment of truth, dictated that the two challengers would
split the anti-incumbent vote, allowing Dixon to waltz into his
third term. But the mostly male core of analysts didn't figure on the

sustained anger of women that resulted from Dixon's vote to confirm Judge Thomas. Analysts believed Democratic women turned out in force and significant numbers of Republican women took Democratic ballots in an effort to eliminate Dixon. But the gender spillover went beyond the Senate matchup. For example, in Cook County, where women ran in 19 contested races, 14 were won by the female candidate.

Virtually overlooked in the postgame commentary was the fundamental role African Americans played in the outcome, not least due to voter registration efforts that included a young South Sider named Barack Obama. As one political observer said:

> The black vote was Carol's "Michael Jordan" and the women's vote was her "John Paxson." You're not even in the game without Jordan, but Paxson will give you the three-pointer to win it. Without the African American foundation, the women's vote, surprising as it was, would not have guaranteed Carol's victory. That's why Carol was the perfect candidate for the situation. Had a white woman run, the conventional wisdom would almost certainly have prevailed, and Dixon would be on his way back to Washington.

Still, Carol showed remarkable strength statewide, winning Chicago with 51 percent, suburban Cook County with 40 percent, and the collar counties with 38 percent. Dixon took the 96 downstate counties, as expected, with 49 percent of the vote, but Hofeld's 31 percent and Carol's 20 percent combined to deny Dixon the majority downstate that would have ensured his reelection. This was the crux of David Axelrod's widely quoted analysis: southern Illinois was where Hofeld's statewide TV ad buys paid off. For Carol Moseley Braun.

Velma Wilson had a pleasant postelection surprise. "The day after Carol won, I was in the office, and four or five people 'just stopped by' to drop off $1,000 checks. People we'd never heard of before!"

"After just a week or so, we began to get two to three thousand pieces of mail a day," said Desiree Tate, who continued as Carol's scheduler. "Everybody wanted her. And early on, we couldn't sell her to anybody! Lots of these were press requests, and for all intents and purposes, our press secretary was no longer functioning. She took a week's vacation right after the primary!"

Virtually every national print and television organization, and not a few from abroad, wanted the woman who was positioned to make history in Illinois. Just like in the fairy tales she had enjoyed so much as a child, in a twinkling, Carol Moseley Braun became a star, an instant celebrity. Money started rolling in. Everybody wanted her, and there was no press secretary, so once again, the indomitable Sydney Faye-Petrizzi, who had been Carol's "body person," accompanying her everywhere, came back off the road to handle the media.

It was stunning to me, walking down the street and having people yell, "Carol! Hey! We love you, Carol!" It happened overnight, and frankly, it was just a little scary.

I am an affectionate person, and hugging and kissing people I know well and care about are natural expressions for me. But now, perfect strangers, people who would give a male candidate a handshake, would think nothing of grabbing me and giving me a kiss. And the last thing in the world you want to do is rebuff them.

Then, it wasn't long after I became a "celebrity" that I began to get heat from my Republican opponent, Richard Williamson— echoed, I might add, by the press—for being a mere "celebrity"! And that's ironic because at the same time, I was also criticized by several political professionals for not getting right out on a national fundraising tour in order to capitalize on my newfound—ta-da— celebrity!" [Celebrity being a lame political put-down that you will recall was used by Republicans in 2008 against Obama.]

But I wanted to catch my breath after the primary, and Kgosie and I had to put together a new organization. I wasn't going to win a seat in the United States Senate by kissing everybody in Illinois.

Because, you see, the primary election reality was that Dixon had been soft, women had been angry, and Al Hofeld had been rich enough to help Carol out, however unintentionally.

It was a historic victory, but not because she had won by a landslide. Now the campaign had to recognize some hard demographic facts. African Americans constituted 13.5 percent of the statewide voting-age population and Latinos about 7 percent. To win, and assuming that Carol could expect 95 percent of the black vote, she would still need two-thirds of the Latinos and 41 percent of the white vote.

Was the state of Illinois ready to send a black female senator to Washington? There was absolutely no way to make that assumption.

Carol later told me that this cold reality struck her as she was singing and swaying to the music on primary election night:

Maybe it's a woman thing, that old-fashioned practicality, or maybe it's just me, looking for the next obstacle. But there I was, with this huge victory and people around me were shouting, "Yeah! This is wonderful!" And all I could think about was what it was going to take to translate this moment into an actual Senate seat.

PART II

Carol Moseley Braun represents the redemption of the American political process.

—SENATOR TOM HARKIN, IOWA

CHAPTER 5

Kgosie

ALTHOUGH CAROL HAD AGREED on the book project in April 1992, it had become clear that I was not going to get the necessary access without Kgosie Matthews's imprimatur. As for the ease of securing an audience with him? Well, he might as well have been an African prince!

During my repeated visits to campaign headquarters—now occupying the ninth floor of an under-rehab art deco building that towered over the rumbling El tracks at Lake and Wells—I had become well acquainted with the attractive young woman I thought of as Kgosie's doorkeeper. Elizabeth Nicholson is 5'9" with those sweet Irish looks—a faint sprinkling of freckles, long, light red hair, and a ready smile. Liz also had a charming way of telling me no and inviting me to keep trying. Then one morning she called and said, "Yes."

Matthews escorted me into his office, where Carol's brand-new, 29-year-old press secretary, David Eichenbaum, sat at a conference table, clearly prepared to discuss some campaign problem other than mine. Said Matthews to Eichenbaum, startling us both: "This is Jeannie Morris. She'll be assisting you in the press office." The young press aide, a slender six-footer who seemed mature beyond his years, gave me a look I was to see again and again in the course of the campaign. He gazed blankly at me, blue eyes wide and mouth slightly open. But behind the mask, the question almost surely was, "What the hell is going on here?"

The mental process behind Eichenbaum's blank expression, I would learn, was this: whatever is presented, the first reaction will be neutral and unsurprised. Meanwhile, an excellent brain will analyze the situation at hand and, harnessing well-developed verbal skills, will devise a response that may or may not have anything whatsoever to do with what the hell is going on.

Eichenbaum had come to Chicago directly from the recently defunct Paul Tsongas presidential campaign. Before that, he had served as press secretary for Connecticut congresswoman Rosa DeLauro, and before that, as press aide to Senator Carl Levin, and before that, David Eichenbaum had been a struggling actor. He'd crammed in a lot of experience since graduating from Michigan University, where he had majored in English literature. Acting and writing would serve Eichenbaum well on the Carol Moseley Braun campaign.

In this case, however, the press secretary didn't get much beyond, "Oh? Hello." All that David Eichenbaum knew about me was that Carol was cooperating with me on a book. And he thought that was a very bad idea.[13]

Now I had the campaign manager's tacit endorsement. But gaining the confidence of the senior staff would be another challenge altogether. Unlike Carol and me—and even Kgosie—these recently recruited and more experienced politicos knew what kinds of things can happen in a major campaign, and they didn't like the idea of someone hanging around taking notes.

I was a reporter by profession, of course, but I was here because I'd convinced the candidate that her historic campaign must be recorded: *not reported* but recorded. Although we agreed that some future book might come of this, I was thrilled to dive in and swim upstream without any promise of compensation. My husband had been a professional football player—a Chicago Bear—and living the untold stories of the NFL subculture, along with my

---

13 Eichenbaum is today a leading Democratic strategist and ad maker, having helped elect governors, US senators, and members of Congress. He was communications director for the Democratic National Committee for Bill Clinton and also advises campaigns overseas.

compulsion to write, had led me into sports. But my favorite game had *always* been politics, seeded as far back as early adolescence when I joined my mother in the 1950 California Senate campaign for Helen Gahagan Douglas.

Helen! A woman! Running for the US Senate!

Douglas's opponent was a man my mom called "Tricky Dick," although his signs read "Richard Nixon." The Nixon campaign relentlessly painted our candidate "pink," which is, of course, a lighter shade of "red"—not a great color during what would become the McCarthy era. Nixon won by 20 points, but I was hooked. Now, decades later, I was all in, my political/feminist instincts fully charged. But as you will read, despite the fact that Carol consented to let me pursue my ambition—and I was physically present throughout the campaign—like most involved, I was at times inside, other times outside, yet always the observer, taking those notes.

June 4, 1992. Washington, DC.
The single purpose on this day was to raise money. "After that primary," Carol laughed, "I'm like Scarlett O'Hara. 'As God is my witness, I'll never be hungry again!'"

This would be the first full day Carol and I would spend together, and I was to learn a great deal about money and politics and about the multilayered individual that is Carol Moseley Braun.

I arrived ahead of Carol at La Colline, a Capitol Hill restaurant where she was scheduled to meet a dozen or so representatives of federal employees' unions in a private dining room. Their political action committee (PAC) was called the Fair Coalition.

The room held a somewhat uneasy assortment of people who were sipping juice and struggling to make conversation. But the atmosphere shifted immediately when Carol walked in. Sensing that no one was really in charge here, she seemed to naturally assume the role of hostess.

Seating ourselves around a large table, Carol suggested that everyone introduce themselves. Then, unlike so many featured guests who tend to disdain food (making others, who just might be hungry, uncomfortable), Carol attacked her meal with gusto, all the while telling us about her background, explaining how her positions on various issues grew from her experience, and inviting comments and questions—which she got. Rather than simply attending a lunch to hear yet another candidate, these people got to know Carol, and, I'm sure, most left feeling that she learned about them and their concerns as well.

In terms of age, gender, and race, these union reps from the government's crazy-quilt bureaucracy were an unusually mixed group, and when Carol said, "I see my candidacy as the maturing of democracy," there was an appreciative assent: Yes, indeed. And about time.

Carol had demonstrated the intimate, informal, and inclusive style that is natural to her but that frequently catches people off guard. I was to see this again and again: first surprise, then pleasure, and then they were hers. In this case, by the end of lunch, it was clear that the check would be in the mail.

When we left the restaurant, a light rain was falling, and Tina Stoll, the Washington political fundraising consultant who had organized this visit, apologized for not having brought an umbrella. Carol was apparently unfazed by the rain. I was to learn that, while Carol was meticulous about her appearance, she was never overtly fussy. Her hair was in a weatherproof bun, her white linen suit fashionably wrinkled. She'd been on the run since a dawn appearance on *Good Morning America* in New York. The question to Tina was: where to next?

The answer was that we needed a taxi or we were not going anywhere. And standing between our little group and the taxi stand was the cowboy senator from Wyoming who had so arrogantly belittled Anita Hill during the Thomas hearings—Alan Simpson. Tina asked Carol if she'd like to meet Senator Simpson. Now, you might think that as an aspirant to that exclusive club up the avenue, Carol would have chosen to be introduced to one of its senior members. But, no. Carol just looked at Tina with a raised eyebrow that said, "What? And unmake my day?"

In the cab, Tina commenced to brief Carol on our next stop, an appointment with a PAC man who represented a group of the country's independent insurance companies. Tina got a few words past her introductory sentence when Carol exploded. "Tina, I read the material you gave me. I don't want to see him. I'm against virtually all the positions these guys hold. We had constant trouble with them in the Illinois legislature. They *want* health care to be expensive...." The candidate was on a tear.

Tina had been trying to interrupt. Clearly, she thought Carol had something to learn about PAC money. "Just hear me out," she said. "As an individual, this guy is a Democrat at heart. Richard Williamson's been in to see him, has courted him on the issues, but he thinks you're gonna win. He doesn't want to be on your bad side. And if he possibly can, if he can find a way, he'll support you."

Grudgingly willing but unconvinced, Carol entered the offices of the Independent Insurance Agents of America.

Women have some choices that men do not, or think they do not have, when it comes to meetings of this kind. Most men tend to grab the conversational lead, and Carol let that happen when it served her purpose. She could then assume the initiative whenever she wished—or not at all.

So the fact was, while Carol was supposed to be going into this meeting to sell her*self*, she assumed the attitude that *he* was the one who had to do the selling. Although Carol complained, and legitimately so, about the "presumption of incompetence," her advantage was that people who met her for the first time were burdened with a whole portfolio of assumptions, and her reality inevitably knocked them off balance. This was to be one of those times.

This PAC man demonstrated several attitudes we were often to see. First, he was at pains to let Carol know that he grew up in a big city and a poor neighborhood—"almost a ghetto," he said.

I'm sure that would not have been part of his opening remarks to Senator Simpson.

When he asked Carol how her race was going, she responded by telling him about her opponent's first series of radio ads that were both racist and sexist—"$147,000 worth," she said, throwing in a number because, of course, numbers attach to most everything in Washington. "The ads are totally irresponsible," Carol added.

"Irresponsible?" countered the PAC man, who was, by now, at least talking like a Democrat. "This game can get vicious. Are there any pictures of you with Winnie Mandela? These guys are going to have you connected with those beatings in South Africa before they're through!"

PAC man then went on to lecture Carol about the Senate, which, he said, lately had not been displaying the comity that had once been its hallmark. "When you come to the Senate," he said, "you are going to have to climb a mountain of condescension."

I was glad no one was paying any attention to me because I couldn't suppress a smile. Condescension? So far, this conversation had been rife with it! Of course, Washington itself is the Capital of Condescension, a city that condescends to its own country—to a whole world, for that matter.

But Carol had her own way of dealing with this, so accustomed was she. Laughing, she said, "Oh, I know all about condescension." And she launched into a story about her freshman year in the Illinois legislature and her dealings with an old-time downstate rep named Webber Borges.

"I'd written a bill that had to do with family support services, and, not yet understanding how the system worked, I did all my research, then created an analysis for each member of the House demonstrating the individual benefits for his district. It was a huge job, and when I was finished, I put each individual report in an envelope and personally visited every member."

"When I delivered his," Carol continued, "Webber Borges patted me on the hand and said, 'Very good, honey, but this don't have a chance.'"

PAC man laughed. Carol was a perfect mimic.

"Well, my bill passed. And some time later, the old gentleman came by my desk and said he'd voted 'no' as he'd promised, but he'd almost changed his mind because, he said, I was 'the second-nicest colored lady he'd ever met. I would say you're the first,' he went on, 'but the first nicest has been working for my family for 40 years!'" Now Carol laughed heartily.

This had been her longest contribution to the conversation, and she'd worked up quite a twinkle by this time. "Oh, yes," she concluded, "I know all about condescension."

PAC man laughed, too, but I don't think he really got it.

As we stood to leave, he said, "You noticed, Carol, that we didn't get into specifics here?"

"I noticed," Carol replied.

"May I say your door will always be open?"

"That you may," Carol smiled.

It was an interesting meeting, but as we left, I couldn't help thinking: Is this the way it starts—money baits the trap—the incestuous, ravenous maw defined by the Washington Beltway? Is this the way those who had lived so firmly outside its influence are gradually sucked in?

I was excited about the last event of the day, a celebration held by Harriett Woods and her National Women's Political Caucus to introduce many of the candidates for Congress to Washington. Just that week, California Democrats had nominated Barbara Boxer and Dianne Feinstein. Patty Murray, a Democratic contender in Washington, was to attend as well. Geographically, this was an impressive spread: Northwest, Far West, Midwest. Women were on the political move across the country.

At the reception, the sense of history infused the room. Assuming the quarterback position for the evening was the diminutive (until she started talking) Senator Barbara Mikulski of Maryland. A box had been provided for the senator to stand on so that she was respectably visible over the podium. Nodding to candidate Barbara Boxer, just below her, Mikulski declared, "For anyone under 5'4", boy, have I got a platform for you!"

Later, when a photographer hired to record this historic event asked, "Will you girls bunch closer together?" Woods responded, "These are not girls; these are senators." And when another pleaded, "Would you mind moving back?" Mikulski clenched her powerful little fist and said, "You bet your life we mind. We are never moving back."

When introduced, Carol received a tremendous ovation. The first of the women candidates to win nomination, she had also deposed one of the two Democratic senators who voted to confirm Justice Thomas, a fact that helped raise her national profile. But unlike the women who preceded her on the platform, Carol, as was her custom, did not dwell on the Thomas hearings except to point out that what energized her campaign was less the issues of the inquisition than the nature of the senator-inquisitors and the obvious fact that "they do not represent us! We represent vitality, honesty, and a new energy! That's what this campaign is about. There is strength in diversity, and we haven't yet begun to tap it!"

Cheers and applause. They loved her.

And so did the press. Since we were in the heart of the capital, it was reasonable to assume that the dozens of people with microphones and notepads seeking interviews with Carol after her speech were members of what I'd heard called the "jaded Washington press corps." I know jaded. It means that you dread covering the assigned person or event because you know there will be the same old questions, the same old bullshit answers, and you are going to have to find a new angle, a fresh way to make a tired story interesting.

Rather than listening to the candidate, I stood behind Carol and watched the reporters. Clearly, these folks had left their "jade" at home. Their faces were intent, their bodies were energized, and they smiled a lot. These people were interested in what Carol had to say. Carol Moseley Braun was a living, breathing, fresh angle.

On the way to Washington National Airport (now called Ronald Reagan Washington National Airport) for our return trip to Chicago, I rode in a cab with Kgosie Matthews. I would have been astonished at the time (not to mention discouraged) to know that this would be one of only two private meetings he and I would have during the course of the campaign.

Kgosie was worried about a profile the *Chicago Tribune* was working on. He said a reporter named Frank James had been asking his friends and former associates a lot of questions. I wondered what Matthews was worried about. The only possibly damaging rumor abroad about the campaign manager was that he was sleeping with the candidate.

Back in Illinois, the $147,000 in ad buys Carol had discussed with the Washington PAC man was creating quite a stir. Williamson's first ad was to run for two weeks on 26 radio stations statewide. Using a female announcer, it said:

You've heard a lot about Carol Moseley Braun.

But just who is she?

She's part of the Chicago Democratic machine.

She was Harold Washington's voice as a state legislator in Springfield.

While there, she voted two times to raise her own pay, twice to raise her own pension and to raise your taxes 11 times.

She voted against penalizing welfare cheats, and she even opposes the death penalty.

Who is Carol Moseley Braun?

Well, she was a Jesse Jackson delegate to the national convention.

She's given lucrative contracts to former campaign supporters.

And she's run in 14 elections in 14 years.

Who is Carol Moseley Braun?

Well, after all else is taken away, she's just another big-government, far-left Democrat.

Don't be fooled....

Carol Moseley Braun: just another liberal machine politician.

Paid for by the National Republican Senatorial Committee.

WILLIAMSON: Authorized by Williamson for Senate.

This early campaign attack ad was arguably not only the first but also the biggest mistake the Williamson campaign would make. It set about defining Carol before revealing anything about Richard Williamson, except, perhaps, that he was mean-spirited. The Republican candidate's press secretary, David Fields, claimed that such action was necessary because Carol had been "on a honeymoon with the press."

Rather than disrupting the honeymoon, press reaction to the obvious racial overtones of the ad forced reporters to snuggle a little closer to Carol.

At the *Chicago Sun-Times*, Lynn Sweet wrote: "Braun has supported a variety of liberal candidates—male, female, black, white and Hispanic. By highlighting only her association with two blacks,

Washington and Jackson, the latter unpopular among Illinois whites, Williamson's ad exploits race."

Basil Talbott, the Washington correspondent for the *Sun-Times* and an old Chicago political hand, pointed out that it was impossible to be "part of the Chicago Democratic machine" and linked to Jesse Jackson or Harold Washington, both of whom "campaigned ardently against that machine." Also, in reference to the "liberal tag," Talbott reminded his readers, "insofar as the machine had an ideology, it was conservative."

Mark Miller of *Crain's Chicago Business* wrote that "Carol Moseley Braun did vote for at least 11 tax increases in her 10 years in the Illinois House of Representatives," each and every one of them "proposed in the early 1980s by former Gov. Jim Thompson—a Republican in name if not in deed, the last I heard."

The saturation of the ads, and subsequent print follow-up, allowed Carol to point out not only that the taxes cited were a Republican governor's tax increases but also that they were caused by Reagan administration cutbacks (loftily called, "the New Federalism") that shifted responsibility for many programs to the states and cities—and Williamson had been a member of the inner circle that designed those policies.

While it was not inaccurate to call Carol a "traditional liberal," the Williamson ad gave the Braun campaign an opportunity to say that calling her "a far-left Democrat" was wrong. The campaign responded: "Carol is talking about a number of economic proposals that would be considered to be far from liberal but are very middle of the road and moderate: investment tax credits, enterprise zones, and targeted capital gains cuts."

The lasting damage to the Williamson campaign was due less to the substance of the ad than to its tenor, especially the linkage to Washington and Jackson, those "scary black men" from Chicago. People were sick of negative campaigning. "Williamson is like the mediocre general who fails to understand when strategies of the past begin to fail the present," editorialized the Decatur *Herald & Review*.

The Braun camp had not yet aired any ads and would not put up a negative commercial until the late innings of the campaign when an old error would surface, tightening the score and forcing Carol to limber up her hardball.

On Friday, June 26, 1992, *Chicago Sun-Times* gossip columnist Michael Sneed ran the following item:

> Creative wallpaper in the Kgosie korner: A friendly memo attached to a wall Thursday at the headquarters of Dem senatorial candidate Carol Moseley Braun seeking suggestions to improve the campaign netted one big inscription: Please FIRE campaign manager Kgosie Matthews.
>
> History: Braun's former press secretary Al Miller quit, reportedly over Matthews' "style," just before the primary election. Braun has told insiders she considers Matthews "my savior." But according to a source close to Braun: "Nothing could be further from the truth. This guy could alienate Eleanor Roosevelt." Stay tuned.

Carol became convinced, undoubtedly by Kgosie, that her ever-faithful Sydney Faye-Petrizzi had not only put the note on the bulletin board but had also leaked the item to Sneed. This had to have been a painful conclusion for Carol to draw. No one had been more loyal than Sydney, and Carol surely remembered the long, strenuous hours and exhausted laughs they'd shared during the primary. They were true girlfriends.

Carol heard about Sneed's column from Barbara Samuels, who got the news from Sydney. Kgosie had been accompanying Carol on what Carol called her "forced march," a fundraising trip that included stops in eight cities, concluding in Los Angeles with an event held by the Hollywood Women's Political Caucus and headlined by Goldie Hawn and Barbra Streisand. Barbara Samuels met Carol and Kgosie in LA while Sydney was back in Chicago.

"I picked up the papers at 6 a.m. and saw the 'Fire Kgosie' item," Sydney later recalled. "I waited as long as I could. I guess it was about 5 in the morning in LA when I called Barbara at the Beverly Wilshire. I said, 'Listen, there's an item in Sneed. I'm calling you because I want you to hear it from me so you can be the one to tell Carol.' And I read it.

"'Holy shit!' Barbara said, when I got to the 'fire Kgosie' part. 'This is not going to be a good day.' And it wasn't."

"I can't pretend about this. I hated Kgosie from the first time I laid eyes on him," Sydney confessed, "but I would never have done anything to hurt Carol's candidacy."

Sydney had been the first campaign aide to feel the tension created by the unique relationship between Carol and Kgosie. She recalled, "It was Gus [Fordham], so loyal and wise, who kept me straight. With Gus driving, the three of us would be in the car for hours—me working on the schedule, going over the mail, handing Carol the appropriate briefing papers—or giving her wet wipes so she could clean up after reading six newspapers. That part was great.

"But Carol would constantly be on the phone with Kgosie, and it was clear something was up. I'd say, 'Gus, what the hell is going on?' I could tell she wanted the relationship, but I got nothing but negative energy about her *from him.*

"I would get these feelings, 'that son of a bitch!' and Gus would say, 'Sydney, don't fool with it.' Gus knew that I would fall on a spear for Carol—as would he. But Gus also taught me that 'you can't interfere between a man and a woman.'"

"Several times, Kgosie got out of line with me," said Sydney, continuing her version of events. "And a couple of those times, I called it to Carol's attention and she intervened. After one confrontation, Carol had a fight with Kgosie over me, and she called me late that night and she told me that she was going to take care of it, that she loved me, not to worry about it. This was right before Election Day, in the primary. She started crying on the phone. It was a very stressful time.

"All along, I would tell her, 'It doesn't matter what anyone says or what he does to me, Carol. I think he's an asshole, but I won't leave you, no matter what. Kgosie can't hurt me enough to make me leave.'

"But Carol could."

"On Sunday, June 28," Sydney continued, "Carol and I were scheduled to go together to the national NOW convention, currently in session at the Chicago Hilton, and then to march in the Gay Pride Parade. Now it was Friday afternoon, the day the item appeared in Sneed, and I was in the office, working on Carol's files, and I was not happy," said Sydney. "I'd given up $100,000 a year, worked for nothing from October until January; we'd won this great victory, and now—when things were really going great—I'd been separated from my best friend.

"The phone rang, and Desiree Tate said it was Carol for me from California. I picked up the call in the office Carol and I shared. 'Hey!' I said. 'What's up?'

"Carol said: 'I just want you to know that I know you have been a continuous source of leaks to the media and that you are on notice. If you do one more thing, you're out.'

"I couldn't react. I was numb. I couldn't believe that she had said this to me. Then I got hysterical. Then I called my husband, Richard, and said I was coming home.

"I had been so stunned that she thought I would do such a thing that I'd had no response. And the longer I thought about it, the more berserk I was going. I started trying to call Carol back in California. Willie Brown, speaker of the California State Assembly, was hosting a fundraiser for her, and I knew she was going to San Francisco on Friday night, but she hadn't checked in yet at the Hyatt Regency, so I left a message.

"I didn't hear anything. So two hours later, I called Carol's room at the Hyatt again, and he answered with this very dull voice, 'Hello.'

"'Hello, Kgosie. It's Sydney.'

"'Yeah?'

"'I'd like to talk to Carol.'

"'She's not here.'

"'I left a message for her....'

"'Yeah.'

"'I'd like to talk to her.'

"'I'll tell her you called.'

"'Did she get my message?'

"'Oh, yeah, she got your message.'

"'Well, where is she?'

"'I don't think that's a concern of yours.'

"'I need to talk to her.'

"'Well, I guess she doesn't want to talk to you.'"

Sydney continued, "On Saturday, I called Barbara Samuels in San Francisco and left a message for Carol with her. Still no call. I knew I couldn't just show up for the NOW thing on Sunday morning without having heard from her. After all, she had questioned my loyalty, insulted my integrity. Finally, I wrote something down and called and read it over the telephone. 'It is with deep regret that I have to tell you this, but I'm resigning from the campaign. You haven't called me back, so I won't be there for you tomorrow. I wish you all the best.'

"After all that, after everything we'd been through together, I resigned to Carol's answering machine. I'm telling you, my heart was broken."

The NOW convention on Sunday, June 28, was well covered by the press, and when Carol showed up without Sydney, the woman who had been her shadow since the previous October, it did not go unnoticed. In a column dealing with the Braun campaign defections and Sydney's categorical denial that she'd leaked the memo story, the *Chicago Reader's* Michael Miner wrote, "A political reporter we talked to said Faye-Petrizzi knew how to keep secrets, and her image inside the campaign was of a lady whose devotion to the candidate approached sycophancy."

Sydney's phone rang all day Monday as her friends in the Chicago press called to find out why she hadn't been with Carol on Sunday. By Monday afternoon, reporters also learned that Kay Clement had resigned as chair of the steering committee and that her son, Adam Clement, one of the few people who could sign checks for the campaign, was gone as well. The week before, finance director Jan Hensley, who'd been with the campaign just long enough to set up the recently completed national tour Carol called her "forced march," had also quit.

It was clear by this time that Carol Moseley Braun was going to be able to raise vast sums of money with comparable ease; in other words, it was a finance director's dream campaign. But the core problem developed when Matthews insisted upon a system whereby only he and treasurer Earl Hopewell, who answered only to Matthews, knew precisely how much money came in and from where. For the finance people, this made follow-up and re-solicitation difficult, if not, in some cases, virtually impossible. In fact, toward the end of the campaign, Braun fundraisers who remained were actually reduced to referencing Hopewell's Federal Election Commission reports to find out whom they should nudge, thank, or re-solicit for contributions!

This situation was intolerable for Hensley, who, as a veteran political fundraiser, had her professional reputation to consider as well. Hensley was also not pleased, she told certain staffers, with the way Kgosie Matthews had let his hand rest on her knee during a lunch they had together.

But because their relationship had been both long and personal, for Carol, the schism with the Clements was more serious than losing Hensley. Although Kay Clement was the single person who had launched Carol's political career, both women admit their relationship had never been smooth. "Kay and I are both stubborn and can be headstrong and have strongly held opinions," Carol said, adding, "but I've always felt a real love for Kay and her family, and they are very much a part of my life."

The final fight, though, was not between Carol and Kay but rather between Kay and Kgosie. And although Clement did not confirm her resignation with the press until late June, the key confrontation took place shortly after Carol's primary victory.

"John Rogers [then chief executive officer of Ariel Capital Investments and chairman of Carol's finance committee] and I requested a meeting with Carol to talk about how the operation might be shored up for the general election," reported Kay Clement. "We'd hoped to do it without Kgosie, but Carol wanted him there."

"Just as I was leaving the house to go down to the recorder's office for this meeting," Kay continued, "Sue Purrington called and said that *People* magazine was trying desperately, but without success, to get through to Carol. They wanted to put Carol on the magazine's cover, to do a major piece. I told Sue I was on my way to see her now, and I took the name and number of the person from *People* who had been trying to reach Carol.

"So while we were sitting in her office, waiting for John Rogers—myself, Carol, Kgosie, and Carol's assistant at the Recorder of Deeds, Sue Bass—I said, 'Sue Purrington has this message from *People* magazine,' and Carol said, 'Oh, good,' and started writing down the number.

"Kgosie just looked at me and said, 'Kay, that is not the way we do things....'

"I said, 'What?'

"He said, 'We go through channels.'

"I just exploded. I said, 'Kgosie, I am so tired of you! I have done nothing but answer phone calls complaining about this campaign. You've alienated so many people. You've got to straighten yourself out. This is impossible, the way you behave!' All the time I was yelling, Sue Bass was saying, 'Don't do this to the recorder. Don't do this to the recorder!'

"Kgosie put on his coat and stomped out.

"When John arrived, I told him, 'John, I'm sorry. I think I just blew our meeting. Kgosie and I had an argument.'

"But Kgosie was hanging around in another office, and Carol got him back.

"So John Rogers and I, he as finance chairman and I as steering committee chairman, went down our list of suggestions, discussing them with Carol, who was making notes. Kgosie sat across the room from us on a sofa saying things like, 'We've already thought of that. We talked about that months ago.' John and I never mentioned getting rid of anybody. Just, as I said, shoring things up, adding some more experienced professionals.

"But I heard later that Kgosie told Velma Wilson and Desiree Tate, both of whom are African American, that John Clay, who, as head of the lawyer's committee, had raised a lot of money for Carol but had no part in this discussion, and I wanted these two women fired! Totally untrue! John Clay is white. John Rogers, who is black, wasn't mentioned. Not that Rogers wanted anybody fired, either. But this racial stuff, after all our years working together, was absurd and destructive. I was furious with Kgosie."

Adam Clement got into what his mother called "a bruising battle" with Matthews over issues that had nothing to do with Kay's complaints. He left the campaign, he said, "because Kgosie was taking over every aspect of the finances." Clement had signed three blank checks in February, during a period when the campaign was in a hurry for money. Then, in June, he found out from campaign treasurer Earl Hopewell that one of those checks was being "investigated." Clement was angry that he hadn't been informed and told Kgosie so, along with the fact that he would not sign any more blank checks.

But for Matthews, the sticking point with Adam Clement was something else altogether. Clement had asked Hopewell why Matthews was being paid as a consultant. But the way Matthews heard it from Hopewell, Clement had asked *how much* Kgosie was being paid. And that was Kgosie's beef: what right did Adam Clement have to inquire about the campaign manager's salary? (Matthews's salary, a matter of public record as it must be reported to the Federal Election Commission, was $15,000 per month).

The bottom line was that both Kay and Adam Clement—at different times and for different reasons—advised Carol that it was in her best interest to get rid of Kgosie Matthews. And that was not about to happen.

The *Sun-Times* headline on Tuesday, June 30, read, "Braun's Staff Again Hit by Resignations." Reporter Lynn Sweet quoted only press secretary David Eichenbaum: "It's a campaign. People come and go."

True enough, but hardly what the hell was going on.

As for Carol, she was able to rationalize the losses, to explain and, thus, absolve her campaign manager.

Kgosie is temperamental; you can't get around that. I am going to try to be objective now in saying what I think are the three things he had going against him. First, he was young, 35, and for running a statewide campaign, that's pretty young. Second, Kgosie came out of nowhere as far as the Chicago community was concerned. So, because nobody knew him, he was kind of a shadowy figure, and mystery is always interpreted negatively. And third, I think people—especially my longtime personal and political friends— were more than a little chagrined that I imposed such confidence in Kgosie.

And just think of the communities and constituencies that combined to elect me, people Kgosie had to deal with. When have white feminists sat down at the table with black nationalists?

Regarding the opening round in the fight with Kay about going through channels, that comes of the fact that Kgosie is so process-oriented. And the process he's comfortable with demands a hierarchy. He gets crazed if things do not go according to process.

Around this time, I was beginning to make excuses—mostly in my own head, not something I discussed—for the way Carol excused Kgosie for his many counterproductive behaviors. What did "process" mean to Matthews? In this defense of Kgosie Carol actually answered that question. "Process" meant control. "Process," as Carol described it, was not only a need for complete control over the campaign's finances but surely a device to cover Matthews's own insecurities. He was a smart guy. His years with Jackson had taught him how chaotic campaigns can be, and he wanted none of that. But here's the mystery: what was his *personal* goal? If Carol won—and the chances looked pretty good at this point—Matthews would earn a free ride forward in American politics, and yet he had no problem alienating not only individuals but also whole constituencies!

The sad irony here is that Carol was spending so much energy excusing her campaign manager when what she clearly desired from him was the kind of emotional support she deep-down recalled that her little brother had once provided, remember? "Johnny was my social life, my protector. He was everything."

But getting back to Sunday, June 28, and that painful dispute with Sydney, like so many campaign days, it was a roller coaster ride. We'd returned from the California trip the night before to find Sydney's message, and I knew I wasn't finished with the press on this one. Also, I would miss Sydney, but I realized the breach could not be mended.

So, with this personal turmoil as background, first I went to NOW and got the most overwhelming and astonishing reception I had ever received up until that time.

Later, Carol told me she was almost frightened by the degree of adulation she felt when she walked into her first event of the morning, the final meeting of the three-day convention of the National Organization for Women. "I can't imagine myself reacting like that to anybody. People were just going wild!" she said. And they *were* wild.

The next day's headline read: "NOW Greets Braun as Conquering Hero," but that did not begin to describe the scene.

The Sunday plenary session was held in the International Ballroom of the Chicago Hilton and Towers, with 1,500 delegates, mostly women, sitting in sections marked by the standards of each individual state, much like a national political convention. The crowd was juiced before Carol arrived, having just heard a rousing address by NOW president Patricia Ireland.

I think a great deal of the emotional explosion that occurred when Carol walked into the room on that Sunday morning came from a sort of chemical combination that had never before found expression. It had a cathartic feel. A Googly moment, you know? Like that ubiquitous search engine: something you never knew how much you needed until it was there.

The outpouring was a political mix with both personal and organizational ingredients. This was an audience of informed women. They knew Carol was a divorced, single woman. They knew she had won against all odds. The personal ingredient, the "Yeah, sister!" factor, was that Carol had flat-out spanked an arrogant bastard, the only senator in the whole bunch who would be directly punished for violations against Anita Hill and by extension, this group felt, all American women.

The broader ingredient in the mix had to do with a demonstration of real political power and each member's pride in the knowledge that, without Sue Purrington and her Illinois women, Carol would not now be a candidate for the United States Senate. Furthermore, NOW had been the earliest—and almost the only—national organization to support Carol's primary candidacy with real money. Thus, as the first of the women candidates to win a Senate primary, Carol was NOW's baby. As she entered the convention hall, hundreds of women, some standing on chairs, shouted ecstatically: "Carol, Carol, Carol!"

The candidate's speech was a match for the ovation. Carol had an off-the-top-of-the-head talent for tailoring her material to fit an audience, and though I heard her talk countless times, I was never to hear this particular set of inspired talking points again.

Carol took phrases represented by the letters "CW" as her theme, and the first of these was "colored water." She told a Jim Crow story about her little brother Johnny throwing a fit because their mama wouldn't let him drink from the "colored" water fountain at the train station when they arrived to visit relatives in Montgomery, Alabama. Later, Carol and her mom realized that young Johnny expected the fountain would spew rainbows. "They can no longer fool us with colored water!" declared Carol. "We want the water that is there for everyone. Why should I be limited? Why should you? Why should anyone?" she asked, bringing down the house.

"CW stands for conventional wisdom. And the CW told me, 'Carol, you can't win this primary without millions of dollars. And Illinois women shouted, 'Oh. Yes. We. Can!'

"And CW is for courageous women, women who will nurture this society back to health. It is said that Hope has two daughters: Anger and Courage—anger at the way things are and the courage to change them. Anger needs courage to make it work, to fight off the forces that would intimidate us. In Illinois, hope lit the spark that started the flame that took this nation by storm—and we ... will ... not ... go ... back!"

Well, you can just imagine—I will tell you tears were running down *my* face.

After the session was the most crowded Sunday press conference I'd attended since retiring from the Michael Jordan beat. Carol consistently drew more attention than most politicians, but the following day, Monday, June 29, was the day the Supreme Court was expected to hand down its decision on the Pennsylvania case that could restrict abortion rights or, worse, outright kill *Roe v. Wade*.

Carol sat down with Patricia Ireland to discuss with reporters the possible outcomes of the Pennsylvania decision. Ireland said flatly, "We will simply refuse to obey any unjust laws that restrict women's freedoms and women's lives."[14]

Privately, Carol agonized over questions like abortion. She said, with moral certainty, that she herself would never have an abortion. At one time, a member of her extended family, someone she loved dearly, had gone through the trauma of a secret abortion. When Carol found out about it much later, she was very hurt by that experience. She should have been consulted, she thought. She would have wanted to help.

But the law of the land, for Carol, was another matter entirely. Saying she did not think the court would overturn *Roe*, Carol added, "I don't think they have the nerve to send women back to second-class citizenship. We have not had to labor under that for a generation. I will not concede that. I call on everyone to support the Freedom of Choice Act, to affirm at the national level that women will not go back."

Carol's left shoulder pad slipped, peeking out from under the yoke of her dress. (Where was Sydney with a safety pin?) Because a number of photographers were snapping pictures, one woman piped up to point out this wardrobe malfunction to Carol, who was unembarrassed and grateful. "These damn things," she said of shoulder pads. "I can't wait 'til they go out of style."

Checking the reaction to Carol's disarmingly candid behavior, I looked around at the three-deep semicircle of people surrounding her. Everyone was smiling, everyone related to her comment, including a male photographer I knew who would certainly protect Carol in this matter. A subtle reality that many folks rarely

---

14   The court did indeed approve four of the five provisions in the Pennsylvania law in deciding *Planned Parenthood v. Casey*, striking spousal consent as giving husbands too much power but upholding the 24-hour waiting period, informed consent, and parental consent provisions of the law. In a 5-4 decision, the court affirmed the essential holding of *Roe*, reiterating a previous challenge to the law: "If the right of privacy means anything, it is the right of the individual, married or single, to be free from unwarranted governmental intrusion into matters so fundamentally affecting a person as the decision to bear or beget a child."

recognize is that publications can play hell with candidates depending on which pictures they choose to print. (Today, the photo would undoubtedly have been tweeted nationwide along with a snarky comment!)

Finally, a reporter asked Carol: "If the court decision expected tomorrow does not change anything, lets *Roe* stand as it exists today, is there any concern that the impetus you've enjoyed in the election will slide?"

"No, no," Carol said, looking earnestly into the reporter's face. "This candidacy is about a whole series of issues—choice, humanity. It's about democracy, giving people hope. If there is a victory, we will celebrate that victory and face the challenges that still confront us."

And my thought was this: If Alan Dixon said these words, would we believe him? No, he'd sound ridiculous. Orrin Hatch? Paul Simon? No. It takes this color, this gender saying she truly believes this election is "about democracy, giving people hope" for us to believe. Herein, I thought, lay the key to Carol's success: to call her candidacy merely symbolic was an understatement. This was a highly substantive symbolism. If this woman is in the chase, maybe there is hope for women and minorities on a whole range of issues.

Afterward, we stopped by the Hilton Café to sample the brunch buffet—Carol, Kgosie, and I joined by Leah Myers Smith, Carol's campaign coordinator for the St. Louis suburbs along the Mississippi in Illinois, and Lynn Sweet, the irrepressible *Sun-Times* reporter who never ever runs out of questions.

Carol had taken me aside and briefly explained Sydney's absence, but she skirted the subject with Lynn. It would be Tuesday before Lynn had the story.

The conversation at the brunch table centered on white sales. Yes, shopping for linens. It started with Carol's complaint that she couldn't do such things anonymously anymore and segued into each person's describing the last great sale she'd encountered. Kgosie was not an active participant in the conversation, but he did appear comfortable listening to Carol discourse on this domestic subject. As for me, I thought: Did we not just witness an incredible couple of hours featuring the "Year of the (liberated) Woman"? Are we not in the middle of a historic campaign for the US Senate? Are we talking about sheets and towels here?

But that's the way it was to be with Carol Moseley Braun. She lived in the real world—where people frequently come into contact with sheets and towels.

While Carol and I and the others were enjoying lunch and discussing white sales, several campaign workers, including Barbara Samuels, were waiting for Carol at the kickoff point of the Gay Pride Parade.

Carol had always been very sensitive to the intolerance that gays and lesbians had to endure. The June issue of *The Advocate*, a national publication dedicated to gay and lesbian issues, published an anecdote that illustrated Carol's comfort with demonstrating how she felt about people and their issues, rather than just talking about them.

> Senatorial candidate Carol Moseley Braun made quite a splash at last winter's big fund-raiser in Chicago for Impact, the Illinois gay and lesbian political action committee. It wasn't because of anything she said, because she didn't make a speech. In fact, she showed up too late to be introduced with the cavalcade of attending celebrities. But when the band started playing, Braun was one of the first to hit the dance floor. Her partner in all the swinging and twirling was Christie Hefner, the comely publisher of *Playboy* magazine. And it wasn't until Hefner's boyfriend cut in several songs later that Braun, laughing and clapping, was finally pulled away by her campaign detail to head out to her next engagement.
>
> "I didn't want to leave, I was having such a good time," says Braun, months later the surprise Democratic nominee from Illinois for the U.S. Senate. 'The only problem was that Christie and I couldn't figure out who was leading."

Illinois's gays and lesbians worked hard to elect Carol because her positions on their issues were well established. As a legislator, with no particular evidence of a significant gay and lesbian population in her district, she nevertheless had sponsored a gay and lesbian civil rights bill, in addition to the first state antidiscrimination housing bill that specifically covered gay men and lesbians. Carol had also introduced the first hate crimes legislation in Illinois history.

Carol told *The Advocate* that she did not see gay marriage as a radical issue at all. "'My aunt married a white man in the 1940s. Until *Loving v. Virginia* (1967), when the Supreme Court struck down all the anti-miscegenation laws, that marriage was illegal. And that was absurd. Who's to say this woman can't marry this man? How is that different from saying this woman can marry this woman or this man can't marry this man?'"[15]

On this topic, Carol told me the following:

Kgosie is more conservative than I am on these issues, and at the same time, he is not altogether sympathetic with my spiritual bent, and we were airing this one out at one point, and I said to him, "If we start out with the proposition that the Lord works in mysterious ways, and mere mortals don't know what the grand plan is, who's to say that the apparent increase in homosexual behavior is not a function of God deciding that the planet is over-populated? Well, think about it! If you're a believer, that is not an irrational thought.

I threw that out to Kgosie for the sake of argument, but fundamentally, my position as it relates to this issue is simple: I believe that if a person is black or white or gay or straight or handicapped or whatever, our challenge is to facilitate that individual's ability to contribute in a positive way to society.

South Africa, Kgosie's native land, historically is the classic example of wasted human resources. What a tragedy when a country can only rely on the contributions of one-fifth of itself—all people cut from the same mold. The bottom line is, personally, I can't be

---

15   More than 20 years later, our country is finally catching up with Carol's instinctive, humanist view on this issue. However, at the time, freely expressing this view also showed political courage as most of her constituency would disagree, especially when it came to gay marriage, and especially in the African American community.

what I want to be if someone who's gay is cut off from being what they want to be. And the big picture is that a society cannot possibly realize its potential if individual members are limited in their right to growth and fulfillment.

While it was not clear that all Illinois politicians had views on gay and lesbian issues as strong and well thought-out as Carol's, a number of them believed it to be at least expedient to show up for the Gay Pride Parade.

Barbara Samuels arrived to find Bill Weeks, campaign liaison to the lesbian and gay communities, pacing the pavement and looking "very stressed." The cars were lining up, getting ready to go. "Oh my God, do you know where Carol is?" he asked.

Barbara understood the seriousness of sending off an empty convertible with a Carol Moseley Braun banner on it. "You might as well send a hearse," she said. She remembered a time when Harold Washington missed a parade, and his car was booed for the entire parade route.

"What are we going to do?" Weeks wailed. This was a big deal. The community represented here had worked hard for Carol. She was a genuine hero.

"I said, 'I know what we're going to do,'" Barbara remembered, laughing. "I threw my hair up, put on my sunglasses, and jumped in the car, just as it took off. And for three blocks, I got a feel for what it was like to be Carol. I was waving. People were shouting, 'Hey Carol. God, we love you!'

"I was in some jeopardy of being discovered, however. Dawn Clark Netsch, years in the state legislature, was in the car in front of me, and she turned and it was like, 'What? Who are you?' Then a Channel 7 cameraman came up to the car to get a shot, and I said, 'Don't *do* that!' and pulled off my sunglasses. He said, 'What? Where's Carol?'

"We were laughing so hard in the car, and then we heard this big crowd noise build up behind us, and here came Carol, sprinting down the street, running the parade route to catch up, and people cheering her on. Carol hopped in the car, and I said, 'Boy, am I glad to see you.'"

That was the fun part of the parade. But something happened a few blocks later that frightened Barbara in a way she had never been frightened before.

"We were talking and Carol was waving, and suddenly, out of the crowd, here came this maniac, screaming, spitting, calling names, 'You don't deserve this office, you bitch. You don't deserve this office!'

"When Carol turned around, she just froze. This madman was right there, at the car. He had a big American flag, and he threw it on us—at one time, I was completely covered—but he was trying to get it around Carol, all the time screaming this hatred.

"In retrospect, it couldn't have lasted more than 10 seconds before we speeded up and got out of there. But it was the longest 10 seconds of my life."

That moment changed the campaign for Barbara: "There were people on rooftops, hanging out of windows, and suddenly, they didn't look so friendly anymore. Any one of them could make my son an orphan! And I thought about how vulnerable Carol was, and how our boys, Greg and Matt, are together all the time. What if some monster decided he wanted to pick her off? Carol kept smiling and waving, but we talked about how weird this change of feeling was. We were scared out of our minds. I said, 'I love you, Carol, but I will never do this again.'"

The man who attacked Carol, Gary Steven Foster, was arrested and charged with assault but eventually released. Sometime later, he was rearrested after threatening to kill presidential candidate Bill Clinton and his daughter, Chelsea. At that time, three psychiatrists, one of them Foster's own doctor, told Secret Service agents that Foster was "psychotic, delusional, and possibly dangerous."

The incident at the Gay Pride Parade changed things for Joe Moseley, too. A homicide detective who worked out of Chicago's Area 1 Violent Crimes Division, Carol's younger brother had been his sister's bodyguard from the outset of the primary. A handsome man in his thirties, Joe could easily have played himself in a TV cop drama. But Joe now became consumed with concern for Carol's safety, although initially, it was Edna Moseley who charged him with protecting his big sister.

Joe recalled, "Even during the primary, my mother felt that Carol's safety was paramount, and she asked me to take that responsibility, which I was happy to accept. She said, 'Joe, you go take care of my baby!' I said, 'But Mama, I thought I was your baby!' She said, 'You were, but right now, Carol needs you.' So at that point, I went to work."

Joe gathered together a small group of friends from the Chicago Police and Cook County Sheriff's Departments who volunteered their time to protect Carol. Depending on individual work schedules, Joe could call on nine officers, chief among them his close pals Edwin "Nick" Fizer and Lester Bailey. However, in June, shortly after the Gay Pride incident, Carol began to receive death threats, and at that point, the Chicago Police Department officially assigned one of Joey's volunteer officers to Carol. She was Patrolman Anita Ashton. And while Joey and his people continued to cover events, Anita became Carol's constant shadow and trusted bodyguard (and my all-time favorite cop).

Joe showed me one of the letters Carol received, this one hand-delivered to campaign headquarters, a fact that in itself was alarming.

> Braun
> Just because you are black you think we suppose to kiss your ass. You need a brick on your head like Martin Luther King. It will be coming soon. It might wake up your brains. You go around kissing all the white asses for votes.
>
> KKK

"I don't discount anyone," said Joe. "That's the difference between the casual observer and someone responsible for security. If you think it can't happen, that's when it does."

"Look," Joey continued, explaining where the strength of his passion came from, "Carol will become the highest elected black official in the country; she's female and she's educated. Now you can put these qualities in any order you want to, but the bottom line is she antagonizes the shit out of many members of our society. It comes down to two words," Joe Moseley concluded, "nigger bitch."

Detective Joe Moseley earned his living on the street. He understood things his sister didn't even want to know.

The much-feared article on Kgosie Matthews—the one he had mentioned to me days before during our DC cab ride—appeared in the Chicagoland section of the *Tribune* on July 1 with the headline, "Braun's Manager Knows Success and Controversy." The first 14 paragraphs dealt with the controversy part, mostly a rehash of Braun campaign defections. As Matthews had refused to speak to reporter Frank James for this article, in the interest of adding some balance, the writer had to call up an old quote: "'Everyone who manages a campaign gets criticized for his management style, he [Matthews] said last winter, 'it's a non-issue.'"

After reciting Matthews's impressive family history, James got to his Jackson campaign experience.

> Those familiar with Matthews' role in Jackson's 1988 campaign say he was a cross between valet and road manager, packing Jackson's suitcases and making sure things went according to schedule. Matthews was very protective of Jackson, as he is with Braun. Reporters particularly annoyed him.
>
> "He had nothing but disdain for the press. He called them dogs and animals," said Del Marie Cobb, Jackson's 1988 press secretary.
>
> He also had run-ins with campaign staff. Cobb said she and an assistant, Denise Lee, were in Matthews' doghouse, but she was not sure how they got there.
>
> One day, when the campaign bus pulled up to the charter plane and as Lee was getting off the bus, she slipped and lay sprawled on the tarmac. Matthews, next off the bus, stepped over the woman's prostrate body, refusing to help her to her feet, and got on the waiting plane, according to Cobb.

This was a chilling description, particularly for those who had seen demonstrated Matthews's perfect manners. James was able to find one Matthews fan. Prominent Chicagoan Joseph Gardner had worked with Matthews on the Jackson campaign and was now a member of Carol's steering committee. Said Gardner: "Kgosie has no problem telling people no. Carol doesn't need another politician as a campaign manager. She needs a no-nonsense, crack-the-whip type, and Kgosie fits that bill very well."

Gardner's assessment was at least partially correct. Certainly, Carol needed someone to say no for her, given as she was to trying to please everybody. And as for the crack of the whip, in Kgosie Matthews's hand it did, indeed, get the candidate's attention.

CHAPTER 6

Black and White and Family

*I*T WAS IN LAW SCHOOL *that I met Michael Braun.*

I was working at a Kroger supermarket, living at home, and dealing with all the chaos that involved. But it was tax law that threw me—and threw me together with Mike. Actually, it wasn't entirely a coincidence. My girlfriend Esther Largent suggested that the way to get through tax [law] was to study with somebody smart, someone on Law Review *would be nice. Her suggestion was quickly followed by a solution. She introduced me to Mike.*

We began by just studying together. He would come over, we'd hit the books, then maybe go to a movie or something. Pretty soon we were dating. And then—we just fell in love. It was a classic young love kind of thing. But what I think I appreciated the most about Mike was that, especially in the beginning, he was very protective of me. And I had never felt protected before. So having someone looking out for me, for once, was different—and irresistible. That was very important to me.

My family and friends—they were absolutely shocked: "Carol, of all people, with a white guy!" I'd always had white friends, but he was my first white date. People were shocked because I was pretty political at the time. And Mike was so white, a WASP, white Anglo-Saxon Protestant, from a New Jersey suburb. But then, there was that flower child in me: Mike and I would end racism and save the world.

But mostly it boiled down to one thing: I loved Michael Braun, and he would take care of me. I was much more traditional than the course my life had taken would indicate.

So Mike and I were just fine, but what we had to grapple with was our families. My dad, who had spent several years in California, was now back and more stable—relatively. He and Mike didn't hit it off at first. And even later, after we were married, they had a huge argument one time, and my dad got a gun and said he was going to shoot Mike. So Mike said to me, "Your father is threatening my life!"

"Well," I laughed, "that just goes with the territory." And eventually they came to terms. But my dad was appalled at the outset that I would marry white. I think he was afraid for me. Which may not have been unreasonable.

It was Christmastime, and Michael wanted to take me out East to meet the folks. He assured me it was all arranged. Mike had this little Toyota, and we were going to drive. So we were going across Ohio, headed for Westfield, New Jersey, when Mike just casually mentioned, "Oh, by the way, you're going to stay at Shelly's, not my parents' house."

At first that made sense to me. We're not married yet, and we don't want to dishonor the situation, so I stay with his sister, he stays with his parents—not a big deal.

So we were driving along, and I was mulling it over, and as we pulled up to a tollbooth, I asked, "Michael, how many bedrooms does your parents' house have?"

And he, without thinking said, "Six."

"Now wait a minute. Six bedrooms? There's your mother and your father—even assuming they've got separate bedrooms—and your grandmother is there...." I said, "Michael, who else is staying with your parents besides you and your grandmother?"

He said, "Nobody."

I said, "Michael, that's four bedrooms. What about the other two? Why am I staying at Shelly's?"

So then he started this long, convoluted explanation that his mother had told his grandmother that I was Shelly's friend, and he was bringing Shelly's friend to spend Christmas with them. All this because his mother thought his grandmother would be too shocked about this whole thing.

I listened. Then I said, "I'll tell you what. I don't need this. If I'm going to have to be brought in with a bag over my head, you can just turn this car around and take me back home. My mother and the rest of my family are already upset that I'm not spending Christmas with them. Why do I want to drive all the way to New Jersey to go through this stuff?"

So Mike said he'd work it out. And we stopped at a pay phone, and he called his mom, then came back to the car and said, "It's all cleared up. You can stay at our house."

On we went, arriving later than we'd expected, so when we walked in the kitchen, they were all there and excited: "Oh Mike, we're so glad to see you!" And on the kitchen counter, I noticed a neat little stack of blankets.

Girls notice these things.

When I got Mike alone, I asked, "Are you sure you have this worked out with your mother? Are you sure she thinks I'm staying here and not at Shelly's?"

"Oh, yes, yes. It's all worked out."

Nighttime came, and it was very apparent to me that Mrs. Braun was still determined that I was going over to Shelly's. So I said, "Look, Michael, I'll tell you what. Instead of having an argument about this, why don't you take me to the airport, and I'll just go home?"

So they all went in another room and talked and talked. Finally, Mike said, "OK. You're going to stay." They put me in a guest room. We got up the next morning, and everything was fine.

Throughout all this, Mrs. Braun was very nice to me, and so was Mr. Braun. He was something of a horticulturist, and he took me down to the basement to show me how he propagated seedlings and explained his hobby to me. We went around to visit relatives, and when we got back and walked in the kitchen, there were the blankets sitting on the counter again!

"Michael," I said, "those blankets are on the counter, and I'll bet you dollars to doughnuts that if you go upstairs and you go in the guest bedroom and the guest bathroom, you'll discover that your mother has changed the linen, refurbished the bed and the bathroom."

"No, no, no." But he went, and she'd changed the linen, put new towels in the bathroom, and all my stuff was straightened and neatly stacked, ready to be moved.

"OK. That's it. I'm out of here." And I ran upstairs and started packing. I put everything together and was about to leave when I heard a raucous argument starting. Then it quieted very fast, and I guessed the family had moved to another part of the house. I'd told Michael I was not coming downstairs again, that I wanted him to come up and get me and we'd go directly to the airport.

So I was just sitting there when there was a knock at the door. It was John Braun. "Carol? May I come in?"

He sat down, and he looked straight at me, and he said, "Carol, my son loves you very much, and I love my son very much. And anyone my son loves, I love." John said, "If you have been offended at all by anything Doris has done, please understand that she was just trying to make this situation smooth for everybody and meant no offense. And I'd like you to come downstairs and join us for dinner, and I'd like it very much if you didn't leave."

Mike's dad was so sincere and so straightforward, I said, "OK." And when I joined the others, Mrs. Braun looked like—well, discomfort doesn't begin to describe it. But she was straightforward, too. She apologized, "I'm sorry if I offended or insulted you."

Now it was my turn. I said, "Frankly, I was insulted. I didn't mean to cause you a problem, but it wasn't my idea to come out here. I thought I was invited." Doris then began to explain about her mother: "You've got to understand. She's old, I don't want to upset her."

Well, Grandma might have been old, she was in her eighties, but she wasn't stupid. I'd visited her in her bedroom, and she was sitting up in her bed, with this pretty little bed jacket on. She was very nice—and funny. She told me stories about "the colored girls" who lived in the town where she grew up. I did not find this at all offensive because I understood the era in which she was reared, and I knew that she was trying, the best she knew how, to relate to me. Later, Shelly told me her grandmother had suspected all along. She'd told Shelly: "I think Michael and Carol are sweet on each other."

So I said to Doris, "I don't think your mother is deluded about any of this."

You have to understand," she pleaded. "If you children are happy, then I'm happy for you. But what about your children?"

"They'll be black, of course," I shot back. It must have just killed Doris—my brashness, probably, more than the idea of black grandchildren.

But to her everlasting credit, to their everlasting credit, there was never another discussion of race. They handled the situation with integrity and genuine affection. The Brauns were wonderful in-laws and adoring grandparents to Matt when he was born.

When Michael and I talked about it later, he said that his family had always been the liberals in the community—in the sense that they were not bigoted—and they were the moral voice, the social conscience, among their set of friends. So now his parents had to come to grips with what they'd stood for all those years. And they did so with dignity and honor and, eventually, I'm sure, with pleasure.

Michael was the one who made adjustments when it came to in-laws. He married himself a very bizarre black family. As one person familiar with our household said, "Going over to Mike and Carol's was like walking into a daily sitcom."

As June melted into July, I had yet to travel the campaign trail with Carol, but my request to do so was sitting on Kgosie Matthews's desk. I got the call on the morning of July 3. Matthews said, "You can fly to Carbondale for the weekend with Carol. Be at her house, 6740 South Oglesby, at 1:30 this afternoon."

Just a block off the lake, Carol's building was a Chicago classic with rococo flourishes, a condominium on each of seven floors. Carol and Matt, who was 14, lived on the fifth floor.

The lobby entrance was paneled in a dark mahogany that Carol said was too gloomy for her taste. It annoyed her every time she walked in the door. The cost to refinish the wood, however, was $10,000, and all seven owners had to agree to spend the money— something that was not going to happen. For this and other reasons, Carol had listed her condo for sale. The fact that she was required to keep the place in shape to show was just another of the problems a candidate without a wife had to think about.

I rang the doorbell next to "Braun," and Matt answered over the intercom. I said my name.

"Who?"

I told him again.

"Well, my mom's not home."

"Kgosie told me to meet her here at 1:30," I responded. "I'm going to Carbondale with her."

"OK. Come on in."

Matt, a handsome kid, tall for his age, was dressed in a T-shirt and shorts. Although he didn't know me, had not been told to expect me, was home alone, and had no idea about his mother's schedule, Matt appeared perfectly at ease. I was carrying my laptop, and I suggested that if he could find me a table and chair, I had some work I could do while I waited.

Matt led me through the kitchen into a combination pantry and breakfast nook where the sun streamed through a window over the table. "Everybody likes to work in the nook," he said, teaching me in the space of a sentence something about what it's like to be the son of a politician.

The nook was decorated, as was the kitchen, with Carol's collection of African American memorabilia—an Aunt Jemima cookie jar, Little Black Sambo—images that were common once but have now disappeared from our culture. Carol also has lovely antique silver and some arresting original art. The apartment was spacious and had views of Lake Michigan from a set of windows in front of which sat a baby grand piano.

We were supposed to catch a private plane at Meigs Field, Chicago's small, lakefront airport, at 2:30—but that hour passed with no sign of the candidate.

Matt and I had time to get acquainted.

He told me that he and Kgosie "had a big fight last night." Matt called the campaign manager "the 'K' Man," or "The Kos." He said, "'Kgosie' means something like 'awaiting the king' in African."

Matt didn't seem particularly anxious to get back to whatever he was doing when I interrupted. He asked me what my business was, and I answered, "Until recently, television sports." The 14-year-old nodded, unimpressed. "I don't find sports that interesting," Matt said.

Then he asked, "You ever read Kurt Vonnegut?"

"Sure."

"My dad just gave me *Slaughterhouse-Five*. It was great." He said he liked stuff that was a little crazy.

He went to get another book he'd enjoyed, called *Time Enough for Love*, by Robert Heinlein. Matt assured me that I'd like this book, too. "It's not about love," he said.

Then Matt turned to a section he really thought was special where Heinlein pauses the plot and plops in gems of wisdom as uttered by his character, a fellow named Lazarus Long. Matt had circled his favorite gems.

He read: "'If you are a part of a society that votes, then do so. There may be no candidates and no measures that you want to vote for, but there are certain to be ones that you will want to vote against. ... By this rule you will rarely go wrong.'"

Matt looked up and smiled, showing his braces. Then he continued: "'If this is too blind for your taste, consult some well-meaning fool (there is always one around) and ask his advice. Then vote the other way. This enables you to be a good citizen (if such is your wish) without spending the enormous amount of time on it that truly intelligent exercise of franchise requires.'"

Then Matt read me one he didn't get: "'Never frighten a little man. He'll kill you.' What do you make of that?" he asked.

"I think it's true," I said. "He might not mean 'little' in the physical sense, or even "kill" in the violent sense. It's 'little' like weak, pinch-souled, without imagination. That kind of little man will kill you because he doesn't have the intellectual resources to fight you." I didn't want to get into a discussion of the Napoleon complex.

Matt nodded. "Oh, I get it," he said.

Matt had one more quote he wanted to read. He'd circled it for Kgosie, he said. "'A committee is a life form with six or more legs and no brain.' The Kos will like it," Matt laughed, "because he's always fighting with the steering committee."

When the door buzzer rang, I felt a great sense of relief, though not because I wasn't having a good time with Matt (by then, he'd tried, without success, to engage me in a computer game and showed me new ways to use my new laptop).

But it wasn't Carol. It was Darlene Mackey.

Darlene was one of a handful of campaign members who genuinely loved Carol. As Catherine Mackey's daughter and Marsha Moseley's best friend, she'd virtually grown up in the Moseley household.

"Marsha and I were about six years younger, and, I remember, Carol was out a lot, always involved in something. But when Carol walked in the house, she was full of excitement and everything sort of revved up," said Darlene. "And she was generous. She would take Marsha and me places, include us in the field trips of this community group she worked for. Once I was at the Moseley's when Carol arrived in the kitchen with $150! She'd just cashed her first paycheck for something, and all she could talk about was what she was going to buy for the house. Tables. I remember, she was going to buy end tables for her mother, Auntie Edna. Nothing for herself."

Darlene had a tough adolescence. "I finished high school, but I wouldn't have if it wasn't for Carol's mom. I would have been on the street earlier if Auntie Edna hadn't been there for me," said Darlene. After a couple of harrowing years where she would only occasionally check in at home, Darlene first joined the Black Muslims, then had a spiritual experience that eventually led her to become an ordained minister. Now a believer in hands-on Christianity, Darlene was working with the homeless in New Mexico when she got the call to return to Chicago.

Darlene is a sternly disciplined woman who was in charge of the campaign's ministerial outreach, an important constituency for Carol Moseley Braun. It's not always easy to coax a smile from Darlene, but when Matt brought her into the nook, she was almost giggling. I knew nothing about the weekend plans. All Kgosie had said was "Carbondale," but Darlene had heard we were going to spend the Fourth of July on a farm. Maybe there would be horses and we could ride. It was clear that Darlene and Matt were fond of one another, and, I then discovered, Matt was going with us, too. This was going to be a fun trip.

Carol soon arrived and immediately commenced to scurry around, packing her things and trying to find clean clothes for Matt. Her housekeeper, a 70-year-old named Candy, had been ill, and Carol, knowing Candy would resent anyone taking her place, had tried to keep up with the cleaning and laundry by herself, which was, of course, impossible.

Finally, with Gus Fordham driving, we headed for the lakefront and Meigs Field. It was a beautiful day, but there was one thing we'd all forgotten: this was July 3. A significant portion of the city's population would be gathered at the Lake Michigan shore for the Chicago Symphony's free concert and a fireworks show.

Chicago is a wonderful summer city. With 26 miles of parks along Lake Michigan and beaches, marinas, and free entertainment events throughout the season, many residents (and people really live in Chicago, 2.8 million of us at the time) do not even consider taking an out-of-town vacation in the summer. Of course, most people can never afford to leave, and that's why the entertainments and festivals are so healthy for the city.

Meigs Field was a general aviation airport built on reclaimed lake land, shielded from the Loop by Grant Park but not more than 10 minutes from dozens of corporate headquarters. It was a savior of an airport for those who owned or could afford to charter small aircraft, not to mention those who used some 20 daily commercial commuter flights.[16]

There was only one road on the tree-lined peninsula that ends with the Adler Planetarium but accesses Meigs, and on that busy holiday in 1992, we found it blocked by a phalanx of Chicago police officers. It is a perfect place to view the fireworks because here, the lighted city becomes background for the show, and the area was already jammed with revelers.

Gus, who got out to argue with the patrolman, was getting nowhere. Finally, the sergeant in charge came over to see what the fuss was about. "I have Miss Carol Moseley Braun in the car, and she is late for her airplane," Gus pleaded. The sergeant, an African American woman, leaned down and scanned Carol, Darlene, and me. She appeared to have no idea which one of us might be "Miss Carol Moseley Braun."

---

16 In the middle of the night of March 31, 2003, Mayor Richard M. Daley, who wanted more parkland, sent bulldozers onto the field to carve big x's in the single runway, thus ending the airport's life—and a battle the mayor had been waging since 1994. More people were pleased than pissed. Chicagoans love those "big shoulders"!

"Let me see an ID," she said.

Carol reached into her bag and handed the woman her passport. "OK," said the sergeant, an attractive woman despite her stern countenance. She then signaled a patrolman, a burly young blond fellow, to lift back the police barricade and let us through. Something about that scene, the respectful way the young white man followed the orders of his superior, a black woman, brought to my mind the old cliché: Chicago is "the city that works." (Well, mostly.)

Seated comfortably in the six-passenger Cessna on our way to southern Illinois, Carol explained to me the somewhat unusual circumstance that would find us spending the holiday weekend in a private home.

"John Rednour was one of the 'good old boys' who stuck with me when I made a run at getting slated for the lieutenant governorship in 1985. John supported Alan Dixon in the Senate primary—all the guys down there did—but he and I have been friends since '85."

Carol was smiling as the plane landed, and there was John Rednour.

Rednour was a tall man, maybe 6'4," in his late fifties, ruddy-faced with basset-hound eyes, and a slow manner that, I was soon to discover, belied a sharp intelligence. Carol greeted John with a big hug and did not apologize for being late, nor did John ask what had caused the delay. Following speedy introductions, John hustled us into a waiting car, and we were off to the Carbondale City Hall.

It was about 8:30 when we arrived and found Senator Paul Simon holding the crowd for Carol by conducting an impromptu town meeting. The senator gracefully introduced the candidate—then fled.

If you run a line west from Norfolk, Virginia, take it a little south of Louisville, Kentucky, and continue west, you'll hit Carbondale, Illinois. "Downstaters," Chicagoans call these people, and many are southerners in manner, speech, and tradition, even though Illinois is counted as a northern state. Much of the area is closer to Little Rock than Chicago.

No African American had ever been sent from this part of the state to the state capital, Springfield, or to Washington, nor had a woman ever been elected. Perry County, where we would spend the weekend celebrating the 217th birthday of the United States, had never even put a woman in countywide office.

The political conflicts between Chicago and the citizens of this area, huge geographically if not demographically, are legend. But this is what makes Illinois politics fascinating.

Illinois had elected Republican governors for more than two decades, but both its senators in 1992 were Democrats. Until Bill Clinton came along, Illinois had not gone for a Democratic presidential candidate since 1964. Even more to the point Carol made about Illinois being a paradigm for the nation, the state had voted for the winner in all but two presidential elections in the previous 100 years.

In the course of her Carbondale remarks, Carol said: "Winning in southern Illinois is important for the message it will send." True enough, given the region's political history, it would be an astonishing message. And sustaining that support would also be the key to Carol's long-term political viability.

Carol was a big hit and following a standing ovation, virtually the entire audience stayed and sought an opportunity to speak to the candidate. It is in these individual, post-speech exchanges that it becomes clear that from the most idealistic citizen to the most pragmatic, politics is all about "me."

Darlene stayed at Carol's elbow with her notepad, writing down invitations, collecting business cards, and promising responses. A slightly bent, elderly lady came up to Carol with tears in her eyes, hugged her warmly, and said, "I am so proud. This is such a big deal for me." The woman was not so much saying she was proud of Carol, but rather, she was proud of "us," of what we might be on the brink of achieving as a people—or, perhaps, as women. "Proud" was a word we would hear again and again as we traveled the state.

Nevertheless, not a few of those milling about Carol were like the man from the Illinois Corn Growers Association who handed me a large envelope that contained information, he said, that Carol should study in order to understand the positions of the Illinois agricultural community. "Dixon has been a very good friend of ours," he told me. "We'd like Carol to understand our problems—ethanol and all."

It was late when we finished at Carbondale, and Darlene and I were anxious to see this farm of John Rednour's. Carol had told me John was a longtime national Democratic committeeman, and indeed, it was clear from the few hours we'd spent together that the man pulled a lot of weight in these parts, but we didn't hear much from him about horses—or even corn or soybeans.

It turned out that we were headed about 30 miles north of Carbondale to Du Quoin. I'd heard of Du Quoin because it had fairgrounds that for many years had been home to the Hambletonian, one of the country's top harness races. As we drove, we learned that John, who, up until this time, had been taciturn to say the least, was not a farmer after all but that he owned a bank and a construction company, among other things.

As we sped through the thick, fragrant night on dark and empty roads, we had no feeling for where we were—only that just beyond the reach of the headlights was a country void. And we were starving. Darlene asked if there was any chance we might pass a Burger King or McDonald's, and John just laughed. "Wanda will fix y'all somethin' when we get home," he said. Wanda is John's wife.

Perhaps because he sensed our nervousness about the speed at which we were traveling, John, who, with Carol in the front seat had grown loquacious, told us a story.

"I was travelin' up to Springfield this one time," he said, "late for a meetin' of the State Police Review Board, of which I am a member, and these two officers pulled me over. Man and a woman. They git out of the car, swaggerin', you know, like they do. And they says, 'What's your hurry, sir?'

"And I says, 'I'm on my way up to Springfield to fire a couple of assholes just like you.'

"And they stopped right there and smiled real nice and said, 'Well, then. Have a nice trip!'"

I was still trying to puzzle out the message in that tale when we arrived at John's home.

The Rednour place was big all right, a gorgeous colonial mansion actually on the Illinois State Fairgrounds. And it had a twin mansion right beside it! Two stunning homes, each set on five groomed acres. As we drove up the curving driveway, we could see that John Rednour had a big old swimming pool, but there wasn't a horse in sight.

"That's the governor's place," John said, indicating the other mansion. "State owns it. Governor stays there when he's at the fair." That would be Republican governor Jim Edgar, who, John told us later, is a "nice enough fella," but they don't socialize. Clearly, John's house was the more meticulously maintained of the two.

We entered John's imposing home through the kitchen door, and while there stood a country table for 10 and a breakfast nook, both were foodless. I figured a meal must be hiding somewhere as we had been expected well before dinnertime. "Wanda's down at a grandchild's birthday party," John explained, "but I'll show you around."

The house had 22 rooms, John told us as we trailed behind him. He was proud of his home—and especially of his wife. "Wanda done it," he smiled, when we admired a framed needlepoint. The mansion, from the industrial strength kitchen in the basement ("We sometimes have hundreds for brunch on the lawn during the fair") to the crocheted detail on the window shades, was testimony to "the complete homemaker." Frilly, pink, silk-flowered, and immaculate, it was a *house* called Wanda.

Although Carol had known John for years, he, like so many others, was anxious to explain that he'd been very poor (he started with an outhouse and now can choose among eight bathrooms) and had come from nothing and nowhere. Well, not exactly nowhere— Cutler, Illinois, actually, a small town just a few miles west of Du Quoin. "We'll go there on the way to the Steeleville parade tomorrow," he said.

Wanda arrived, all energy and charm, bright blue eyes, brown hair framing a lively face. "Y'all hungry?" she asked. We must have looked it. Like magic, our dinner came out of Wanda's multiple refrigerators, into the microwave, and onto the vast table. It was delicious.

Each of our rooms had beautiful country furniture and attached baths. John told us we had a full schedule tomorrow and would leave the house at 8 a.m. sharp. We tumbled into our skirted and canopied four-posters.

As I began to doze, my brain considered the situation we were in, one that occurs over and over in a campaign: you simply lose control. Once we got off the plane in Carbondale, we belonged to John Rednour, who had arranged this whole weekend with the help of other area Democrats. And I wondered if this was one of the deep-down factors in Carol's resistance to campaigning. You couldn't tell it; she was uncomplaining and downright ebullient, not to mention the perfect guest, but still, it was almost in the way she just gave herself over to the situation, dealt with the exception to what I had otherwise observed was the rule: except for the degree to which she bowed to Kgosie, Carol needed to feel in control. I thought: this is the only way she can tolerate being "run" by others. She just shuts down, settles into the bubble, and lets the tide carry her. What was it she had said once? "I just don't let negativity be a factor in my thinking—or feeling." Certainly during a campaign situation like this, that was a positive thing, but when that characteristic devolved into denial, as it sometimes did, it was not healthy at all.

As promised, we drove through Cutler, population 400, on the way to Steeleville. John said he'd like to point out the house he was born in, but it had burned down. "My dad was an alcoholic," John told us, "and we were one step ahead of the rent collector. Seems like no place we lived lasted long after we left it.

"Wanda was born here, too. There were 11 children in her family. She grew up on one side of town; I was on the other, but we both lived on Buttermilk Creek. She was 16 and I was 18 when we got married and left. But I remember when I was in the eighth grade, our class went on a field trip over there to the Du Quoin fairgrounds. And I saw them two big mansions. I come home, and I says to my ma, 'I'm gonna own one of them houses someday.'"

The Steeleville parade was uneventful. More interesting was the ride back to Du Quoin. At one point, we drove by an idle coal smelter, empty coal cars lined up on the railroad tracks. Said John, "We make high sulfur coal here, and the acid rain legislation has killed the business." Perry County, John said, had 20 percent unemployment, which certainly must affect his banking and construction enterprises.

Later, passing through downtown Du Quoin, which clearly evidenced the area's economic stress, John pointed out his bank to us, then a second one. He said he'd made an offer to buy the second bank but was outbid by "the big boys" because Illinois now allowed branch banking. While in the legislature, Carol had voted for branch banking because, she said, given our restrictive state laws, US banks just could not compete with those abroad.

But John countered that the result was that "now when some fella comes into the branch bank for a loan, his papers will be sent to Chicago or Tokyo, and nobody who makes a decision will have any idea of what kind of a risk—or benefit—this man might be in his own community."

Another time, we got into a discussion about labor-management problems. John, differing with Carol—who spoke for labor (in the context of a Caterpillar strike, then in progress)—told her that on one of his bridge construction projects, workers' compensation insurance ran him $60 a day per man. He explained how these more-or-less hidden labor costs stifle business.

Even though they were friends, in the course of very casual conversation, it had become clear that Carol and our host had some fundamental differences. John and his neighbors depended on the coal industry; Carol was an environmentalist. John had lost out on a business deal as a result of a banking bill that Carol supported. Carol had a 90 percent labor rating when she was in the state legislature, while John thought many management problems went unrecognized.

It was obvious that John Rednour had not gotten to where he was without knowing how to deal. He made it clear that Alan Dixon had been a good friend, and so, now, he hoped, was Carol. But I sensed there was much more here than the politically obvious. Finally, a question that had been rising in my mind found voice. "John," I asked, "why are you a Democrat?"

"Because Republicans believe that everyone in this country can help themselves," he told me. "They think if a man has his bootstraps, that's enough. And it just ain't true. There are people in this country who can't help themselves. And those that has, has got to help those that can't get. Democrats believe that. Republicans don't."

Big John (that's what Wanda calls him) and Wanda have four children, all of whom live within five miles and are at the house regularly. Sunday morning, Little John (who is bigger than Big John and has a littler John at home) came by for breakfast, and Wanda spread peanut butter on his pancakes, then cut them in tiny pieces for her 31-year-old son. "I've done it for him all his life," said Wanda.

All in all, it was a delightful holiday weekend. Darlene and Wanda struck up what was to be a lasting friendship. Matt and I swam in the big pool, and John let Matt drive his Corvette around the deserted fairgrounds (which sure as hell beat riding a horse). With the Rednours gathered around, the supper-table stories were funny and sometimes inspiring, but the topper that had tears of laughter running down our faces was Wanda's:

"We were on a trip staying at a real fancy hotel, and I usually wear just old pajamas to bed, but this time I brought along a real pretty nightgown, you know, shimmery, nice. Well, come mornin' and John is in the bathroom shavin'. Now I'm real regular, and when I gotta go I gotta go. So I has to go. So I says, 'John, you hurry up now. I gotta go.'

"So finally he gits out, and I sit on the stool [Wanda wiggles in her chair like she's making herself comfortable], and I think, this is gonna be a stinker, so I light a match, you know, like you do. Well, it's mornin' you know, and I'm not good in the mornin' but I kinda spread my legs [she shows us] thinkin' I'm gonna drop the match through this little V into the toilet.

"But the match hits that little puff of hair down there, and I'm on fire! And John yells, 'What's the matter Wanda?' And I yell, 'My crotch is on fire!' He loved it. He said, 'I knew you was hot, honey, but not that hot!' Boy, did it stink!"

John Rednour's final story of the weekend, though, was the shortest and sweetest. "A few years back, during President Carter's administration, me and Wanda was at the White House, and we was just standing there, looking around at all the people, the president and first lady and all, and I give Wanda a poke, and I says, 'We come a long way from Buttermilk Creek, ain't we, Wanda?'"

I laughed with everybody else, but I thought: No, the real value here is that you haven't strayed too far from Buttermilk Creek, John Rednour. And you haven't forgotten.

John and Wanda and their kids were, on the face of it, a portrait of many Republicans' version of family values, a realization of the American Dream: smart white man takes advantage of the system and his community's resources and, with hard work and the solid, creative support of his wife, becomes wealthy, spending his final years in material comfort, contributing back to his community, surrounded by his healthy children and grandchildren.

Carol had bootstrapped her way up, too, but through an entirely different world of challenges. She and Matt represent a family with equal values, and now, I hoped, equal opportunity to go the same distance.

Though John and Wanda Rednour's journey from Buttermilk Creek to the mansion on the fairgrounds could not have been easy, Carol's personal journey, unlike the generally upward curve of her political career, had been fraught with pain and grief.

Mike and I separated right after Christmas in 1986, and our divorce was final the following August. At the time, I thought it was what I wanted, but the divorce was much, much more difficult than I anticipated, psychologically, financially. In the end, I had to live on a quarter of my former resources, but the awful part was how deeply it hurt Matt. Matt had been a happy, secure, even sheltered child, but if you could see pictures of him taken at the time—he was so sad.

There were certain aspects of our marriage that were very traditional, and although it may surprise some people, I was happy with that. Mike was the first person who ever wanted to take care of me, and that was comforting. I didn't really know how comforting until I lost it.

I suppose I'm still looking at this traditionally, but I believe our marriage fell victim to my career. I think that had it not been for my career, I would still be married. The more I got into politics and began to develop new skills, even a new vocabulary, the further Mike and I grew apart. In the beginning, we lived in the same world. Over dinner, we could sit and talk about deposing a client. But now I'd want to discuss ways to bail out the Chicago schools or where to put infrastructure money or who was currently being ground up by Mayor Daley's machine—and Mike was still deposing clients.

Also, of course, I was away so much and not there to be his partner, so he had a lot of time by himself. Then when he started his own firm, he developed a very close relationship with his law partner in terms of business, and when another woman came into his life, the woman to whom he is now married, I was pretty much displaced all around. I felt betrayed, on the one hand, and it was painful, but it was not like Mike set out to hurt me. There was just no room for me, so the question became, why are we still married?

But those years, 1985, '86, were the toughest years of my adult life. My dear brother Johnny died, I lost my bid for lieutenant governor, my mother had her first strokes, then had to have her leg amputated, my father died, the divorce and all that entailed, and always, always worrying about Matt. Suddenly, I was just out there, with all these people looking to me as their primary caretaker.

I think if it hadn't been for my spiritual rebirth, I would have cracked up. There is an admonition in the scriptures, "Lean not to your own understanding." To use a secular analogy, I think of The Hitchhiker's Guide to the Galaxy, *where he falls out of the spaceship and discovers that if he resists, he might be hurt, but if he stops fighting the fall, he'll be OK. I'm not sure what the end game is because I never set out to order my path the way it seems to be going. But there seems to be an internal map and [a] still small voice that speaks to me when it must. I haven't a clue as to what may be the next step, but I'm not worried.*

CHAPTER 7

Stardom: The Democratic National Convention

Sunday, July 12, 1992

This was not my first Democratic National Convention. I'd been in Los Angeles in 1960 when John Kennedy was nominated. I was 25 years old and had been selected by the California host committee to be a member of a squad of women called the "Golden Girls." There were 100 of us, two for each state. I was assigned to Pennsylvania but deserted my delegation when offered a post as hostess to the podium holding area, the convention's greenroom, as it were.

My most exciting personal memory was being caught in a mob on the convention's final day, bosom to belly with the brand new presidential nominee. JFK didn't give me a big hug, like Clinton was to give Carol when he ran into her on the night he was nominated in New York. No, Jack Kennedy simply stopped, put his hand on my arm, smiled down at me, and said, "Hey, hi, what's your name?" I can still feel my heart pounding.

Clinton and Carol Moseley Braun had some pretty important business here this week, and thanks to a friend, Democratic national committeewoman Marjorie Benton, I had a room in the Le Parker Meridien, where Carol and her small coterie of workers were also

ensconced, along with the 195-member Illinois delegation. But I
had no press pass, no credentials, and no invitations, just a few
friends from Chicago for guidance—and a nose for news.

I was not approved for this trip by Kgosie Matthews. In fact,
the first time I ran into the campaign manager and asked if I might
accompany Carol to a certain event, he reminded me—rudely, if
correctly—that he had more important things to worry about. On
the other hand, Carol had said, "Jeannie, you just check with Des
[scheduler Desiree Tate] and come along whenever you want." Problem: how to hang out with Carol and avoid Kgosie? Solution: none.

Monday, July 13, 1992
Carol spoke to the Illinois delegation at 8:30 a.m., arriving amaz-
ingly fresh from an earlier appearance on *CBS This Morning*. I
knew she had been rehearsing her speech the night before, around
11 p.m. at Madison Square Garden, because I was there, trying
without success to get in.

Carol's address, which she was to deliver to the convention
that night, had apparently been gutted by whomever was holding
the stopwatch at the rehearsal. Carol thought she was at three minutes, they timed her at five, then told her she had just two minutes.
Laughing, Carol told the assembled Illinois delegation: "You can
expect something tonight like, 'Hello! I must be going....'"

Apropos of Carol's point, my friend Bettylu Saltzman, who was
a delegate, whispered to me that the women candidates had originally been scheduled to speak tomorrow night until someone discovered they would be competing against Major League Baseball's
All-Star Game and switched them back to tonight.

The convention brain-trusters, in rearranging the lineup, had
decided to let Jesse Jackson bat against the All-Stars on Tuesday.
While Jackson had been able to muscle the '88 Democratic National Convention, '92 belonged to the women.

Carol would be the first of six women candidates to speak that
night. This was officially explained by the fact that she had been the
first female senatorial candidate to win a primary. But that didn't
matter as much as the fact that she was the most dramatic symbol
of *change*, the Democrats' (familiar?) buzzword—which was even

less important than the fact that Clinton's victory could turn on Illinois, just as Kennedy's had in 1960.

Clinton notwithstanding, considering the way political convention planners can bury speakers in a weeklong agenda, Carol could not have asked for more. The candidate from Illinois would hit the air at the top of prime time.

Carol's speech was more appropriate than spectacular; actually, it was appropriately unspectacular. "Safe" was how one of the Illinois delegates described it the following day. Carol looked wonderful, all in white. She seemed nervous, but maybe that's because I was so nervous for her.

Carol spoke from the floor of the convention, standing at the microphone before the Illinois delegation:

> I have come a long way in my life from the South Side of Chicago. I stand here this evening overwhelmed by the magnitude of the opportunity God has given me.
>
> My mother worked in hospitals and my dad in law enforcement. Both had to struggle to give our family a chance to succeed. Tonight I stand here as a living testament to the hope and faith of my parents who believed, as I believe, that America is the only country in the world where I would have had this chance. The chance to speak freely as a woman of color. The chance to be heard in the forging of a new American agenda. The chance to make history....
>
> This country is challenged to recognize that in our diversity is our strength. Quality and excellence have many faces, many voices. We grow stronger as a nation when these faces are seen and these voices are heard. ...
>
> The people of Illinois lit a spark that rekindled the faith of this nation.
>
> I am proud to stand here tonight with the other women candidates for the United States Senate. We are proof that each person can make a difference. And together, we will win.

Carol's speech was bracketed by spontaneous standing ovations, and this wasn't the usual sign-waving, cheerleading demonstration staged by convention organizers. Expressions of pleasure and pride filled the faces of conventioneers. For voters watching back home in Illinois, perhaps even more significant were the glowing remarks made by television commentators following Carol's appearance: tacit pundit endorsement. Also, unlike most of the women who came after her, Carol's entire speech was carried live on all of the stations covering the convention. It was a big night for the candidate. Carol Moseley Braun graduated from political celebrity to genuine star.

Marjorie Benton told me the next morning that Carol had circulated in the Illinois delegation after her performance "for reassurance," which she got. Some delegates, however, were carping about the fact that the delegation had not been provided with Carol Moseley Braun signs to wave around, reinforcing the conventional wisdom that the Braun campaign was disorganized. Senior staffer Steve Cobble, a political person who was both wise and creative, said not having signs was good. "Who needs it? Having all that visual hysteria behind her would make Carol look like just another candidate. As it was, she looked beautiful, almost ethereal. It was perfect."

Later, Carol told me how her speech had been written. It was yet another case of Carol reacting instinctively to a serendipitous meeting.

At a campaign event on the Friday night before the convention—with her speech still unresolved—Carol ran into a young African American woman who was an editorial writer for a major newspaper (whose name Carol would not disclose for obvious reasons). This woman was understandably thrilled about Carol's candidacy, and Carol just spilled on her.

I told her that in addition to being terrified about getting up in front of the national convention, I was crazed, because I hadn't been able to organize the points I wanted to make in a way that satisfied me.

She and I really hit it off, and we just kept talking about the speech, and I told her there was a copy of it in the car. So we went out and sat in the car. And she made some terrific suggestions with regard to structure and form. Then we decided we had to get this on paper. So we went over to the campaign office, and there was Kgosie, and I

introduced him to this woman and said, "We're working on my con-
vention speech." He just sort of hunkered down and went back into his
office and closed the door. I said to myself, "Uh, oh. I know he's upset."

My new friend and I then sat down at the computer and worked
out the whole speech. This woman was a skilled professional writer
and editor. She identified with me in every way. She was a perfect
collaborator. At about 10:30, we shook hands and she left. I wrote
her a thank you note, but I never saw her again.

Now I had to face Kgosie. "You just don't do that, dragging people
in off the street to write the most important speech of your life!"

Actually, Kgosie, yes, I do.

That man and I are a study in opposites. He is, as I've said, a
process guy. But my feeling is, if the process isn't working, why not
look for creative ways to change it?"

Tuesday, July 14, 10 a.m.

Carol flew to Baltimore with Kgosie for a noontime speech, so I
went up to Desiree's suite, guessing (correctly) that the atmosphere
might be a little more relaxed with both the candidate and the
campaign manager out of town.

This was the nerve center of the Carol Moseley Braun campaign in New York. There were three women: Desiree Tate, who
was handling a myriad of other details in addition to scheduling;
Stephanie Holtz, a bright 25-year-old who had taken over the national segment of fundraising when Jan Hensley quit; and Elizabeth Nicholson, Kgosie's assistant.

Liz combined a sharp mind with an easy smile. She had a master's degree in social service, and when she was unable to find a job
in her field, she had come on the campaign as a temp, assigned to
do clerical work. But Liz's talent and energy clearly demanded more
responsibility. Because Kgosie was so frequently out of the office, Liz
had taken over a number of administrative duties. Matthews, who
was happier to be on the move than anchored to a desk, ran much of
the campaign (and, as it turned out, his life) by cell phone.

Three male senior staffers from the campaign were also in New
York: communications director Jeremy Karpatkin, on loan to the
Carol campaign from Senator Paul Simon; Steve Cobble, who, with

the departure of Hensley, had added "fundraising coordinator" to his title of political director; and press secretary David Eichenbaum, who, from all appearances, was having a very stressful week. Cobble, a Woody Allen look-alike whose gentle cynicism could relax almost any situation, was a stabilizing force, famous for his total wardrobe of three sweaters. He had the best one on that day.

Right now, Stephanie, her dark hair falling about her face and a phone squeezed between her ear and shoulder, was relaying a message from David to Desiree regarding a satellite news feed scheduled for Carol late that afternoon: "David said he assumed Carol knew about it, and it was scheduled," reported Stephanie.

"Huh?" said Des. It was the first the scheduler had heard about this particular addition to the schedule. Apparently, Eichenbaum had told Matthews, and nobody knew whether or not Kgosie had informed the candidate.

Des, also juggling phone calls, was busy denying a credential to a guy she later described as "just a little old lawyer from Chicago" trying to con his way onto the convention floor. Meanwhile, Stephanie was calling printers, attempting to get donor cards printed for a fundraiser the next day. They'd forgotten to bring a supply from Chicago.

Liz, who is pure Chicago Irish, began cursing a recalcitrant fax machine while Des was now informing someone from *Essence* magazine, who was worried about Carol bringing too many people to their luncheon the following day, that the candidate would only be escorted by the campaign manager, "Kgosie Matthews ... K - G - O - S - I - E ... HO-see ... Oh, don't worry about it. Everybody messes it up."

It was a chaotic scene, but how could it be otherwise? An incredible spotlight had been turned on the woman these people served. All each of them could do was handle one invitation, one supplicant, one worshiper, one reporter, one problem, one disaster at a time.

Reflecting the downside of stardom, Carol was getting critical as well as laudatory attention. An article that morning in a feminist convention publication called *The Getting It Gazette* discussed rumors among the delegates that Carol Moseley Braun was "self-destructing." Wrote Celia Morris, "As the stories go, she's stiffed friends in high places, insulted key elements of the Democratic coalition and alienated some of her most dedicated workers."

The article went on to rationalize that "disorder is something that comes to all campaigns." It then detailed the chaos and defections that had plagued the Ann Richards and Dianne Feinstein campaigns, pointing out that both Richards and Feinstein got tough, cleaned house, and turned their campaigns around. Finally, Morris sought to lecture Carol Moseley Braun: "So now it's Braun's time to take hold, be brutally honest with herself, and make the decisions she must to win."

The not-so-subtle message from the feminists was "Sister Carol, you gotta fire his ass!" The article was a measure of how widespread the rumors about Carol and Kgosie's relationship and its effect on the campaign had become in the political community.

But Carol was not going to fire Kgosie Matthews, nor would any associate get by with making such a suggestion. While Matthews may have "insulted" key Democrats and "alienated" workers, the buck stopped with Carol. She would frequently try to smooth things over, once going so far as to gather combatants into a group hug, but when it came to the nut-cutting, Carol would stand by her man. The part of Carol that needed him desperately would continue to undermine her political judgment as well as separate her from those who would serve her best. One Carol would not, *could not*, follow the excellent advice of the other Carol: *If the process isn't working, why not look for creative ways to change it?*

As far back as mid-primary, speculation about Carol and Kgosie's relationship had been rampant among Chicago political people (today, it would have been all over the Internet). Since a national convention is nothing if not a cauldron of gossip, Carol and Kgosie—after Bill and Hillary and Al and Tipper—easily qualified as the most talked-about political couple in New York.

So I was not at all surprised at what David Axelrod told me when I ran into him on the convention floor. The *Washington Post*, he said, was preparing a story "dealing with the nature of the relationship between Carol and Kgosie." For a moment, silence reigned between us. Axelrod is a former newspaperman. He knows you get your best answers when you throw something out there and then shut up, hoping the object of your query will follow a natural human compulsion to fill the void. I suspected David had been asked to confirm the rumor by this *Post* reporter (which I was sure he did not do) and was now asking me to confirm it as well. We both, of course, knew it was true, that Carol and Kgosie were, indeed, "involved," but we kept to the steps of the dance.

"Look," I responded, "whenever a man and a woman work this intimately together on a project at this level of intensity, there are those rumors."

Then it was my turn to ask a question. "To your knowledge," I asked, because Axelrod knows Chicago Democratic politics like a fished-out lake, "has Carol been flat-out asked whether she and Kgosie are having an affair?"

"Yes," said Axelrod, "and she accused that person of spreading vicious rumors."

"Vicious" was an unfortunate characterization. Carol might soon need to stand up for her right to her personal relationships.

It was later confirmed that the *Post* had, indeed, been working on a relationship story but with little more than unsubstantiated gossip to go on, decided to give it a pass. With a wet finger held almost as high into the wind as any politician's, publishers are sensitive to their readers' mood swings. The romantic involvement of two single adults, even if they were candidate and campaign manager, was nothing compared with the Clinton/Gennifer Flowers story,[17] which the public had clearly demonstrated that it did not feel was relevant.

In fact, the romance rumors did not make print until writer Gretchen Reynolds mentioned them as part of a long *Chicago* magazine profile that appeared three months later, in October.

---

17 Just before the New Hampshire primary, former Arkansas state employee Gennifer Flowers revealed that she'd had a 12-year affair with Bill Clinton. This was followed by a widely viewed (50 million) *60 Minutes* segment featuring Bill and Hillary Clinton, in which both debunked the charges. Years later, Clinton admitted to having had sexual relations with Flowers "one time" in 1977.

Wrote Reynolds, referring to Carol: "She will not discuss her private life. But friends, campaign workers and observers agree that the candidate and her campaign manager appear to be romantically involved. 'They're an item,' one woman said. It was the talk of the [Democratic National] convention.'"

Carol believed, and the evidence suggests she was correct, that she would never have remained in the Senate race but for Matthews. And then Carol fell in love. Eventually, she confessed:

Well, you know the African prince story, Betty Magnus telling me that this guy, whose name she never could pronounce, was interested in me, and then Kgosie coming to Chicago and taking over the campaign.

I think the first time I related to having any romantic feelings for Kgosie was right before Gloria Steinem came to Chicago. We were out of money, and I was scared, and I just broke down. I said to him, "Kgosie, I can't go into debt. I have to take care of Matt. Even assuming I get a job, if this doesn't work, I could never pay off a big campaign debt."

I was crying. I was exhausted. But mostly, I was scared. And he put his arms around me and said, "I am not going to leave you in debt." I believed him, and it sobered me, and I felt his strength. He just said, "Don't worry."

Then Gloria came and gave us $1,000, and a number of people she touched contributed, and we made it.

So now I've figured out this man is really interested in me, and I see him as a pillar of strength and then, when I won, well, it was just the greatest thing since sliced bread. And by that time, I was totally smitten.

We just spent so much time together, and by the time we were on the "forced march," our big fundraising expedition in June, I knew there was a real relationship. Then, by Election Day, I had the sense that this was not going to end.

There were rumors all along, I know. But it was a great source of strength for me that Kgosie was so protective. Considering the traditional culture he comes from, this was perhaps as much a gender role as a matter of him playing out his duties as campaign manager.

*I don't believe our relationship affected the campaign until the end,
when Kgosie was accused of sexual harassment.*

And at the very end, of course, he did leave me in debt.

Wednesday, July 15, 10 a.m.

Carol was scheduled to appear at a Voters for Choice rally at the
Hilton at 10 on Wednesday morning. Arriving shortly after 10,
I caught Gloria Steinem speaking to the largely female audience
and rationalizing the cosmetic remake of Hillary Clinton—contact
lenses, bleached hair, a more fashionable wardrobe. Steinem said
that traditional relationships still favor the male 70-30 to 60-40 and
because that "ideal" exists, Hillary had to play down her "self" in
order to help Bill win the election. "Political wives," said Steinem,
"now play in a 90-10 game." But, she added, the good news is that
what the nation will see and benefit from in the Clinton White
House is a revolutionary concept: a 50-50 marriage partnership.

Once again, Carol's tardiness worked to her advantage. She
didn't so much "arrive" as she "entered," this time looking stunning
in soft black, unadorned except for her characteristic long beads
and subtle earrings. As Carol approached the stage, the audience
whispered and then rose to a standing ovation. Political people
being nothing if not adjustable, Senator Tom Harkin, who, at the
time, was saying that bringing up "family values" every four years
was the "Republican version of leap year," immediately introduced
the Illinois candidate, saying to a resounding cheer, "Carol Moseley
Braun represents the redemption of the American political process."

Warming, as she always did, to the audience of women, Carol
launched her speech by relating that her favorite sign in the recent
march on Washington had been "'Menopausal Women Nostalgic
for Choice.'" She then told the personal stories of three people,
friends of hers, who had pre-*Roe* abortions, each with a tragic ending. It was an intimate, moving presentation, and Carol finished to
another standing ovation.

As she moved out of the hall, surrounded by fans and reporters, one woman shouted to Carol, "Bill Clinton told the Democratic Women's Caucus yesterday that if he won Illinois, it would be
because of Carol Moseley Braun."

"He did?" Carol said, looking pleased. She then responded to questions about opponent Rich Williamson's campaign tactics, saying, "He's throwing mud balls." But when press secretary David Eichenbaum broke in with a request that she do an interview with the BBC, Carol said, "No!"

There was no particular reason to blow off the BBC, but with Illinois reporters present, Carol felt the need to make the point that she was tending to statewide business. The local press, always the great leveler, had begun to suggest course corrections.

The *Chicago Tribune*'s lead editorial the previous day, headlined "Carol Braun, Superstar," began, "No one seems to remember the last time that a Recorder of Deeds of Cook County was the toast of New York." Going on to chastise Williamson for dismissing Braun as a "hack," which, the editorial emphasized, she is not, the *Tribune* cautioned Braun to sit lightly on her pedestal and remember that the election is "about who should replace Dixon, a Senate workhorse whose moderate positions pretty closely reflected the state."

Wednesday, July 15, 6 p.m.
Despite the fact that the female political candidates were the ostensible stars at the EMILY's List party, it was interesting to observe that the person who got the most fawning attention upon his arrival was Ted Kennedy. From a distance, I watched the women pressed around him, smiling, touching—adoring—asking to be photographed with the senator.

Certainly Kennedy (who, virtually alone,[18] had elegantly defended Anita Hill during the Thomas hearings) was a legislative friend to women, but I found the adulation disconcerting, and so, it appeared, did the senator. Sweating profusely, Kennedy pulled out

---

18   Kennedy, addressing Anita Hill, who listened to this positive message with the same engaged equanimity with which she had borne all the nasty stuff:
      "I know it's been a long day for you, Professor Hill. I want to pay tribute to your courage in this whole procedure, to your eloquence and dignity. I think it's been important to millions of Americans who tomorrow will think differently about sexual harassment."

a hankie and mopped. "Nice to see you," he said expressionlessly, over and over again. Oh, sure.

The EMILY's List party raised $750,000. It was the largest single fundraiser for women ever. If, as the saying goes, "money talks, and bullshit walks," then 1992 truly was to be the "Year of the Woman."

Carol missed the more intimate VIP reception that preceded the EMILY's List program but arrived in time for a triumphant entrance at the main event. As usual, the Illinois candidate won the ovation prize. Also, as usual, the Chicago papers featured her late arrival, saying that the campaign explained she'd been meeting regarding "a fiscal report due today."

Wednesday, July 15, 11 p.m.
Validating Bill Clinton's confidence in Carol's ability to help him in Illinois, the presidential candidate's media guru, James Carville, got word to Kgosie Matthews as to when and where Clinton would enter Madison Square Garden for an "unscheduled" appearance after his nomination Wednesday evening.

Thus, Carol just "happened" to be leaving the hall as Clinton was entering, followed, of course, by live television cameras. "Hey, Carol!" hailed the new presidential nominee "Well, Bill!" the happily astonished senatorial aspirant responded, and the two naturally affectionate candidates met in a grand national embrace.

If Bill Clinton was up for the convention Oscar, Carol Moseley Braun was most assuredly a shoo-in for Best Supporting Actress.

Thursday, July 16, 1 a.m.
An hour or so after the televised Clinton/Braun moment Wednesday night, Carol walked into the Parker Meridien bar, where I was having a drink and late snack with Bettylu Saltzman (now famous for having predicted, right around this time in 1992, that Barack Obama would be the first African American president of the United States); Marilyn Katz, a Chicago consultant who does a lot of political work; and Chicago alderman Mary Ann Smith. Carol sat at an adjacent table and whispered to me from behind the potted palm that separated us, "Marilyn Katz said in the paper today that my campaign was disorganized—shall I confront her?"

"Why not?" I said, giving Carol bad advice that, thankfully, she did not take. Politics is all about seeing who can brew the biggest tempest in the smallest teapot. Katz was just repeating the conventional wisdom, which, it seemed to me, was fairly accurate. But I would be inclined to support another bit of conventional wisdom that says the term "campaign organization" is, in and of itself, an oxymoron.

Thursday, July 16, noon

The delegates—make that the nation—were abuzz in the morning with the news that Ross Perot had quit the presidential race. When I stopped by Braun campaign central, Desiree Tate, still in her bathrobe because events had moved too fast to allow her time to dress, was saying to Kgosie Matthews: "Now, you have told Carol about Mayor Daley's lunch at the Boathouse, because I don't want to hear later that she didn't know about it...."

"Yes," Matthews assured Des, his expression implying that Carol was not planning to attend anyhow. At the other end of the couch, opposite Des, Liz Nicholson was applying eye makeup while carrying on a phone conversation. Matthews, apparently in a congenial mood, talked about a place he'd found where designer clothes could be purchased wholesale. "You ought to go down there," Matthews said. Des gave him an incredulous look, "Oh, sure! I don't even have time to put on the clothes I've already got!"

David Eichenbaum appeared to be at his wit's end. A phone to his ear, he was begging someone for passes that would admit him immediately to Madison Square Garden. Carol was scheduled to go on live television inside the stadium with news anchor Allison Payne at the top of WGN's noon news. That would be 1 p.m. in New York, and it was already 12:20.

Finally, David found someone who would give him four temporary passes into the Garden and invited me to tag along. Matthews went off to find Carol while David and I went down to the car. It was now obvious that we would be late, and David was frantically trying to reach Allison Payne to let her know. It was also clear from a conversation I'd overheard that David had been instructed to tell Payne that she was not to ask Carol about the withdrawal of Ross Perot from the presidential race.

Perot's withdrawal was the story of the day, I thought. How could Payne not ask a senatorial candidate that question? Also, I knew—and I knew David knew—that it was a very bad idea to tell a reporter what you would or would not like her to ask.

David continued to try to reach Payne in the car—which he finally did—at about two minutes to high noon in Chicago. But it was still lunchtime in Manhattan, and we were looking at grid-lock between the Parker Meridien, on 56th, and the Garden, 22 blocks south.

At about 1 p.m., Carol strolled out of the hotel looking cool and elegant. I complimented her on her appearance, especially her hair. "It takes an hour," she said. And for the millionth time, I thought about how much harder this business is for women candidates.[19] When Matthews showed up, we took off like a snail in a bog.

In the car, Carol reminded David, "No questions about Perot now...." David looked uncomfortable, and I wondered if he really had conveyed that difficult message. I couldn't help speaking up: "Carol, Allison *must* ask you about Perot."

"I know," said Carol, who really did understand the reality, even though she resisted it. And then Carol explained that she was wary of getting into what was "Clinton campaign territory." She didn't want to play into the "too big for her britches" criticism that, fol-lowing the "Carol Braun, Superstar" *Tribune* editorial, had become this week's press message in Illinois.

We had to stop by the Ramada Inn for the passes David had begged and so got into the Garden with about 20 minutes left in WGN's hour-long show. Upon entering the stadium, we were im-mediately accosted by an Illinois delegate with her family in tow, who stopped Carol for an autograph and a photograph. Carol,

---

19   When I met Carol in Chicago in 2011 to try to convince her to revisit her story with the perspective time might offer, she refused. But the one (and only) thing she mentioned about the first draft that she'd read 20 years earlier was the fact that I'd commented too frequently on her groom-ing—specifically, her hair. "Don't you know that 'hair' is the third rail for African American women?" Truth was, I hadn't given it a thought. I was just constantly amazed at how beautifully dressed and put together she always looked, considering the pressures she was under.

gracious, as always, behaved as if she had all day. David looked like he was going to hemorrhage.

When we finally get to WGN's anchor location—a platform built about halfway up the grandstand across from the main stage—Allison Payne was vamping, chatting to her Chicago counterpart on the air live. There would be no way—in case he hadn't done it before—that Eichenbaum could now deliver the "no Perot" message.

Allison motioned Carol over, saying, "Carol Moseley Braun has just arrived," and telling her audience about Carol's triumphant week in New York as Carol slipped the ugly headset over her carefully coiffed hair. Then Allison asked, "How do you think the Perot withdrawal will affect the Clinton candidacy?"

"Well," Carol said, "that's not my focus. I'm thinking about all those people who have worked so hard for Mr. Perot who are going to be so disappointed—I hope not disillusioned—but certainly disappointed." Carol gave a good solid, local-angle answer, including a subtle appeal to Perot voters, then Allison switched gears on her own.

Beside me, David breathed, "Thank you, Allison. Thank you."

Afterward, David thanked Payne for changing subjects, so apparently she did get a message. The reporter responded, "We'd talked about Perot enough already in this broadcast. Our audience is older and largely female, and they want to know about Carol."

Suddenly we noticed a stir on the platform across the way, and there was Bill Clinton walking on stage with a huge grin on his face. We could see the grin because the stadium cameras were live, and Clinton's close-up image appeared on the two monster screens that flanked the stage. Then Hillary appeared, and both began to receive instructions. Tonight, the nominee would deliver his acceptance speech, and this was the rehearsal.

Carol and I walked out together discussing neither Clinton nor Perot but rather the stories that had appeared in the morning Chicago papers. As of June 30, the Braun campaign had raised close to $1.8 million compared with Williamson's $516,502. Carol—who remembered every individual who ever told her "you will not be able to raise enough money to run for the US Senate"—was downright gleeful.

Thursday, July 16, late evening

Al Gore's speech was surprisingly stirring, I thought, and Clinton's a little long and woolly, but finally, there up on the stage before us, were the newly anointed first and second Democratic couples, hand-holding, swaying to and fro as Fleetwood Mac urged us not to stop "thinkin' about tomorrow." The inescapable message: across the nation, a new generation—boom-boom, boom-boom, boom-boom.

As I contemplated the tableau before me, I couldn't help thinking of what Senator Bob Kerrey had said about his having no chance for the vice presidential nomination: "'Bill and Hillary and Al and Tipper' had such a nice ring," he said, "but 'Bill and Hillary and Bob' just wouldn't do."

The ring of it aside, I thought Senator Kerrey was probably wrong about the substance of his comment: America was now the baby boomers' country, and the electorate would surely accept a bachelor vice president or president.

Carol's "singleness," playing well behind her "blackness" and "femaleness," had not been a factor at all in the campaign. Nevertheless, I loved what Senator Barbara Mikulski had said regarding the proposition that a political woman simply could not win in the man department. "If you're married, you're neglecting the guy," said the firebrand from Maryland. "If you're divorced, you couldn't keep him; if you're single, you couldn't get a man; and if you're a widow, you killed him!"

Now Carol appeared on the stage and was hugged by Bill and trailed by the other candidates, including all the female senatorial aspirants. Balanced by color and gender, the group on stage formed a pretty people picture, carefully composed. And, as someone said in contrasting the Democratic convention to the Republican, it did "look much more like a country than a country club." What with the music and balloons and all, the Democratic convention planners had produced an exciting finale.

I found myself wishing that it was real.

CHAPTER 8

Race and Religion

I T WAS MIDNIGHT. We were driving back into the city from Ravinia, the outdoor music theater in suburban Highland Park on the far North Shore. Peter, Paul and Mary had given a concert during which Peter Yarrow, after a short, impassioned speech, brought up the houselights and introduced Carol. Many in the audience stood and cheered, but not all; a significant number of concertgoers sported that politely pinched look that said: "This is not what I paid to hear."

In a sense, Carol was being paid to listen; we'd come to Ravinia for money, not music. Following the event, the famous folk singers, whose songs defined the youth of most of the attendees, hosted a $125-a-ticket reception. Yarrow and Mary Travers, both of whom spoke, told us how Carol embodied the realization of their closely held beliefs. Like their music, the artists' words held poetry and passion, and not a few had to wipe away tears.

Carol shook hands and smiled and was photographed, but I could see she had her eye on the lemon squares that topped an elegant dessert table. We hadn't eaten all day. As the witching hour approached and we prepared to leave, Carol whispered, "Grab a couple of those for me, will you?" I didn't have to ask the candidate what she meant.

Now Carol was in the backseat of Gus Fordham's Lincoln, polishing off the lemon squares, wishing she had a cup of coffee, and massaging her cramped feet. She'd begun the day on asphalt 14 hours earlier at a ribbon-cutting ceremony on the South Side, then hit the floor of the Chicago Board of Trade, followed by the gleaming surfaces that pave the Sears Tower (now renamed Willis Tower). After that she got to return to her campaign office, where the floors were covered in what might charitably be called fuzzy cement. Then it was off to a fundraiser on the blessedly comfortable oriental carpets of a luxury Michigan Avenue apartment, where the candidate never even had a chance to sit down. Next came the concert, and after that the reception, held in a brightly stripped tent erected over—asphalt. Not a great day for wearing high heels.

But it had been a excellent day in another sense. On the front page of that morning's *New York Times*, right under the date, July 29, 1992, appeared a wonderful picture of Carol in a tasteful, smiling embrace with Bill Clinton, who had made a quick stop in Chicago's western suburbs the day before. Below the photo the headline read, "Black Woman's Senate Race Is Acquiring a Celebrity Aura." The story, a long feature by Isabel Wilkerson, had clearly been in preparation for some time. I suspected that it never would have been a front-page piece but for the stunning and seemingly serendipitous convention photo op. Newspapers can be seduced by the visual thing. (Now even more than then!)

Carol was laughing. "Can you believe it? Front page, *New York Times*—and a puff piece to boot!" But I was uneasy about this kind of noncritical attention. Writers are always subject to attacks of Journalism 101 guilt and might turn on Carol later. A diet of sweets will hold reporters for a while, but sugar crashes are inevitable.

Many, like Ira Cohen, the veteran progressive thinker who headed the campaign's issues department, knew it was time to go deeper on the issues. Ira, a burly bear of a man, was a quiet fellow who worked long hours and said little, but from the crew of eager young people who labored under Ira's guidance (and adored him, incidentally), I learned that detailed position papers on the economy, education, health care, crime, agriculture, energy, and the environment had been in preparation for some time. The problem was that Carol kept kicking them back to the issues group, unsatisfied with the way the material was presented. "If she'd just tell us what she wanted," one young woman wailed, "we could do it." This curious process, which caused no small amount of angst on the campaign staff, continued until late October when a full set of issues papers was finally distributed to the press.

For me, the issues mystery was finally cleared up in one sentence uttered by Kgosie Matthews in a senior staff meeting he had invited me to attend in early October. "I don't like taking positions on issues," said the campaign manager, "because then you have to defend them." The fact that Matthews pressed for issues papers he demonstrably did not want added to the surreal aura of the campaign.[20]

Yet, despite the lack of detailed, bound-and-printed information, on the stump and when asked, the candidate was very clear about where she stood and what she wished to see accomplished on the relevant issues, particularly domestic problems, with which she had a great deal of legislative experience and that were much on the public mind during this election season. While Carol admitted that she had some things to learn about foreign policy and defense, she was explicit regarding the principles upon which her decisions would be based. The public was not misled about where Carol Moseley Braun stood. The press, in this case, did not care to forage; it wished to be fed. Thus, to the end, issues were an issue.

Nevertheless, Carol's legislative record was clear and her lead so substantial—at least until mid-October—that despite the universal disagreement of staff and journalists, Matthews's "no detailed positions" position, if frustrating, was, in fact, tactically insignificant. What was going on "out there" was exactly expressed by one woman quoted in Wilkerson's July 29 New York Times piece:

---

20 On the other hand, there were those in the campaign who thought that as long as Carol was being buoyed along by her popularity and candor on issues as they came up, why complicate things by getting into weeds that could tangle?

> "She's me," Diane Valleta, a white woman from the
> Chicago suburbs said of this black woman from the
> South Side. "She represents everything I feel, every-
> thing I want to be. I'm so locked into her that what
> she says is unimportant."

Later in the *Times* story, another woman was quoted whose attitude went far to explain the success of the campaign's fundraising
strategy. Described as one of the women "waving checkbooks" at
the candidate, 31-year-old registered Republican Julie Weber said,
"I can't give enough. I couldn't wait to write her a check."

Carol's intelligence, outward confidence, and personal charisma had much to do with these typical reactions, the passions
en*gender*ed dating back to Carol's tough stand during the Thomas-Hill face-off, an issue still very much alive in the land. Yet these
were expressions of feelings, not of thought, and were therefore
vulnerable to incidents that might stir countervailing emotions.

The campaign's first financial goal, to annihilate Richard Williamson
in the fundraising department, had been achieved in June. Interestingly, a Steve Cobble memo to Kgosie Matthews dated August
15, 1992, estimated that through fundraising events and what were
proving to be remarkably successful national telemarketing and di-
rect-mail efforts, the campaign would eventually raise $5.3 million.
Missing the mark by more than $1 million, Cobble had underrated
the power of what Ann Lewis, former Democratic National Committee policy maker, characterized in July as a "national candidacy."
Said Lewis: "Women around the country feel emotionally and politically invested in this [the Carol Moseley Braun] campaign."

"What meeting that first fundraising goal achieved," Cobble
said, continuing his analysis, "was to negate the well-known fact
that Carol had not been able to raise money in the primary and to
show the political world that this very special woman could draw
more money than a rich, white, male Republican attorney from
Kenilworth, a suburb with one of the highest per capita incomes
in the nation." Not to mention, according to the *Chicago Tribune*,
that Kenilworth—for the fifth straight year—ranked number one
nationally in "social status," whatever that means.

"So this fundraising achievement gave Carol tremendous credibility going into the convention," said Cobble, "and by the time the convention was over, she was a star.

"I remember asking Celinda [Celinda Lake, then of the Washington polling firm Greenberg-Lake, was the Braun campaign pollster][21] what we will have to do in September so that the Republicans will have to write Williamson off, and she said, 'If you report two million for the quarter and she's 25, 26 points ahead, he's finished.' Republican funders would take one look at the disproportionate numbers in Carol's favor and say, 'Nope, not throwing any more money down this rat hole.' And it would be all over for Richard Williamson."

Meanwhile, back on the campaign trail, Richard Williamson continued his effort to reduce Carol Moseley Braun to a set of stereotypes.

When an individual spends her or his adult life in Chicago politics, she or he will inevitably accumulate some baggage, and Carol, while less culpable than most, had, nevertheless, collected a small cartload that Williamson tried mightily to exploit, mostly under the general heading of "cronyism."

For example, during her 1988 race for recorder of deeds, Carol had borrowed $30,000, interest-free, from a PAC controlled by her friend Billie Paige's lobbying firm, Shea, Paige & Rogal, Inc. As the press pointed out, interest-free loans to campaigns are not unusual, and the money was paid back in three installments over the following 17 months. Then, on Carol's recommendation, the Cook County Board awarded Paige a $30,000 lobbying contract in 1991.

While it was not unusual for city or county interests to be represented by paid lobbyists in Springfield, the recorder's office had never had such an advocate. "I had weekly and monthly reports from her [Paige] on a whole slate of matters," an angry Carol responded to the implication of Williamson's charge that the contract was a political payoff. Carol said that the fact that the loan and contract numbers were the same was "just coincidence." Indeed, among other

---

21   Still active in Democratic politics, Lake is now president of Lake Research Partners.

things, Paige had worked successfully to get the legislature to repeal the hated—and outdated—Torrens system used by Cook County to record land title transfers, an act that was widely praised both editorially and by the real estate and construction interests affected.

As for how much punch Williamson's charge carried, the *Chicago Sun-Times'* coverage was typical:

> In his continuing effort to make ethics an issue in their campaign, Williamson said the contract shows Braun is "part and parcel of the old-boy network that is not acceptable to the people of Illinois."
>
> "I don't approve of the old-boy network," said Williamson, a partner in the law firm of Mayer Brown & Platt, which has been a major recipient of "pinstripe patronage" government legal business. Williamson himself has performed work for the Illinois Housing Development Authority, one of Mayer Brown's public clients.

"Pinstripe patronage" is a mildly pejorative description of the long-standing tradition that city businesses get a lot of city business, and where you stand in this gravy train frequently depends on whom you know—or to whom you have contributed—in City Hall. Upon his election in 1983, Mayor Harold Washington set out to see that alms to the rich were more equitably distributed. And herein lay another Williamson issue, this time a bond issue.

Always, as she said, "keeping her shingle dusted," Carol had accepted a small amount of legal work throughout her legislative career and even during her stint as Cook County recorder of deeds. But in 1983, she became the beneficiary of Washington's affirmative action when the mayor declared that the city's lucrative bond work would no longer be awarded to all-white legal firms. Trouble was, there were no African American bond lawyers out there. So Washington pointed to attorney insiders Earl Neal, Albert Terrell, Senator Richard Newhouse, and Representative Carol Moseley Braun and said: "Thou shalt be bond lawyers." And, of course, this being Chicago, it came to pass.

Either directly or indirectly, from 1984 through 1991, Carol drew income through various firms, Sidley Austin, Braun & Rivkin, and, finally, Jones Ware & Grenard, for work on city bond issues. The *Chicago Tribune*, in an editorial on January 12, 1985, opined that the "new patronage" might not be all bad in that it opened up opportunities for minorities, adding, "The real scandal here may not center on who has received the business but on why some lawyers can make so much money for so little labor."

Carol agreed.

It's ridiculous. I knew nothing about the bond business going in, but I learned, did the work, and took the money. The critics are correct about the system. Much too much money goes to these legal firms for what is essentially embroidered boilerplate stuff. There is a technical piece—knowing what the market will bear, making sure the revenue flow is in place to pay off the bonds—and the people who count those beans probably do earn every dime. But in terms of the firms involved, everybody in a bond deal gets a percentage, not based on the complexity of it but based on the size of the offer—and what it comes down to is just a bunch of lawyers sitting around a table pushing paper at one another. So I was one of the paper pushers.

Was this illegal? No. Was there a conflict of interest in regard to my other responsibilities? No. Was this a cup of gravy spooned into the minority community by Mayor Washington? Absolutely. In February of 1984, city corporation counsel James Montgomery directed law firms doing business with the city to hire four—four—minority lawyers—four places at the table where the gravy is served. I sat down. It tasted good—partly because I knew that if it hadn't been me, it would have been some guy who looked like Richard Williamson.

It was 8:30 a.m., too early to be waiting for Carol outside of Spiaggia, an upscale Michigan Avenue restaurant. Hell, the stores didn't even open until 10! I glanced down at the briefing paper I'd been given by the campaign scheduling office the evening before. Carol would also have a copy. "This is a regular board meeting of the Chicago Development Council. There are 80 members, big owners and developers of downtown Chicago real estate. There will a big turnout because you are coming. Their meeting will begin at 8 and you will speak at 8:30. Most of these people have to get to their offices by 9-9:30."

I looked down the near deserted avenue, searching for either Gus's black Lincoln or the blue Jeep Cherokee, which meant that Matthews would be at the wheel. To pass the time, I went back to the briefing paper: "Passive-loss Rules. Under the 1986 tax code, all limited partnerships in real estate are considered passive, and investors cannot take tax deductions for losses, no matter how 'active' an investor is in the property … they are against this provision of the current code. We support the current passive-loss rules."

Oh boy, much too early in the morning for this shit—and late on top of it.

I stepped inside for a moment. Kathleen Murray, an ace fund-raiser, was standing outside the door of Spiaggia's posh private dining room with zoning lawyer Jack Guthman, a staunch Democrat and, at the moment, a very pissed-off Carol supporter. Guthman was Carol's sponsor for this event and did not fancy being embarrassed in front of his fellow Rich White Men. Inside the room, the suits were beginning to twitch; a few left quietly, but most were anchored by curiosity.

Shortly after 9, Carol bustled in looking only slightly less tense than Guthman. Murray decided it was time to breathe again. I slipped into a chair at the back of the room.

Combine annoyance and testosterone, then temper it with a veneer of courtesy, and the result is a distinctly suffocating atmosphere. Clearly, Carol was feeling it; she was not her usual upbeat self. Then, the sometime Democrat and president of the huge and (politically) well-connected Stein & Company developers rose with a question.

"Carol," Richie Stein said, "I think there is substantial money that would come your way from Democrats, but people are hesitant because of three questions I'd like to pose to you. One, there is considerable concern over Louis Farrakhan and his anti-Semitic attacks, and we'd like to be clear on your position regarding him. Two, there is a fear that you might be under pressure to support a black candidate for mayor in the next election, and three, what about Williamson's charge that Mayor Washington threw you $100,000 in no-bid bond work you weren't qualified to do?"

Before Stein finished the question, Carol's eyes were flashing. Richie had found her starter button.

Up went three fingers. "One, I have consistently and will always condemn racism in all its forms. Regarding interests concerning the Jewish community, check my record. For one, I am a strong supporter of Israel. Israel is the only democracy in the Middle East. I believe our foreign policy should follow our values. But I will not, and should not be asked to, denounce any individual."

One finger folded crisply, the other two were still raised.

"Two. What kind of question is that: 'Will I be under pressure to support a black candidate for mayor?' I support Richard M. Daley, who *is* the mayor, and he supports me. Furthermore, I am not known for succumbing to interest-group pressure."

Two down, a tough one to go.

"Three. At the time Mr. Williamson refers to, with over 600 black lawyers in Chicago, none were listed as bond counsel. Mayor Washington learned that in a study he had conducted regarding minorities in city government. He appointed four black attorneys, myself as one, as cocounsel to work with certain law firms. I worked with Sidley Austin.

"For my opponent, referring to 'no-bid' bond work is a deliberate deceit. As an attorney, himself, specializing in government practices and with a firm that does significant work for the city, he knows very well that such work is not put out for bid. One more thing: I did the work, and I did a good job."

Carol was up and running, and the rest of the session went smoothly. For me, this was another moment among many—the first being her courageous dissent on the appointment of Clarence Thomas—that showed what an important senator Carol would be. As a politician, she was so much more than the symbol (black, female) that people saw first. She was super smart and tough; she understood the issues and, best of all, had no problem confronting power with the truth as she saw it. She'd just stood up in front of some of the wealthiest, most influential men in the state and kicked ass. I could not stop smiling.

Despite the fact that Carol had been a staunch ally of Jewish interests throughout her career, she continued to have problems for one reason and one reason alone: she was black. Indeed, at the time of this exchange, her opponent, Richard Williamson, was running an ad with yet another deceitful line, this one implying that she was a supporter of renegade African American congressman Gus Savage. Savage's parting shot upon being defeated in the recent March primary was still fresh in the minds of Carol's Jewish constituents. Said Savage: "We have lost to the white racist press and to all the racist, reactionary Jewish misleaders."

Williamson's ad, after repeating the tired refrains about tax increases and Jesse Jackson that the public had been hearing for months, now added "[Braun] was there to sponsor a resolution calling Gus Savage 'a model of public service, integrity, and dedication to his fellow man.'" And so Carol had done—*in 1979* when Savage, one of her Hyde Park constituents, had been a newspaper publisher and civil rights leader—many, many years before Savage was elected to Congress and eventually revealed his bitterness.

Nevertheless, as the *Chicago Jewish Star* reported in June 1992, "Braun has been the target of a subterranean whispering campaign seeking to link her to support for forces unfriendly to Israel." Political correspondent James D. Besser went on to report that Wisconsin Republican senator Robert Kasten, in a speech to the American Jewish Committee, had suggested that Braun was "allied with what some Republicans are now imaginatively calling the 'Jesse Jackson-Louis Farrakhan wing' of the Democratic Party."

Despite the fact that Carol had consistently supported Israel, despite the fact that she had introduced a resolution condemning the racist remarks of Minister Louis Farrakhan in the Illinois legislature, despite her well-publicized sponsorship of a hate-crimes bill, in July, the *Star* reported that "the whispering has taken its toll among Jewish voters—a key constituency for Braun in November.... In their eyes, Braun is guilty by association—because she is black, because she is liberal, because she worked with Jesse Jackson in a city where Jackson was a major political force."

But mostly, because she is black. Carol told me:

I do not deal in personal denunciations, I've made that clear. I wouldn't denounce Eddie Vrdolyak, even if the lieutenant governorship depended upon it; I wouldn't denounce Farrakhan, even if it meant the Jewish vote. But what really frosts me is the implication that I should have to answer for Farrakhan or Gus Savage—or any-one else—just because our skin is roughly the same color! William-son is Aryan, white. Do I ask him to explain David Duke? Do I say to Richie Stein, "OK, Richie, what about Ivan Boesky?" just because they're both Jewish businessmen?

Carol said something to me when I first joined the campaign that still haunts me. I don't remember what exactly sparked her comment or precisely how I responded, but somebody must have made a nasty, perhaps racist or condescending remark to her and I reacted dismissively, saying something like, "He's an idiot. Don't let it bother you." Carol turned on me, angrily, her eyes flashing, and said: "You are so damned color-blind, Jeannie. You just don't get it. Some Alabama redneck would understand better than you do!"

I was stunned—and sorry. Pondering her instinctive rage, I did "get it," at least intellectually, but could I feel it deeply and emotionally as she did? I would never have the audacity to claim that. I asked Carol, when she had time, to talk about herself in terms of race. One day, she did.

At Chicago Law, I undertook to help form the first Chicago chapter of BALSA, the Black American Law Students Association.[22] *Some members of the faculty thought this a challenge to the liberal tradition of the university. Chicago Law had always admitted a few black students, and certain officials saw BALSA as a repudiation of the school's good intentions.*

I'll never forget the day I was called on the carpet by one of the most formidable members of the faculty. Soia Mentschikoff was a scholar in her own right, but she was also married to an even more famous legal scholar, Karl Llewellyn. Mentschikoff was a large woman of stately demeanor who would—and on occasion, did—terrify a student with a glance. She functioned as the unofficial dean of women. I was in awe of her.

---

22 The organization is now known as the National Black Law Students Association.

As I entered her office, I was prepared to be challenged about my activities on behalf of BALSA, but I was not prepared for her approach. Dr. Mentschikoff said to me, "Miss Moseley, you must remember you are first a University of Chicago law student, then a woman, then a black. There is no need for this separation based upon race."

My response was instinctive: "No, Dr. Mentschikoff. I am first a black, then a woman, then a University of Chicago law student. And this is not so because I would define myself in that way but rather because that is how the world sees me, how my realities are shaped."

This exchange effectively ended the discussion between Dr. Mentschikoff and me, and I and others went on to form the first Chicago chapter of BALSA. But I think a clue to the confusion about race in America lies in this well-remembered incident and in the dual perceptions it illustrated. Whether one cares to acknowledge it or not, for black Americans, race (and its sidekick, color) is a defining issue of existence. I think white Americans have difficulty with this notion: aren't blacks perpetuating separation by this continual reference to race? Haven't we done away with segregation? Isn't that enough?

The truth is that the separation is not perpetuated by black ethnic pride but by the myriad encounters and situations in which the society as a whole acknowledges the "differentness" of people of color. It is how we are perceived by others that shapes the reactions that many well-meaning whites find so disturbing. When I walk down the street, I am perceived by both whites and blacks alike as a black. It is a threshold, defining issue.

I remember an incident that happened years after finishing at U of C, when I was working as an assistant United States attorney. I'd left the office late and was attempting to catch a cab. Several taxis passed me by, empty ones with no passengers. The predilection of cabs to refuse passage to blacks was based upon a presumption that the driver would be required to go into the feared ghetto. After several frustrating minutes standing on the street attempting to hail a cab, a police car drove slowly by.

The police officer on the passenger side of the squad car leaned out and yelled at me, "Hey, you! Give up that corner!"

I was too tired to immediately recognize the implication of what the cop had said to me, and I continued to try to flag a cab. By and by, the police car returned, and the policeman, even more rudely than before, said, "Hey! I told you to give up that corner. If you're still there when we come by again, I'm takin' you in!"

The Chicago police officer didn't see a U of C law school graduate on that corner or a US attorney; he saw a black woman on a street corner at night. With Mayor Daley's recent order to crack down on prostitution, that was all he needed. I was angry, but I was also exhausted, and when a cab finally stopped, I went home.

But one does not forget. Nor was my experience unusual. It remains commonplace among black Americans, no matter how privileged or accomplished, to be stigmatized by the still extant stereotypes associated with race and color. "It doesn't matter how big you get, you're still a nigger," is a familiar part of the lexicon of blacks. Whites overhearing such statements note the voice of victimization and that in itself short-circuits understanding.

My grandmother's generation used to say things like, "You may be my color, but you're not my kind" as a way of making class distinctions within the black community. The issue of color had such a pervasive and restrictive role in her time that among blacks, there were very precise delineations about who was worthy to associate with whom. The "house nigger/field nigger" reference of old was much too broad; there were Creoles and Guiches and folks who clung to being Indian. And there were infinite gradations of skin shade, hair texture, nose structure—not to mention the more obvious distinctions of wealth and occupation. The irony of it all, of course, was—and in many places, still is—that to whites, color and race were not class distinctions at all; they defined a caste.

This aspect of caste, in connection with Jim Crow segregation, remains largely responsible for the historic inability of black Americans to accumulate wealth and, more importantly, to be able to pass that wealth on from generation to generation. This is yet another area that seems to mystify white Americans. How is it, they ask, that after all these generations in this land of opportunity, the blacks have not been able to pull themselves up the economic ladder as have other immigrant groups? The answer is clear: question virtually any apparently successful African American, and you will learn that, on an economic scale, her or his parents lived somewhere between poverty and the lower middle class. It is after that struggle that capital accumulation begins. And, for most, the struggle continues.

Generations that preceded mine point with pain to the theft from its black originators of the "policy" gambling game, first by the Mafia, then by the state. "When it was ours," the old folks say, "it was illegal. Now they've got it, and it's called the lottery." Whether the industry was aviation, or surveying, or the construction trades, the perpetual frustration of black Americans in attempting to break into, sustain, and advance in the economic mainstream is another defining aspect of existence.

With the fall of state-supported segregation came the end of the more rigid limitations of caste. Integration has meant that some black Americans are now afforded an opportunity as never before to participate in the American Dream. But frustrations remain, and they will, as long as old ways of thinking remain, old habits, old memories.

There is debate in the African American community today about the virtues of assimilation; there are those who fear a loss of pride in our special heritage. I disagree with that. As our democratic institutions mature, I think we will find that liberty and individualism, including racial and ethnic distinctions, need not be lost as those who have been historically disadvantaged begin to swim in the mainstream. I know that learning to live in the white world, for all its challenges, enriched my life. It all comes down to ignorance and lack of personal contact between the races, and it will be solved by the racial integration of all of our institutions because then we will know and judge one another as individuals.

Going to church and then a picnic is a lovely way to spend a sunny Sunday in July, unless you are campaigning for the US Senate, which meant that on this particular Sunday, we were flying from Chicago to Champaign and going to four churches, two picnics, and a county fair.

I picked up Darlene Mackey in a cab, and we arrived at Meigs Field at around 9 a.m. Carol showed up a few minutes later, snorting and fuming. "I've had it. I told him I was going to quit," Carol complained. "They've just got to stop scheduling me like this."

Trailing the candidate and looking dapper and relaxed in his Calvins was Carol's campaign manager and, today, chauffeur,

Kgosie Matthews. He had a little smile dancing on his normally stern countenance.

Darlene and I glanced at each other. This was a fairly routine litany, and apparently Kgosie had been catching it all the way to the airport. Matthews appeared unfazed. He didn't have to speak at four church services this morning; he was going to work in the office. "At least that's what he says," Carol laughed as we climbed aboard the little plane. Moments later, as we soared over Chicago's sparkling lakefront, turning southwest, I thought about the strains created in a relationship when one person is accountable for her or his time—and the other is not. It was a bumpy ride.

Champaign County, home of the University of Illinois, was one of the few downstate counties to cast a majority vote for Carol in the primary, and Carol never fails to appreciate those who helped her when she struggled in anonymity. It's the flip side of something Steve Cobble had recently said: "Carol is a firm believer in the John Kennedy axiom, 'Forgive your enemies, but don't forget their names.'" Carol remembers names on both sides of the tally. Donna Marie Jackson had been an active supporter during the primary, and she would escort us to our first four stops, all African American churches.

I liked Donna Marie immediately. She was the wife of a local pastor, and the first congregation we would meet was her husband's at the Bethel African Methodist Episcopal Church. Donna Marie told us there would be a larger crowd than usual today "because you are here," she said to Carol and that Reverend Jackson would invite her to the pulpit to speak.

As we entered the sanctuary, we were handed programs. Suddenly, Carol, who had clearly not lost all discomfort with this day's demands, stopped dead in her tracks. She turned to me silently and drew my attention to the cover of the program, which featured a tranquil, full-color photograph of a sparkling stream running through sunlit woods. I looked at the picture, puzzled. "So?" I mouthed. "No," she whispered, and pointed to the bit of scripture, Galatians 6:9, below the photo: "And let us not be weary in well doing: for in due season we shall reap, if we faint not."

Smiling, Carol opened her remarks with this verse, telling Reverend Jackson's congregation that she had begun this day complaining about the demands of her campaign and that today's scripture had met her needs exactly. Then she delivered the short but appropriate speech we had heard in formation on the plane when Carol had asked Darlene—a woman who gets up at 5:30 every morning to read her Bible—to complete a scripture passage regarding faith that Carol only half remembered.

"Faith," Carol said, was what the people had who cast a vote in the primary for a woman who the experts said could not win. "Hope" is what we create when we invest our resources in education and jobs, and "Charity begins where…?"

"In the home!" the congregation responded.

"Yes. And Illinois ranks 48th out of 50 states in federal dollars returned. I will help bring more dollars back home to Illinois."

As we left, Carol seemed relaxed and happy. She'd rediscovered the fact that the harvest was worth the plowing. It was clear the candidate would faint not.

On the way to the Mt. Olive Baptist Church, Donna Marie told us that the Reverend Lundy Savage "is a chauvinist. Even if he asks you to go to the pulpit, don't." Sitting in the backseat with me, Darlene explained that among African American denominations, the Baptists feel very strongly that men are the leaders of the church and women are the workers.

Reverend Savage's church was modern and, thankfully on this muggy day, air-conditioned. It was also packed with beautifully dressed people, a few of whom moved even closer together to give us seats. When Carol was introduced, she walked to the microphone below the pulpit and repeated the remarks she'd nailed in her previous appearance, this time with even more verve. She finished to a standing ovation.

We rose to leave but—oops! The good reverend had arranged a photo op. A photographer appeared in the aisle, the reverend signaled for his wife to join him, and the congregation waited while the preacher got his picture taken with Carol. Apparently to ease the awkwardness, the reverend addressed the assembly, saying of

Carol, "This is a proud black woman—and good-looking, too. It's time we send a good-looking woman up there to Washington!"

I glanced over at Donna Marie. Her face was stony.

Back in the car, Donna Marie said, "He tells his wife what to wear and how to act. She doesn't do anything without asking him." We drove by the magnet school Donna Marie's children attended. "I am president of the PTA," Donna Marie said. "The first black president. I am proud of that."

"So are we!" said Carol. Then the discussion turned to gender issues in the African American community. Carol told us it had been Kgosie who'd said to her, when they'd attended a Baptist church together recently, "That minister thinks he can sleep with anyone in this congregation and she must submit to him." (Kgosie had been around this block with the Jackson campaign.) Kgosie might have been exaggerating, Carol said, but it was true enough in essence. "That idea represents an age-old ethic that has kept black women suffering in silence for generations."

She added, "And this silence is fundamental to the schism among black women brought on by the Thomas/Hill thing. The reason so many African American women lined up with Clarence is that they felt Anita betrayed this tradition that says that women must support their men because black men have enough to deal with without being undermined by their women."

As we drove to our next church, I reflected on a lunchtime conversation that had taken place a few days earlier. There were five of us, all women, two white, three black. We chewed over Thomas/Hill. Then, as often happened, I was asked about how it had been for me all these years as the only woman reporter dealing with male professional athletes. I replied that, in working with Carol, I realized that I'd had advantages similar to those she used as an African American. More often than not, the men you were dealing with had certain stereotypical expectations, and by confounding those, you immediately gained the advantage.

"But the black guys are much more chauvinistic than the white guys," one of the women insisted. I had to say that my experience as a reporter with countless black athletes didn't reflect that. And all three of the black women exchanged looks and headshakes—like I was clueless.

It turned out we were not talking about the same level of male on female conflict. My friends told me that sexual abuse was a serious, unspoken problem in their community, one they were expected not to talk about to a white person, a deeper, more painful aspect of the schism Carol had just spoken of in relation to Thomas/Hill. Now, laughing, one of the women said emphatically, "and the guys from Africa are the worst, the very worst." So, naturally, the conversation shifted back to Kgosie Matthews and the sad irony of his relationship with our candidate.

My participation in that revealing lunch-hour conversation had been pretty superficial, but now my mind floated back to the '60s and the subculture I had married into: my husband had been a professional football player; I was a stay-at-home mom. What I often felt during those years was a suffocating atmospheric pressure, a threatening cloud, always there, bearing down, keeping me well below it in a stability-ensuring but psychologically stifling role.

I know it is arrogant for me to mention myself in *any* context with the supremely gifted James Baldwin—a gay man, a black man, and a literary genius—but Baldwin defined something once in an interview that (for me) explained my later activism, the whole women's movement, the recent reaction to Clarence Thomas, and the uncontained joy so many women found in Carol's candidacy. In reaction to the interviewer's comment, "I suspect most gay people have fantasies about genocide...." Baldwin replied:

> I know from my own experience that the macho men—truck drivers, cops, football players—these people are far more complex than they want to realize. That's why I call them infantile. They have needs which, for them are literally inexpressible ... and that's why they need faggots. They've created faggots in order to act out a sexual fantasy on the body of another man and not take any responsibility for it. Do you see what I mean? I think it's very important for

the male homosexual to recognize that he is a sexual
target for other men, and that's why he is despised.
And why he is called a faggot. He is called a faggot
because other males need him.

I copied that paragraph into my journal at the time with the
comment, "Just substitute 'cunt' for 'faggot,' Jimmy, and we're on
the same page." And "nigger" and "bitch" work, too.

As much as I admired, no, loved, James Baldwin's work, for a
long time, I had a problem with the way he would generalize about
the thoughts, feelings, and prejudices of white people, even though
I knew, also from his writing, there were many whites he admired,
notably the beloved elementary school teacher (he called her Bill)
who led him into literature. But then I realized that what mattered
was not whether Baldwin's generalizations were true or not of a
single individual; rather, he was using his gift to help us all understand how our repressive culture affected every aspect of the
lives of our fellow citizens who happened to have been born with
dark skin. Like Dr. King, he was using the power of words to plead
for understanding and, through that, the true emancipation of all
Americans. Over and over again in his writing, Baldwin shows us
how hate wounds the hater as much as the hated.

Getting personal again, for me, the insight and despair expressed by Baldwin in the paragraph quoted earlier is the "nut
graf" that explains how the women's movement of the 1970s grew
out of the civil rights movement of the 1960s and now the gay
rights movement we are finally seeing today. We all just had to get
our heads up through that very heavy, very male, very white, and
stifling cloud. We're not done yet—not even close—but the atmosphere is improving.

As sister African American feminists, Carol Moseley Braun and
Donna Marie Jackson were really hitting it off, and Carol was completely warmed up by the time we got to our final service at the
Canaan Missionary Baptist Church in Urbana, twin city to Champaign. The Reverend B. J. Tatum had already launched into his ser-
mon, and a rousing one it was. Reverend Tatum took as his theme

the journeys of Paul, and the qualities the preacher expanded upon were determination and dedication. A man who obviously loved the language, the preacher punctuated his declarations with the cry, "Do I have a witness here?"

Reverend Tatum most certainly did, chief among them, Carol Moseley Braun. I glanced at the candidate, who was sitting beside me, content to wait her turn. I thought: Bring on the picnickers, the fairgoers, the outstretched hands, and the redundant questions. This day was not yet half over, but the rest of it was going to be fine.

Carol approached the front of the overflowing church to warm applause. As she took her place below the pulpit, she drew a big breath, smiled, and said, "Reverend Tatum, you were preaching to me. I am, indeed, on a journey. Dedication and determination?" She laughed, then shook her head slightly and sighed, "Yes, I was meant to be here."

CHAPTER 9

Campaign Unrest; The Carolvan

"A FTER LABOR DAY, THE CAMPAIGN STARTS IN EARNEST."
"After Labor Day, there will be no rest."

"After Labor Day, we'll all be so tense, so frantic, you won't believe the fights!"

This was the sort of talk going around the campaign office as August melted into September and the veterans warned the rookies that they were about to enter two months of hell.

In an early September staff meeting, Jeremy Karpatkin (who subsequently left the campaign) warned 30 or so mostly young staffers not to get too complacent about a recent *Chicago Tribune* poll that showed Carol ahead by three to one. He said that by several definitions, Carol is the "default incumbent," which will weigh against her in this election season. Also, said Karpatkin, surveys show that white people who say they are undecided will break nine to one against an African American in the privacy of the voting booth.

Finance coordinator Steve Cobble also sought to simultaneously dampen the fire and fan the flame. "The 30-point lead works against us in some ways," he said, "because it's harder for us to convince some people we need money. But it can work for us, too. There are a lot of big givers out there that want only one thing: to be on the winning side." Cobble then told this group, most of whom were working for little—or nothing but their ideals: "We must raise $75,000 a day. It costs $300,000 a week for statewide TV. And you never know what might happen in October. We may need more."

That was experience talking. But it turned out to be prophecy.

Field director Heather Booth was a conscientious participant in staff meetings. Although she had never run a statewide field operation for a political candidate, Heather was easily the most experienced organizer on the senior staff, and she knew that communication among campaign members was a key to maintaining morale. Sternly disciplined herself, Heather also felt a special responsibility for the youngsters, the rookie political activists. At the Democratic National Convention, one of Heather's disciples, 23-year-old Laura Retzler, told a *New Yorker* reporter who didn't recognize her boss's name, "Heather Booth is a god in political organizing."

It had been a long march for Heather, and unlike so many of her early compatriots who strayed to more conservative paths or simply decided that "me" was more important than "we," in three decades, Booth had not wavered from pursuing her social and economic agenda for America.

Starting in 1960, when Heather helped organize lunch-counter sit-ins in the South, and continuing to the 1964 Mississippi Freedom Summer, when three of her male colleagues were murdered for their participation, to the pre-*Roe v. Wade* abortion counseling service she set up in Chicago called Jane, and to the establishment of the activist training center Midwest Academy, Heather Booth had devoted her life to the struggle for justice and equality. "What led me here, to the Carol Moseley Braun campaign?" she asked, rhetorically. "Everything."

Heather had spent most of her years in Chicago but now made her home in Washington, DC, where her husband, Paul Booth, worked for the American Federation of State, County and Municipal Employees, a generous labor supporter of Democratic candidates. When Heather slept, it was in a studio apartment in a building on North LaSalle Street referred to as "the campaign dorm," where most of the out-of-town workers were housed. But Heather didn't sleep much. From 7 a.m. until 11 p.m. or, more often, midnight, seven days a week, she worked, training and coordinating some 10,000 staff and volunteers statewide.

Said Heather, "In races where African Americans are at the top of the ticket, the drop-off was six to eight points from what the polls showed." Heather was playing this election as if Carol's victory would depend upon each and every one of her people getting out the vote. It was a staggering job. At this September staff meeting, Heather reported that, in a combined effort with the Clinton people, "We will have 1,000 phones working every day from the end of September until Election Day."

Experience had taught Heather never to be overconfident; she'd been battling for inches all her life. "Head Start, for example," she explained, "is one of the most popular social programs ever conceived, with almost 90 percent approval. But in focus groups, if a black person leads the discussion, the questions change: 'Who will this serve? Is this just for you people?' Race becomes a screen, a filter that alters perception, even for people who would never think of themselves as racist."

Heather, who had known Carol for years and would have liked to have maintained their friendly relationship, had been cautioned by Kgosie Matthews (in no uncertain terms, once being reduced to very uncharacteristic tears) not to go directly to the candidate with anything but rather to work through him. By this time, all other senior staffers had been likewise advised, but it was a genuinely painful situation for Heather.

On a personal level, Heather anguished for Carol. Though cautious in everything she said, once, when we were talking about the almost physical revulsion Carol sometimes displayed before tackling one campaign task or another, Heather said, "You must remember that Carol was an abused child, and her reaction to much of what is happening is an extension of that."

"Do you mean that she emotionally internalizes these relentless calls upon her time and energy as abuse?" I asked.

"Exactly," said Heather.

In 1960, Carol was 13 years old. The building blocks, strong, if flawed, were in place, set firmly by her parents: Edna, the fierce caretaker

with a ready smile for all the world to see, and Joe, the neighborhood activist and talented musician who couldn't punish the world
that was punishing him and so brought his frustrations home to his
family. It is important to know that none of the Hysmith or Mackey
children, who were regularly in and around the Moseley home, ever
witnessed an act of violence. It was a family secret.

*As I approached my teens, my father began to descend into violence
more frequently—against me primarily—maybe because I was
more defiant. Johnny got it, too, but he was smart. When he saw
trouble coming, my brother got out of the way.*

*My dad had a police belt, a very wide, heavy leather belt he
beat us with. Johnny and I tried to hide it all the time. We'd stick
it in the garbage or bury it. But my father always seemed to find
it. Once, years later, I went looking for the burial place of that belt.*

Edna and Carol both remember an incident that came toward
the end of the marriage. It was Christmastime, and the plan was to
go to visit Edna's mother who lived at 4169 South Berkeley.

It was cold and snowing, and Joe had been out drinking with
his half-brother Burton Moseley, a Chicago police officer. When
Joe got home, he wanted to put the family in his Ford Fairlane and
drive them to see his parents, Mama Liz and Papa Grant, who lived
in Gary, Indiana. Edna refused. She said Joe was too drunk to drive.
They fought, the children shivering with fear, and when Joe got out
his gun and threatened to shoot his wife, Edna grabbed her kids
and fled. Carol remembers:

*She took us and said we were going to the bus stop on King Drive (it
was South Parkway then). There was so much snow; it was like the
Yukon. We ran across the street and down the alley, and then we saw
him coming in the car. We crunched down behind a fence and hid.
But we could see him weaving, with that shotgun out the car window.
I was carrying a crystal bowl for my grandmother and a doll. I lost my
doll that day, behind the fence, and I never found it again.*

Heather felt she understood the pain Carol internalized and,
no matter what the circumstances, was stalwart in her loyalty to

Carol. While many staffers believed Matthews to be mean-spirited and often downright cruel, Heather defended him. She thought much of his bluster grew out of insecurity, and she admired the diverse campaign he and Carol had put together. When other campaign members complained to Heather about the behavior of the campaign manager, her response was that Carol needed Kgosie and that was the overriding reality. When evidence began to emerge that Carol herself might be an object of Matthews's emotional abuse, it broke Heather's heart, but she would not waver from her goal: Carol could be a great senator. We must get her elected.

As the weather cooled down and the campaign heated up, it became clear to me that Kgosie did not discriminate when it came to choosing targets for his anger. Whether young or old, black or white, male or female, it was not hard to run afoul of the Matthews temper.

One afternoon, I was standing in the hallway at campaign headquarters with Carol's bodyguard, police officer Anita Ashton. Both of us were lounging against a wall, chatting and waiting for the candidate to venture out and join us for a trek through the western suburbs. Anita was the most elegant, graceful, and tastefully dressed cop I had ever seen outside a James Bond film. A tall, lovely, African American woman, she most often wore slacks, perhaps a silk blouse, and always a jacket perfectly tailored to conceal the .357 Magnum tucked beneath her left arm. Anita also had a fascinating history. She was 40 when, on a dare, she took the Chicago police entrance exam and scored an astonishing 99.69. Ordinarily, this would have afforded her automatic entrance into the police academy. Anita, however, was rejected because of her age and gender, she thought.

But times change. Five years later, when Anita was 45 years old, she got a call. Would she like to tackle the Chicago Police Academy? She said, "It was the hardest thing I'd ever done, competing against all those young guys with their great bodies. I climbed walls, I broke a rib—but I passed, and I was in the greatest shape of my life."

Anita was sustained not only by her fine mind and body but also by her wicked sense of humor. On this afternoon, as we stood waiting for Carol, Kgosie passed us without so much as a nod, his face screwed into its usual scowl. "That little spear-chucking son of a bitch," said Anita. "I wish I had a gun...."—a beat— then, "Oh," she smiled down at me, "I do!"

We burst out laughing, an act, Anita predicted, for which we'd pay.

Anita's initial confrontation with Matthews had come when he had given her two days off because he and Carol were going on a fundraising trip to Atlanta. Matthews had asked operations director Marlene Johnson to inform Anita that her bodyguard services were not needed. Anita was downright gleeful at the prospect of two successive days to herself until Barbara Samuels confronted her and asked, "How can you not go to Atlanta? These death threats may be real, and one includes you!"

Death threats? Anita had not been told. It seemed that a week before the Atlanta trip was to take place—and, frighteningly, before Carol's schedule had been made public—there had been two after-hours calls to campaign headquarters in which the caller said "they" were going to "get" Carol in Atlanta. Neither Joe Moseley, who was in charge of security, nor Anita Ashton, who was the candidate's personal bodyguard, had been told about these threats. Both police officers were furious.

Anita's typically straightforward solution was to confront Matthews and say, "I'm going with you to Atlanta." Now it was Kgosie's turn to become enraged. "You can't talk to me like that!"

There were three parts to this fight in three locations. The first, in the car, when Anita informed Kgosie she was going on the trip. The second, later that afternoon, when Kgosie confronted Anita in Marlene Johnson's office and demanded that she "give him respect." Anita's response was, "Wait a minute, you give me respect! This has nothing to do with you. I am a police officer assigned to protect Carol Moseley Braun. Her life has been threatened, and, incidentally, so has mine [one call had mentioned taking out Carol's bodyguard, too]. I must do my job!"

The third and final confrontation took place in Atlanta. Apparently, Kgosie had been in touch with campaign headquarters and learned that detectives had stopped by to collect a too-long-delayed police report on the death threats. This was a step Anita had ordered upon the advice of her district commander. Again, Kgosie was furious. "Who called the police?" he demanded of Anita.

"I called the police. I am the police! Are you crazy?"

Anita sighed. "He hates the police, and maybe that is understandable considering he's South African. Kgosie must have been humiliated a lot because he came over here, and now he tries to humiliate virtually everyone he meets," concluded the lady cop, who had earlier told me, "Women bring a special perspective to police work."

The "Carolvan" set out to visit voters in southern and western Illinois in early September. For those of us on the bus, it was a wacko couple of days. But that had no relevance whatsoever. The Carolvan was a huge political success.

"Within the campaign, the trip was widely regarded as a fiasco because so many people were mad at each other," said Steve Cobble. "But, in fact, it was a great trip. The press we got in the area was awesome. This was a Reagan Democrat part of the state, yet the people were ready to throw the bums out. Carol showed them she was someone they could live with."

Cobble said people in the campaign were mad at each other, but what surfaced in late August and early September was confusion. Indeed, there had been several shake-ups lately. Desiree Tate had been replaced as scheduler by Letitia Dewith-Anderson, a lobbyist for Illinois attorney general Roland Burris's office in the state capitol. Letitia had known Carol during her legislative days and had been working for her as a volunteer out of the Springfield campaign office. Carol and Letitia became reacquainted— and Letitia met Kgosie Matthews for the first time—during the state Democratic convention in August when Letitia served as their hostess and chauffeur. Now, at Matthews's request, Burris agreed to loan Dewith-Anderson to the campaign. This would be Letitia's first experience as a scheduler, a daunting task even for a seasoned pro.

Letitia was an attractive woman with an engaging personality, and her move to Chicago required a considerable adjustment in her personal life as she had a husband and two young children at home in Springfield. I asked her why she was willing to make such a sacrifice for a temporary job. Letitia's answer reflected the depth of feeling Carol's candidacy represented to so many citizens of Illinois: "I did it for my father," Letitia said.

When Letitia was six years old, her mother and father divorced. "My father, Bill Dewith, had been the only boy in a wealthy family, and he was somewhat spoiled and self-centered," recounted Letitia. "The days Daddy was scheduled to pick up my sisters and me [Letitia has five siblings], he seldom did. But Springfield is a small town, and if we needed him, we could find him. And on the days we found my father, we always had a wonderful time."

Bill Dewith, said Letitia, was intelligent and well read, and "he loved to talk. But I never heard him say anything about judging someone—or voting for someone—because of the color of their skin." In October 1991, just about the time Carol Moseley Braun was making her decision to enter the Illinois primary, Bill Dewith was diagnosed with lung cancer. In November, he had a lung removed, and in December, the doctors found malignant tumors in his brain. Letitia's father was told he had perhaps six months to live. "We decided Daddy would move in with us," said Letitia.

"The chemotherapy irritated him, and every day he grew weaker, but he never stopped reading," Letitia continued. "Daddy was thrilled with Carol's candidacy and followed her campaign in both the *Chicago Tribune* and the Springfield *State Journal-Register*. He said that I should go out and help with Carol's campaign, so I did.

"On primary Election Day, I worked at the polls all day, and when I got home, Daddy was listening to the radio, fighting to stay awake. We sat together until the final vote was in, and the announcer said, 'Carol Moseley Braun has upset incumbent Alan Dixon in her bid for the United States Senate!' 'She did it! She did it!' Daddy cried, and then he leaned back on his pillow with the most beautiful smile. It was the same smile I remembered the night I showed up at his house in my prom dress, with my date in a tux. Daddy was proud. He was very proud.

"Then he looked me straight in my eyes with such intensity, and he said, 'We need her in that seat. Letitia, you get out there and help her win that seat. Promise me.'

"'I promise, Daddy. Now get some sleep.' But, as sick as he was, my father wanted me to leave the radio on. He wanted to listen to the good news all night."

"She made it," Letitia concluded her story, "we made it, my father and countless others like him. And I had a promise to keep."

Joe Dewith died in June 1992, and two months later, in August, Letitia was offered a chance to work at the very core of the Carol Moseley Braun campaign as the candidate's scheduler. It was an opportunity Letitia Dewith-Anderson could not refuse.

Former scheduler Desiree Tate was now assigned to travel with Carol. When we met in a farmyard on the second day of the bus trip that had been dubbed "the Carolvan," Des laughed. "Carol put me on this bus to punish me because she thinks I've been punishing her all this time. She wants me to see what it's like on the road!"

But the reshuffling of the scheduling office was not the only change.

Larry Shapiro was on the bus trip, I was told, to work with Carol on "the economic message." The numbers guy was doing issues? Why wasn't Ira Cohen here or his brilliant young assistant, Dayna Bender? Where was communications director Jeremy Karpatkin?

Back in Chicago, I'd noticed that Liz Nicholson was no longer working for Kgosie. She had been, in effect, kicked upstairs and was now serving as Carol's assistant, which meant she took messages and typed thank-you notes. The last time I'd seen Liz, she was underemployed—and seething—but she wouldn't explain why.

Marlene Johnson was the Carolvan's head wrangler. With the title of chief of staff and operations director, Marlene was a disciplinary force around the office, despite the fact that she made frequent trips back to Washington, DC, to attend to her law practice. Not only had Marlene and Carol gone to law school together but, because Marlene was a Chicago native, she also understood the unique nature of Chicago and Illinois politics. Perhaps more important, she was a smart, strong woman with good diplomatic skills, and as chief of staff, she would oversee personnel matters.

Marlene was neither a flatterer nor a word-waster and was well respected by her fellow campaigners. This was the first time I'd seen Marlene out with the candidate, but the word was that Matthews, who'd been accompanying Carol lately, had more important things to do than bounce around the boonies in a bus for two days.

Marlene did not want me on the staff bus, and so I rode with the press. Though we were joined by local media at every stop, our contingent was mostly Chicago people looking for something—anything—fresh. On the second day, the *Sun-Times*' Lynn Sweet found a tidbit and pounced on press secretary Eichenbaum, "I hear Jeremy Karpatkin's gone back to Washington...."

"Yes," said David, explaining that Karpatkin had finished up his work for Carol and rejoined Paul Simon as the senator's deputy chief of staff. And that's what Lynn printed.

When I got David alone and asked what really happened to Jeremy, the press secretary simply drew a finger across his throat—and said no more. Eventually, word filtered out that Matthews had accused Karpatkin of "leaking things to Washington," although nobody seemed to know exactly what was leaked. Months later, another staffer opined, "I think Carol always felt Jeremy talked down to her—and he did. He talks down to everyone, he's that smart. When you get someone like Jeremy, you just need to put that aside and listen to what he's saying. Jeremy was absolutely dedicated to getting Carol elected."

Lynn Sweet, a woman with a thousand ears, most of them to the ground, heard me ask Marlene Johnson if I could get on the candidate's bus. "Maybe later this afternoon," an unsmiling Johnson replied.

"Let me guess," said Lynn. "Your relationship with Carol, once warm, has now cooled." I demurred, but the *Sun-Times* reporter persisted in her theory, part of which was based on her own relationship with Carol—once warm, now cooled. Carol, Lynn thought and I agreed, did not fully comprehend the boost in the applied scrutiny index as she leaped from her roles as a state legislator and county official to being the single Democratic candidate from Illinois for the US Senate. The higher a politician goes, the more isolated he or she becomes, the better the target, and the more people want and need to know.

"I think she thought we were girlfriends," said Lynn. "I always liked Carol, and she was a well-respected legislator. But this is different, and I have to do my job."

Lynn, along with the other reporters who were dissatisfied with the media "gang-bangs" along the way, wanted to get on the candidate's bus, too. Even though the reporters understood that Carol's mission was to hold her lead and that she was doing the right thing politically by charming her way through "Forgotonia," they were thirsting to get the candidate alone and nail her on the issues. "I want her to slaughter me with her knowledge," Lynn said, "and I don't know if she can't or she won't, but I think she can't."

"Have you noticed that whatever she is or is not doing, it's working?" I asked. "'First you win, *and then* you govern,'" I added.

"That's good. I'm gonna steal it."

"Fine," I replied. "But credit George Bush. He's just had a hard time with the second part."

One of our riders was Patricia Smith, a poet as well as a reporter, who'd sold her *Boston Globe* bosses on letting her fly to Chicago and take this trip in order to write a long feature on Carol for her newspaper. While Eichenbaum had been pressing on Smith's behalf for a one-on-one interview with the candidate, he was getting nowhere. So, at one stop, Smith herself went up to Marlene and explained her rather benign assignment.

"No," said Marlene, who must have taken her training at the Kgosie Matthews School of Press Relations.

"But, I came all the way from Boston...."

"NO!"

Finally, late the second day, we all got on the bus, one of those luxury editions outfitted like a lounge, with private quarters in the back. Carol sat at a table with the reporters ranged around her. Lynn asked, "What about all this soft message business? Do you think you're truly addressing the issues?"

Carol replied that she sees herself in something like the role of a preacher who must interpret complicated material for a broad audience. "But I am prepared to talk to you about economic issues if that's what you want to talk about." Carol then began to discuss transitioning the economy out of its Cold War positions.

"But *how* do you transition?" asked Lynn.

Carol replied, "Illinois provides 60 percent of the nation's ethanol. Ethanol is a great example of an industry where jobs and the environment have a symbiotic relationship...."

Lynn had heard all this before and emphatically expressed her impatience.

"Lynn," Carol lashed out, "I am not running for empress here! At some point, I'll have to be accountable, but I can't just wave a magic wand and get us into the 21st century. This country does not have an energy strategy." And then Carol said she was rethinking her long-held position on nuclear power.

Bingo! Something new. Carol had always been antinuclear, a reflection of her liberal Hyde Park background. But Illinois was highly dependent on power generated by nuclear reactors. Taking on another politically sensitive issue, Carol also disagreed with Bush's recent approval of the sale of 72 F-15 fighters to Saudi Arabia, even though 7,000 McDonnell Douglas jobs were at stake in the greater St. Louis area, part of the constituency she sought. The sale would "add to the destabilization of the Middle East," Carol said.

Twice, Marlene had come in and tried to put a halt to the press conference, and twice, Carol had brushed her off. Now Marlene strode up to the driver and told him to pull over. "The press people are getting off!" But we sat by a country intersection, undismissed, while Carol talked about targeted investment tax credits and reduced capital gains treatment, "two topics," Lynn later wrote, "she did not bring up on the stump" in rural Illinois.

In an editorial headlined "A Drive to the Senate Without a Map," the *Chicago Tribune* said on September 17:

> Braun won quick fame with her primary election upset and the possibility that she could become the nation's first black female senator. With a Republican opponent who's obscure by comparison, she has

been exceedingly careful not to do anything that might jeopardize her wide early lead.

Too careful for her own good, perhaps. Braun has a lot of substance beneath the sparkle, but she's not showing it. Instead, she's letting her opponent define her with an exaggerated selection and interpretation of tidbits from her voting record when she was a state legislator representing a South Side Chicago district. ... Across Illinois, most voters know what Braun looks like but not much about where she stands on key issues.

The *Trib* went on to write:

Braun's sins of omission are being matched by those of commission on Williamson's part ... in his paid-media, which is where he has the chance to make an undiluted pitch, Williamson continues down a low road.

His new ad claims repeatedly that Braun refuses to meet in debates. Actually, they're disagreeing on how many—he wants five; she wants two; one is scheduled.

The debate debate raged for weeks, partly because Matthews had, in fact, agreed to five debates with the Republican candidate immediately after the primary, something the Braun campaign never denied but rather acknowledged as a mistake. Now two debates would be scheduled, both in October.

On September 20, the *Trib* published its most recent poll. Wrote Tom Hardy, "Braun was preferred by 58 percent to 24 percent for Williamson among all respondents who said they are likely to vote.... [She] is known to 92 percent of the voters, and their favorable impression of her is unchanged despite the attacks from Williamson."

I was on the schedule the day we flew to Rock Island on the western edge of the state for a luncheon speech. As so often happened, the timing of our arrival was perfect. Lunch and business were finished, the other speeches had been made, and the audience was primed. On this day, Carol spent more time than usual talking about her background, how she grew up, and what that had taught her about our country, its needs, and its vast potential. The mostly white, middle-class audience listened raptly. It was clear that neither the media's nor Williamson's negativity had any resonance here.

Afterward, Carol stood as a long line of people sought to offer a word, ask for an autograph, or seek an embrace. Cried one woman, "Oh, I just love you so much!"

Then a tall, white-haired gentleman had a story for the candidate:

"When I was a child," he told Carol, both her hands grasped in his, "my grandfather planted an oak tree in the yard, and his children all said, 'Why did you plant an oak tree; it grows so slowly?' He said, 'Yes, it does grow slowly, and I won't live to see it grown. But an oak tree is very strong, and it lasts a long, long time.' Carol," the Rock Island voter finished, "you are our oak tree."

There were tears in the man's eyes. He believed.

I wondered if Carol understood this adulation as I did: it was power, real power.

CHAPTER 10

The Medicaid Bomb

I T WAS A POLITICAL MEGAHIT. The mushroom cloud it spawned would hang over the Illinois skyline, dripping its poisons right up to Election Day.

Ron Magers and Joan Esposito were anchoring NBC affiliate WMAQ-TV's news on September 28, the night reporter Paul Hogan broke the story that came to be known as "the Medicaid thing."

Magers read the lead:

> She's the Democratic nominee for US Senate from Illinois. Her primary victory over incumbent Alan Dixon was a defining moment in what politicians are calling the "Year of the Woman." If elected, she'd be the first black woman ever to serve in the Senate. Tonight, in a special report, questions about Carol Moseley Braun's role in a series of events which may have violated federal and state laws and IRS statutes.

Now came the tease, a sound bite from Carol: "I think this, I mean I think this is outrageous; it really is outrageous. It would be different if there was some attempt to cover something up, and there was not."

Magers again:

Is it a question of family finances or is it much more? Illinois taxpayers have been paying for Carol Moseley Braun's mother to stay in a nursing home on Medicaid. Now it appears there was a time when the mother could have afforded to pay for her own care. But Braun apparently took control of some of her mother's money without notifying the Medicaid people and without ever reporting the money as income. Channel 5's Paul Hogan joins us now with this Unit 5 exclusive.

Hogan headed one of the few remaining investigative units in Chicago television news, most having been lost to fiscal cutbacks and the infotainment trend. With a shelf full of Emmys, Hogan had a reputation as a careful, knowledgeable reporter and a kind man. He commented:

Lots of families transfer assets away from a loved one bound for a nursing home. They do it legally, long before their loved one begins receiving Medicaid. Because if you try to do it afterwards, it can be illegal. Our Unit 5 investigation is about what Carol Moseley Braun did. Not about her family. It's about both her conduct and her judgment.

Hogan went on to detail the fact that in 1989, as her share of a living trust, Edna Moseley had received a check for $28,750, proceeds from timber rights sold off the 232-acre Alabama farm that had been in the family for several generations. Said Hogan:

By owning part of the Alabama property, selling timber rights to it, and then collecting a large royalty check for selling those rights, Mrs. Moseley did nothing wrong. It is what her daughter, Senate candidate Carol Moseley Braun did afterwards, that raises serious legal questions tonight.

"The question was," said Hogan, "should that money have gone to offset the cost of Edna Moseley's nursing home care?" He pointed out that Edna had been in a nursing home since 1986, at the North Side's Barr Pavilion since 1989, and that taxpayers had been picking up her costs, less Social Security, to the tune of about $22,000 per year. "It's here that what Carol Moseley Braun did, and failed to do, becomes critical," said Hogan.

Hogan then explained the law requiring that a windfall such as the one received by Carol's mother in 1989 must be reported to Public Aid within five days, at which time there would, in most cases, be an opportunity for a hearing to see whether the money should be applied to nursing home bills. Hogan continued:

> But this royalty income was never reported to Medicaid; both Braun and her mother confirmed that information to us in private conversations last week. Instead, Braun took the check, deposited it in her own bank account, distributed it mostly to herself and her siblings, and then wrote up a legal document, which her mother signed, explaining what she'd done.

The video then revealed that Hogan had copies of the check from the Braswell Wood Company of Union Springs, Alabama, endorsed by Edna to Carol, who then, said Hogan, deposited it in her money market account at the Continental Bank. Then, he said, "Unit 5 *has seen* [my italics] the original legal document written by Carol Moseley Braun, an attorney, and signed by her mother," which provided for the distribution of funds to the Moseley children. The graphic on the screen repeated some of the text of that document, including a line promising that Carol herself "would 'be responsible for the payment of any and all federal and state taxes' on the $28,750."

Hogan continued,

> And though her mother told us, when we met with her last week, that she did not report the royalty check to Medicaid, Carol Moseley Braun said tonight, her mother did report it in a phone call to welfare offices that allegedly went unreturned.

Thus ended the lengthy setup for an interview with Carol that, by the time it was over, constituted a most unusual 15-minute lead story on local news. The Medicaid thing was launched and became a harrowing part of the campaign for all concerned—even for the reporter, Paul Hogan, who died of a massive heart attack the following January. Hogan's partner and chief investigator, Doug Longhini, later described the anatomy of the investigation. And the tale he told says a lot, not only about the personal anguish certain stories can cause conscientious investigative reporters, but also about local television politics.

According to Longhini, "There was a lot of discussion about doing this story over a long period of time, starting in early August. Paul, in particular, had been a very big fan of Carol Moseley Braun's. And I thought she was a wonderful choice. I heard she was going to run right after the Anita Hill thing, and I thought anybody, any senator, who had anything to do with that should have been run out of office.

"But I think Paul had a larger problem, emotionally, with doing the story," Longhini continued. "It was what Braun represented. And he agreed with her on societal issues, as well."

In early August, Hogan told Longhini that he had been contacted by a source, through an intermediary, who told him "something about an inheritance" and a problem with Medicaid. Longhini then went on vacation, and when he returned, Hogan told him that the reporter had again been contacted by this intermediary—and that there were more specifics.

Longhini added, "We were told a fair amount of detail about letters between family members and about the Braswell Wood Company, but we did not have any documents, and we were told we would never have any of those documents. We were going to have to get those documents ourselves. At that point, all we did was call the Williamson and Braun campaigns and ask for income tax statements. It was not clear at all that we were going to move ahead on this."

There was good reason for WMAQ to approach this story cautiously. The African American community in Chicago is a powerful and respected force. For example, in October 1985, upon the firing of a popular African American reporter, the Reverend Jesse Jackson and Operation PUSH had instigated a boycott against the CBS affiliate, WBBM-TV, that triggered a ratings decline from which WBBM had yet to fully recover. When the Medicaid story broke, there were rumors in the local broadcast community that WMAQ had been extremely leery about doing this story in the first place. And, indeed, except for covering Carol's subsequent press conference and one major follow-up—and unlike the crowing that TV often does when it has broken big news—WMAQ soon backed off and let its print brethren carry the story forward.

Longhini said that a possible Braun Medicaid story was first mentioned in a meeting with the general manager of the station, Pat Wallace, and executive news producer Danice Kern in early August when Longhini presented a whole list of possible stories for the fall sweeps period. At that time, all concerned thought the investigation was likely to lead nowhere. "No one was particularly enthused. There was a presumption that we'd find the money would have been declared and taxes paid," said Longhini.

"I wouldn't doubt that there was concern [at the managerial level] about repercussions [from the African American community], but that would not be discussed with Paul and me," Longhini continued. "[Braun] was of such preeminence and popularity and enjoyed such good will. People use—especially when race is an issue—code words. And I presume the code here was, 'We have to be very, very careful on this.'"

In particular, Hogan and Longhini took great care not to have any contact with the Williamson campaign. When the story broke, most assumed that Carol's opponent's people had somehow ferreted out this incident in family history.

"But," said Longhini, "if I cannot dissuade you from the thought that they [the Williamson camp] had something to do with it—and certainly, that thought is appealing—the best evidence is the Williamson campaign's reaction after it came out, which I would describe as completely lost."

And then Longhini added, "It's always the people closest to you that do you in."

Sources reveal a great deal about human character and about motivation in particular. Stated reasons for "shocking revelations" are frequently lofty, but where does the real drive come from?

Longhini, of course, would not reveal Hogan's source in the Medicaid story, nor would he tell anybody the name of the clearly determined intermediary. "But," said Longhini, "these ultimate sources of information are generally never admirable people working from the best of motivations. The good of society, the desire for honesty—the big stuff—is not enough to propel someone forward. In stories like this, the source is likely driven by motives personal, not grand, driven by negative human emotions like jealousy, anger, or revenge for past grievances."

Because Hogan's source had given the two WMAQ investigators so much detail and had assured them that the Braswell Wood Company could easily be tapped for the $28,750 canceled check, it was decided that WMAQ would adopt what had become known (since Watergate) as the "*Washington Post* standard." Longhini said, "a sort of one-time-only special." Producer Katy Smyser, who was a southerner and had the requisite accent, called Braswell and said she was working on tax information regarding Edna Moseley and needed a copy of the check. Smyser had the date of the check, the amount, and so much information about the transaction that the manager she spoke to unhesitatingly dug out the check and sent it to the address Smyser indicated, which was her own home.

Smyser told no lies and would have revealed her identity had she been asked, "But, thank God, she wasn't," said Longhini.

Now Longhini and Hogan had Carol's 1989 and 1990 tax returns, in which nothing was indicated about the December 1989 check for $28,750 or any portion thereof. They had confirmed details of great-grandmother Ollie Braswell's 1962 will (Ollie was no relation to the Braswell Wood Company) and that of her son, Lovelace Bryant, who inherited the property and who died in 1988, leaving a portion of the timber rights to his niece, Edna Moseley.

In an effort (by the source) to propel the story forward, the WMAQ investigative team had also been given a copy of a release and waiver letter Carol wrote for her mother, stating Edna's intentions regarding disposition of the funds and including the declaration that Carol would assume all tax liability. However, Hogan and Longhini's source had forbidden them to actually use this so-called family document. They would need to have its existence confirmed by the candidate.

June 27, 1990

RELEASE AND WAIVER: STATEMENT OF
INTENT TO DISTRIBUTE CAPITAL

In December of 1989, I, Edna Moseley, became entitled to receive the proceeds of a sale of timber from ancestral property. A check in the amount of $28,750 was subsequently received and, at my request, was deposited in an account at the Continental National Bank.

As a handicapped person dependent on Medicare- and Medicaid-supported health services, it is appropriate for me to arrange for the distribution of those proceeds so as not to jeopardize my health care and so as to fairly apportion same between my three living children, Joseph, Marsha and Carol.

First, my daughter Carol, in whose name the account was maintained, shall be responsible for the payment of any and all federal or state taxes, and will seek no recourse or contribution therefore from either me, or Joseph or Marsha.

Second, all debts and obligations previously existing between me and any of my children are discharged and absolved completely. As a part of this distribution, it is my intent to contribute on my own behalf 1/4 of the $8,000 cost of burial of my son, John, and on behalf of Marsha and Joseph, 1/4 each, for a total of $6,000 in reimbursement to my daughter, Carol.

Third, Marsha, Carol and Joseph shall each be entitled to $5,468 of the proceeds. $2,250 of same has been previously distributed to Joseph in the spring of this year.

Fourth, inasmuch as Marsha is presently negotiating the purchase of property, Carol and Joseph have offered until July 1 to lend her, from their respective distributions, the remainder required for her down payment of $10,000.

Last, upon the execution of checks as herein directed, the aforesaid account shall be closed, and the distribution of timber proceeds shall have been fully accomplished. It is specifically my intent that with this act, the matter shall be closed, and no further claims, duties or liabilities shall be heard with respect to it.

(signed) Edna Moseley, 6-27-90.

Now Hogan and Longhini were fairly certain they had a story. The question remained, had Edna Moseley's windfall, as required by law, been reported to the Illinois Department of Public Aid? Because of strict confidentiality rules, this information was not available from the department itself.

The WMAQ investigative team had been working on the Medicaid story for almost two months now without so much as a hint of the impending crisis reaching the Braun campaign. Despite the fact that, from a reporter's point of view, Hogan was about to spring a journalistic coup, he did not feel good about it. "Paul kept saying, 'I just don't want this to be an October Surprise,'" recalled Longhini. Hogan wanted the Braun campaign to have time to recover before November 3.

Nevertheless, it was Thursday, September 24, before Hogan and Longhini felt prepared to go to the candidate. Hogan placed the call. He spoke to David Eichenbaum and said he wished to talk to Carol regarding "a personal matter."

Said Eichenbaum later, "Hogan called maybe three times, and each time, I pressed him to tell me what this was about. Finally, on the last call, he told me it concerned Carol's mother. There was no mention of Medicaid. Each call had been relayed to Carol and Kgosie, along with Hogan's phone number, and in the late afternoon, I finally got a response." But it was not the response Eichenbaum expected or advised. "I thought it was foolish if not crazy to give these *investigative reporters* access to Mrs. Moseley without even asking them why they wanted to speak with her."

"Eichenbaum called back around five o'clock," said Longhini, "and the message was, if we had a problem with Carol's mother, then it was her mother's problem, and we should go speak to Edna. Paul expressed concern," Longhini continued, "saying that we understood that Mrs. Moseley was ill, and we sort of wanted to leave her out of it. Eichenbaum assured him that, although Edna was an amputee, she was mentally pretty sharp, and she could certainly talk to us."

Eichenbaum was just following orders, but in the process had lost another round to the naive—one might even say innocent— candidate and her inexperienced campaign manager.

"If Braun had wanted to confuse us or stop the story, this was a critical mistake on her part," Longhini continued. "Mrs. Moseley was very alert. It was clear that she was not in the best part of the nursing home, and she made a point of how she was the only person with 'two brain cells' working on her floor. She recognized Paul from TV. We told her we were interested in this inheritance and asked her several questions about it. What we got from her was that Carol had handled this matter in its entirety and that she hadn't anything, really, to do with it, that Carol had handled 'whatever' with Medicaid, Public Aid, and in terms of the taxes—that Carol had taken care of everything for her.

"Also, we said that we understood there had been some letters, some family correspondence, and she said yes, there had been some correspondence—and that was a key thing for us."

Longhini was called back downtown from his suburban home that same evening because Hogan had set up a meeting with Carol and Kgosie in the campaign office at 10:30 p.m.

Recalled Longhini, "Hogan was nervous. I was nervous. Basically, we confessed that we were fans of hers and uncomfortable with doing this, but this is where we were in this story." Hogan sketched the outlines and posed the questions.

A substantial discussion of the issues involved then ensued, during which, Longhini said, Carol was forthcoming and cordial, telling the reporters the family background regarding the Alabama property and offering to provide a copy of the relevant will. She also discussed the fact, which, of course, Longhini and Hogan already knew, that Marsha had intended to use her share of the money to buy a condominium. She wasn't sure about what the tax liabilities were or who had contacted Medicaid, "and she said to us clearly, at that point, that she and her sister had not been getting along. She was open and honest about the disputes that had gone on in the family," said Longhini.

Now, because Edna Moseley had confirmed their existence, Hogan was able to say, "We understand there are letters." Carol said, yes, there was a letter, a document, and she would try to find them a copy.

The discussion had centered on relevant events and Edna Moseley's role, but about 20 minutes into the conversation, Longhini said, "We are not here to talk about your mother but rather to talk about you, Carol Moseley Braun, and what you did or did not do.

"And then it struck her, you could see it, literally see it: we were talking about Medicaid fraud, and we were talking about her. It was all there on her face, what she knew, now, she was going to have to go through: 'Oh, my God, this is about me!'"

"And then she began swearing," remembered Longhini, "and at first, Paul and I thought she was swearing at us—which, I'm sure, eventually, she did. But it wasn't us that night. She was swearing at whoever had done this to her."

Months later, Senator Carol Moseley Braun discussed what had been, for her, a difficult time on so many levels.

Isn't it something, that with all the years I've been in politics—and Chicago politics at that—it would be a family thing that became the biggest crisis in my campaign? As I look back on it, with the noble exception of Joey, who has always been there for me, there has not been another family member, even including Johnny in his last years, who has not been a source of great pain to me.

Reflecting on the whole Medicaid thing and the roots of it has made me think about my own development and how I became the person I am. There are two parts of this that seem very important to me.

Ironically, that chaotic existence made the whole notion of family very important to me. I would go to great lengths, for example, to put on a big Thanksgiving dinner and invite the whole family, bring

everybody together, force us to be a family. And all of the arrange-
ments would be perfect, but the party would be a disaster. There
would always be a fight before it was over. So I stopped giving those
parties. Matt is my family, and we are close and always will be.

On the other hand, in the larger context of my life, the family
that was such a source of pain became a source of strength in terms
of dealing with challenges and betrayals and conflicts—dealing with
things people in the outside world did to me or in relation to me.

Because once you've been wounded on a profound level, it's
hard for anybody else ever to hurt you. You build this wall.

And it's made it easier for me to be a lone ranger, guided by my
own light and my own view of priorities, as opposed to the pressures
one gets from others in the political world.

I suppose the psychologists would say that some of this evolves
from being the oldest child of a dysfunctional family, the caretak-
er thing. It's just that, while the others look to me for help, there's
this anger and jealousy and resentment—even more than that, a
hostility that, to me, is bizarre. For example, when Marsha grad-
uated from Yale, the whole family wanted to be there. Mama was
disabled, Matt was little, so Mike [Braun] arranged to charter a
private plane. We must have looked like something, getting off that
plane in New Haven. For one thing, we looked wealthy, which we
weren't!

We sent Marsha money when she was in college and, later, helped
her pay her bills when she got sick out in California. We kept an apart-
ment for my mother after she had her first strokes in 1978. At one
time, we had Mama down at 53rd Street, Joey in a place we owned
across from us on Hyde Park Boulevard, and Johnny's daughter, Toya,
and Matt at home. Mike and I were supporting three households and
never a complaint from him. The trouble around our divorce aside, I
have to say, Mike was wonderful to my family.

In fact, my mother was extremely angry at me for leaving Mike.
Angry and frightened. She saw me as cutting her off because Mike
wouldn't be around to take care of her anymore. There was a pat-
tern of events that I didn't figure out until much later.

Once, around that time, Edna literally attacked me with a knife.
The fight grew out of an incident where she said I did not respect her,
but I know it was more than that. It was deep anger.

Mama was over one day, and I was cleaning out my closet. I'd "grown out of" a few things! And I said to my mother, "Do you think Marsha would like these clothes?" And she said, "Well, I don't see why not. They're wonderful things." So I picked up the phone and called Marsha, who was still out in California.

Marsha wasn't home, but I got her answering machine. I said, "Marsha, this is your sister, Carol, I'm sitting here with Edna, and we have some clothes we thought you might like. Give me a call."

Well, when I turned around, my mother was in a rage. She screamed, "How dare you refer to me as Edna? I'm your mother! As long as you live, I don't care how big you get—and you think you're so hot," and that's when she started coming at me, and she swung her cane at me.

I said, "Mama, why are you doing this? I was just leaving a message on an answering machine!" I didn't know what to do, so I just walked away from her, walked into the kitchen, and the knife was there on the counter. She was yelling and screaming—and she grabbed the knife.

Well that's when I panicked, and I ran and locked myself in the bathroom. But she ran after me and was throwing her whole body against the door and hitting it with the cane. But I've got to confess, at that point I started yelling, "Edna, Edna, Edna, Edna!"

Eventually, Marsha's then husband, who was at the house, pulled Mama away and calmed her down and walked her home. But it was the divorce that set her off. I know it was. I had taken something very valuable away from my mother. I'd hurt her, and she was going to hurt me.

So, well, that's some of the background. Now it's 1989, and Mama is the beneficiary of this living trust. Incidentally, I had advised her against signing off on that timber deal. It made me sick to think of all those trees being clear-cut, and I also felt the family wasn't getting value for such a sacrifice.

Nevertheless, there was a great deal of pressure on her from other members of the family, particularly Auntie Darrel, so Edna went along. When the check came, she asked if I would keep it for her. She said that it was her intention to pay her children back, particularly me for all those years of paying her rent, but she wasn't *sure just how she wanted to distribute the funds. I cautioned her that there could be a problem with that, that she'd have to decide what to do with it and soon. But the money sat there for six months, which the bank records clearly show.*

During those six months, Edna was changing her mind every week about what she wanted to do with the money. It evolved into a huge family fight between Marsha and me, with my mother, I'm convinced, playing one of us off against the other. It was a power position for Edna; she was getting a lot of attention. For the first time since she had her stroke, she was calling the shots.

The details seem too petty now even to mention. Marsha wanted to buy this condo, Joey needed the money, I, of course, had been paying Edna's bills for years, including for Johnny's funeral. At one point, Marsha and Mama even talked about suing me to get the money—went as far as talking to a lawyer. It was ridiculous. I told them I'd turn over the money when a fair decision was made.

The document that we showed to Paul Hogan grew out of this dispute.

I said in the letter that I would take care of any tax problems, but I was sure there would be none, as long as Mama made up her mind in a timely way and I could get the money out of that account. As it turned out, when this brouhaha hit in October and an analysis was done by a tax expert, he found that Edna was the only person who might be liable and that there was not enough profit shown in the timber sale even for a return to be filed. So I was right about the taxes.

But I was wrong about dealing with the Department of Public Aid. I told Mama she needed to report this windfall to her social worker, and she said she did, and I never followed through. I do know how Public Aid works. My understanding was that a Medicaid recipient who somehow came by funds after having been qualified could distribute those funds in certain ways, including repayment of debts incurred. But I should have gone through the process. I took the easy route, not giving the matter enough attention, wanting to get it over with. I just helped Mama draft the letter, wrote out the checks to Marsha and Joey, and got on with my life.

So when Paul Hogan and Doug Longhini said they wanted to talk to Mama, I said fine, talk to her. It didn't occur to me that she'd tell them something that would hurt me. And following that, when they came over to the office, I couldn't figure out, at first, what they were trying to get me on.

And then I realized that they were going to put all this stuff on television, and I was going to have to explain my actions without explaining my family. I was running for the United States Senate in a year when family values were the big deal. But I couldn't do an essay on how hard it was for bright, frustrated people like Joe and Edna Moseley to raise a family in South Side Chicago. Stuff happens. For some dark and unfathomable reason, certain members of my family—at least sometimes—hate me. But the pain, that old, familiar, deep pain—could anyone hate me this much?

Carol had begun to grasp the dimensions of the upcoming problem late on Thursday evening, the 24th. She agreed to be interviewed on Monday, September 28, at Edna's nursing home, asking that all her family be present. Hogan, now fully prepared, dropped his bomb on Monday night's ten o'clock news, and by Wednesday morning, Carol was ready to call a press conference.

The press, of course, was unaware that, for Carol, the past 36 hours had been spent as much anguishing about her family as preparing for the media. The legal problems were put into the hands of Marlene Johnson, who became the campaign's internal counsel on the Medicaid matter, and Carol's friend and adviser, attorney Lou Vitullo.

"I was brought into the loop after Carol's initial meeting with Hogan," said Vitullo. "And it was clear to me that under the Public Aid regulations, Mrs. Moseley was entitled to spend down that money to relieve preexisting debt. I think we could have come up with a better legal result in terms of the amount ultimately paid to settle, but the important thing was to get this matter resolved before the end of October."

"One of the first things I did was to interview Mrs. Moseley," Vitullo continued, "and she indicated to me: one, that the funds had been distributed according to her instructions; two, that Carol was nothing more than a scrivener, somebody who put down notes and distributed the money as her mom instructed; and three, that she [Mrs. Moseley] had made the report to Public Aid. I then asked her, 'When did you notify Public Aid?' She said, 'Sometime just before the holiday in July.' I said, 'What holiday in July?' And she said, 'Well, dummy, there's only one!'

"Edna Moseley was certainly in bad shape physically and, my guess is, had certain emotional problems. But mentally, she was sharp as a tack," concluded Vitullo.

Based on his interview, Vitullo drafted an affidavit that set down the history of Edna Moseley's confinement, first at the Jackson Square nursing home in 1987 and then, after Marsha qualified her for Medicaid in August 1989, at the Warren Barr facility where she currently resided. The affidavit detailed the monies expended on Edna's behalf by her children, principally Carol Moseley Braun. It concluded that the release and waiver was her attempt "to forever discharge all debt and obligations between me and my children to as great an extent as possible." The affidavit was signed, sworn, and dated September 28, 1992, the day Hogan interviewed Carol and broke "the Medicaid thing."

The affidavit was never released to the press. "Carol didn't want to increase the pressure on her mother," sighed attorney Vitullo.

To say the news gathering on Wednesday, September 30, was well attended would be a vast understatement. When he walked into the room and surveyed the wall-to-wall cameras and dozens of reporters, press secretary David Eichenbaum asked, "Hey! Where were all you guys when we had our press conference on the environment?"

Carol arrived on time, dressed in white, and faced the poised pens, rolling cameras, and clicked-on tape recorders of perhaps 80 men and women, who, in all probability—up until now—represented at least 60 votes.

Yet, everything that had brought Carol Moseley Braun here to this moment was in suspension. This was a test.

Carol began with an opening statement that she read forcefully, without a hint of nervousness:

> I have been a public official for 14 years. In that time,
> I voted on some 15,000 pieces of legislation, wrote

hundreds of newspaper articles and made thousands of public appearances. My life has been open to the public. I have always operated on the basic principle that a public official must be a role model for ethical behavior. In fact, I have been honored by many "good government" groups for maintaining high standards for public disclosure and ethics in government.

Carol went on to repeat the details of the Hogan report and re-posed the two questions regarding tax liability—saying her lawyers had advised her that there was none—and her responsibility to the Department of Public Aid. She said:

Concerning the Public Aid Department, in hind-sight, perhaps I should have taken greater control of the fund and reporting requirements. I should have second-guessed my mother, even though she main-tained that her decisions and actions were correct. The buck stops here. I have already, through my law-yers, contacted the department—there is a meeting this afternoon. If there were errors or oversights, they were not deliberate. If there are any corrective actions that need to be taken, I will take them.

It is extremely unfortunate that my mother has become part of this political campaign. I apologize to her and my family for the pain and embarrass-ment that this may have caused them.

Carol left her prepared script, saying, "Now I'd like to give you, before we start with questions, a chronology of what essentially happened here." She then gave a brief history of her mother's care from the time of her first strokes in 1978 through 1986 when she had a second stroke, a heart attack, and an amputation, and the family decided they must put Edna in a nursing home. What had been an agonizing dispute between her sister, Marsha, and herself she covered by saying that the document seen on television Mon-day night had been the result of a "family situation." Unfortunately, Carol was imprecise about the distribution of the $28,750 inheri-tance, and that would cause her trouble later. Questions followed, many questions.

Carol had performed well, presenting her case as candidly as she and her advisers thought she could under the circumstances. At one point, after she'd answered perhaps a dozen questions, Eichenbaum, on Matthews's orders, tried to cut the inquisitors off, but Carol waved him away, insisting that she would respond to any and all questions. And she did.

But a press conference was one thing and around-the-clock dunning was quite another. On October 1, Eichenbaum, Cobble, and media maven Jerry Austin sent a memo to Carol and Matthews, urging that Carol take "an aggressive approach—tackle this head-on and take the offensive." They suggested "live shots (where they can't edit you) and radio call-ins to talk directly to the people." The memo continued, "CMB is this campaign's biggest asset. Yesterday's press conference once again proved that. We need to showcase our strength."

But Carol did not want to talk about this painful subject, and knowing that any other message would be lost in the Medicaid thing, she kept to her campaign schedule and ignored countless media requests.

The following Sunday, the *Chicago Tribune* would report that a poll taken before the Medicaid hit showed that Carol, although she had slipped a bit, still remained 28 points ahead of Richard Williamson. Despite her opponent's relentless (most thought boring) attacks, Carol would now, with one month to go before the election, face the first real crisis of her campaign. How would she handle the pressure? Would she be forthcoming about the details? And further, how would this "scandal," as her opponent now characterized it, affect an electorate that seemed to have fallen in love with this extraordinary African American woman?

Immediately after the September 30 press conference, I accompanied Carol to a previously scheduled speech before a gathering of certified public accountants. Except for the fact that this obscure group found itself with unprecedented press coverage—the media mob having tailed Carol from the campaign office over to the Hyatt Regency—her appearance was unremarkable.

But afterward, I stopped in the nearest ladies room, which I've found is a terrific place to take a temperature: conversation is always candid and eavesdropping is allowed. There, I found five women in various stages of refreshing themselves who had just listened to Carol, and this was a summary of their remarks: "She seemed kinda down. Her speech wasn't very interesting"; "The Medicaid thing was disappointing, but lots of people do it." And when someone asked, "I'm still going to vote for her, are you?" the responses were "Yes"; "Sure"; "Uh-huh"; and "Who else?"

Furthermore, in the days following Hogan's revelations, the media, both print and television, began to do sidebars on the problems faced by families with aging parents. Reporters also consulted experts and, on their own, came to the conclusion that it was doubtful whether Edna, Carol, or her siblings owed any taxes.

Up, down, and across Illinois, newspapers printed letters to the editor, most of them supporting Carol's position and a significant number citing underlying health care issues. A letter from Janet Riehecky of Elgin was typical:

> It is both legal and ethical for a parent to transfer assets to a child. What parent who has worked hard would not want his/her child to have the benefit from that work rather than give that money to the government?
>
> If we had the type of health care system we ought to have in this country, no one would even be asked to bankrupt themselves and their children in order to pay for the health care they need.

If Carol had to have a scandal, if her record was going to show moral vulnerability somewhere, there was probably none better than an incident that involved family, the complexities and inequities of health care, and "the system." Some people who had played by the rules, depriving themselves for an infirm parent, were properly enraged. But although she'd lost her halo, the majority seemed to give a collective shrug, and again, there was a certain "connect," even if it was essentially negative. Carol Moseley Braun was hurt, but not fatally.

CHAPTER 11

Medicaid II

AS FOR THIS REPORTER, in the midst of the campaign's biggest crisis, a request was answered that had been submitted 10 days earlier. When I arrived home late on October 1, I found a message: "Kgosie Matthews will meet with you tomorrow."

Although he had assured me the previous April that he would be a source for a possible book, this was the only time that the campaign manager and I would sit down together for a real conversation. Because Matthews refused to let me use my tape recorder, I offer my notes.

Kgosie was very cordial. Enough so that I almost relaxed—almost. He even, as sort of an aside, mentioned his and Carol's "relationship." I didn't pursue it. I wasn't *that* relaxed. And anyway, that did not seem to be among the things the campaign manager wanted to talk about.

Ever since arriving in Chicago, Matthews had been more or less at war with INC. and Sneed, the *Tribune* and *Sun-Times'* respective gossip columns, both written by women. Kathy O'Malley and Dorothy Collin, who cowrote INC., had this morning fired another shot:

> Caroling: Now that her pedestal is wobbly, look for conservatives (and other enemies) to go after Kgosie Matthews, Carol Moseley Braun's campaign manager.

They'll say he's being paid big bucks and claim that
part of the money is going to South Africa, where his
family is prominent in the African National Congress.

But this time, the "Kgosie Kops" from INC. had been late on
the beat. The day before, their archrival, Michael Sneed, had lev-
eled a powerful preliminary blast:

> Scoopsville ... the Braun report—Egads! (Let's get
> Kgosie?) The campaign manager for Dem senatorial
> candidate Carol Moseley Braun, Kgosie Matthews,
> is one highly paid staffer! To wit: Cash paid: Sneed
> has learned Kgosie was paid $51,577 from April 1 to
> June 29, according to a quarterly campaign finance
> report filed with the Federal Election Commission!
> Get it—$51,577 for THREE months! (The Braun re-
> port was also filed LATE—on July 29.) Cash owed:
> In addition, the report claims Braun owes Kgosie
> $5,123! Whadda deal!

So apparently with this latest barrage on his mind, the first thing
Matthews asked was if I had seen the item about his sending money
to the ANC (African National Congress). My response had two
parts: an actual truth and a political untruth. I said, yes, I had seen
the item, and it seemed pretty far-fetched to me. "I guess the bottom
line is," I said, "if it's your money, you can do what you want with it."
   "Exactly," said Kgosie.
   Well, no, not exactly. If it was discovered that Kgosie Matthews, one of the country's highest-paid senatorial campaign man-
agers, his salary arbitrarily set by the candidate, was indeed sending funds to the ANC, Carol Moseley Braun would be wounded,
perhaps mortally. But I didn't believe the story for a minute. For
one thing, although Matthews's sister was an officer in the ANC,
his dad worked for ANC rival Chief Buthelezi. Furthermore, judging from his lifestyle, Matthews needed every bit of his salary.
   Still refusing to let me tape, Kgosie then launched into a tale of
his fascinating background: his grandfather's exposure to America
and its influence on him; his upbringing in Botswana and England;
the British parliamentary system and its politics, "very different
from America"; and his three years with Jesse Jackson, which were

"not mainstream," he assured me. Kgosie said working with Jackson was a total American political experience.

Why, I thought, was Kgosie Matthews "credentialing" for me at this particular point in time? Was I being played?

I asked him, considering this impressive political background, why he did not respond when attacked for his inexperience.

"Our family ethic is much like that of George Bush's family," he replied. "We don't brag."

And then Kgosie admitted that he had much to learn about Illinois politics and that he relied on Carol, who was very observant and a good teacher. Carol helped him, he said, with the history of alliances and relationships and gave him advice in dealing with people. In relating a story where Carol had described a city-hall functionary that Kgosie was to meet as "a typical Afrikaner," a characterization that had turned out to be absolutely accurate, Kgosie seemed fairly astonished that Carol would have such insight.

I thought, Why would that surprise him? The Afrikaner, for good or ill, is a pretty well-established stereotype.

Also, said Kgosie, he had had to learn to deal with Carol.

"With a woman candidate," I stated, more than asked.

He laughed but denied the implication. Then he told me an anecdote about an old girlfriend, calling it "a relationship that ended a long time ago." He was telling this woman about Carol's being tired and discouraged, and he apparently explained all this to her in a sympathetic way. And the woman said something like, "When did you get so understanding? Why didn't you treat me like that?"

We talked a little bit about strategy. Kgosie said that, besides himself and Carol, Jerry Austin had been the campaign's most important adviser, and he suggested that I talk more with Jerry and Steve Cobble. Sketching the campaign's overall strategy, Kgosie said the important thing had been to raise money in the late spring and then shine at the Democratic National Convention, and he told me that he had urged Carol to ask Bill Clinton for a speaking role.

It was a memorable half hour for me. On the job since the previous April, with a month to go before the election, I had finally been fully exposed to the charm and intelligence of a most unusual and strangely captivating man. Given that it was hell week for the campaign, I wondered about my luck.

At 4 p.m. on this same day, Friday, October 2, Carol had an editorial board meeting with the *Chicago Tribune*. If ever there was a year the conservative-leaning *Trib* would endorse a good liberal, 1992— the "Year of the Woman," the year for real change—might be it.

Unfortunately, it was a good year but a bad week. When I asked Eichenbaum the next day how the meeting went, he replied, "Terrible." The young press secretary was aging fast.

Also on this day, October 2, three staff members dropped doozies on me.

"Kgosie and I were together yesterday," said Darlene Mackey (who, you'll recall, grew up with the Moseley family). "We went to visit Carol's mom. The man truly cares for Edna, I have to say. As we were walking out, Kgosie says to me, 'Do you think Carol really loves me?' I was shocked! But I said, 'Yes, she does.' And then I asked him, 'Do you love her?' And he got very gruff and he said, 'Yes, I love her. I do.'"

The second anecdote was offered by a staffer who had talked to a friend in DC who'd just heard that Kgosie, while on the phone with a political operative who was giving him some stern advice, got extremely defensive and ended the conversation by shouting, "You don't fuck with the guy who's fucking the candidate!"

And from Elizabeth Nicholson, Kgosie's now *former* assistant: "I used to like Kgosie. But all you need to do is cross him once, and that's it. He's mean. And I think he's crazy. I really do."

Oh, boy! Just another day on the Carol Moseley Braun campaign, I thought. Weeks later, I learned why Matthews had called me in: he wanted to know how much I knew (which was nothing) regarding the trouble that was about to break out. He *had* been playing me—and Liz and Darlene, too.

Timing is everything. Carol Moseley Braun's biggest fundraiser of the fall was Monday night, October 5, at the Chicago Hilton and Towers. It would feature a huge screen with a live, closed-circuit television feed from the nation's capital, from which a host of senators, including Joe Biden, Bill Bradley, Ted Kennedy, Carl Levin,

George Mitchell, Jay Rockefeller, and Paul Wellstone, would each take a turn to speak to Illinois Democrats about how excited they were to contemplate Ms. Braun's coming to Washington.

The event was organized by fundraiser Kathleen Murray with help from ever-faithful (if fired) Jeremy Karpatkin, who was back with Paul Simon in DC and had volunteered to herd all the senators together. At $250 a head, the affair would raise over a quarter of a million dollars. The evening featured a good deal of forced gaiety layered over nonstop conversation about "the Medicaid thing." Democratic Party chairman Ron Brown spoke with his usual upbeat enthusiasm. Carol, however, delivered a loquacious but empty speech and was definitely off her game.

Adding to the surrealism of the party was the ever-sunny acolyte Larry Shapiro, who summarized the events of the past week by saying, "As far as we're concerned, we've put this matter behind us. Carol is ahead by 30 points! If the press wants to continue this, that's their problem."

Even as Larry and I chatted in the festive ballroom, the press was, indeed, "continuing this."

NBC had a network crew in Chicago doing a profile on the Braun/ Williamson race. Naturally, the Medicaid thing would be a part of the story. In order to take advantage of the hoopla surrounding Carol's biggest fundraiser, NBC's congressional correspondent, Bob Kur, had a previously scheduled interview set up with the candidate just before she was to address her supporters.

It turned out that Paul Hogan's source had provided a portion of a *second* document, ostensibly a letter from Carol to her mother, that was even more politically damaging than the first. The fragment provided by the source read:

> For the life of me I can not understand why it is my lot to be ever abused by you. In an effort to help you "launder" the timber proceeds and not run afoul of the state regulations, I agreed to handle your $28,750. The money was deposited in a money market account and touched only at your direction. While you are absolutely entitled to an accounting

of those funds, rather than ask me for a statement or accounting, you have—once again— resorted to writing letters which imply that somehow I have failed to properly treat with you and your money.

After much consultation among WMAQ (the NBC Chicago affiliate) news executives, it was agreed that Hogan would ask Kur to present the letter fragment containing the "L" word to Carol at the end of his interview and get her reaction.

In journalism land, this is called an ambush. It's not a fun thing to do, and it's a much less fun thing to have done to you. Hogan and Longhini studied the resultant tape.

Longhini recalled: "[Kur] said, 'Keep the camera rolling' when he was finished with his interview, and he handed Carol this section of the letter we had typed out. The date on it was around the time of the previous letter. It looked like she read it—maybe twice. They were both clearly nervous. She said, 'This is pretty damning.' They went back and forth, but in the end, she was equivocal. She didn't say she wrote it; she didn't say she didn't. Then she stopped the interview."

David Eichenbaum, who was in the room, got a brief look at the typed paragraph and knew the campaign was in for more trouble. Lou Vitullo remembered that he was summoned from the festivities downstairs. "When I walked into the room, Kur still had the camera going, and [Carol] handed me the letter and she said, 'Lou, this is very damning,' and the word 'launder' was in quotes. And I said, 'So what if it's very damning?' And I looked at Kur and I said, 'You really better have your shit together because we've gone through this nonsense with Hogan. We think the story's bogus. You don't play this until you verify your source, or you've got some large problems here.'"

Because Longhini and Hogan decided not to air the Kur interview, this incident was never reported. But in that moment, Carol had no way of anticipating a favorable outcome. Since the interview preceded—by just minutes—her appearance at her biggest fundraiser of the season, well, it's no wonder she was off her game.

———

Kur's ambush, of which most of us were unaware at the time, was part one of a long evening. Part two was the fundraiser itself. Part three was divided into three subparts: in a suite upstairs, Carol gathered several associates, including Matthews, Vitullo, Marlene Johnson, and former Harold Washington adviser Grayson Mitchell, to chew over the latest chapter of the Medicaid thing. Several staffers found the cool and quiet of the Hilton's Lakeside Green Lounge the appropriate place to slough off the evening's stresses, while yet another bunch of us discovered Kitty O'Sheas, a well-known Irish pub in the Hilton that featured live music.

Take a group of exhausted, determined-to-party people, add a little alcohol and a rollicking band, and what you have is something bordering on hysteria. At one point, Kgosie Matthews's exiled former assistant, Liz Nicholson, had David Eichenbaum backed into a corner, bending his ear for 15 animated minutes. All that emanated from the conversation was the frequently spat word, "asshole."

Around midnight, Eichenbaum was snagged by Tom Hardy of the *Tribune*. The two men moved to the side, and suddenly, David left Hardy and walked across the room to grab Steve Cobble ("Come—NOW!"), who joined their conversation. It looked like something was up.

When I asked Eichenbaum what was going on, he would only throw two (impatient) words my way: "It's bad."

How bad was it?

Tom Hardy's piece the following morning was headlined:

BRAUN'S BIG LEAD ERODES

Wrote Hardy: "Although Braun still holds a 17-point lead over Williamson among likely voters, a once-commanding advantage that foreshadowed a potential rout has been sliced in half in the last three weeks." The poll had been taken over the weekend of October 3–4. During the week of the Medicaid thing, Braun had lost eight points, according to the *Tribune*.

"Since media coverage of the story has been concentrated in the Chicago area, where two-thirds of the statewide vote is cast," wrote Hardy, "the events of the last week had less of an effect

Downstate." Indeed, while the Chicago press kept after Carol regarding full disclosure for the remainder of October, the Medicaid story had remarkably little play throughout the rest of Illinois.

And what about Richard Williamson, the Republican candidate who'd been on the mat just a week ago, and who had now been handed a strategic gift? "It's clear who Carol Braun is when it comes to questions of ethics," Williamson told a rally sponsored by the Highland Park and Deerfield Republican Women's Clubs. "She's a machine politician."

In his Monday column, Chicago's inimitable Mike Royko predicted that Carol would win, despite the fact that, "As cops, politicians and reporters would put it: Somebody dropped a dime on her." Richard Williamson, said Royko, had "all the charisma of a plate of cottage cheese."

Tuesday, October 6, was the day Carol was scheduled to deliver her much-delayed economic message. She was to do this at a factory in Rockford. For reasons not evident in their coverage the following day, a host of city print and television journalists chartered planes or drove the 60 miles northwest of Chicago for this event.

We took off from Meigs at 10:30, arriving at the Rockford airport in time for Carol to closet herself with David Eichenbaum in a conference room, ostensibly to do a local radio call-in show. Issues adviser Dayna Bender, bodyguard Anita Ashton, Des, and I waited in the airport lounge, thinking some disc jockey was getting really lucky. Carol and David were in there for an hour.

Months later, I learned that this was the first time Carol had explained her family dynamics to her press secretary. "You should know this because you will have to deal with it," she now told Eichenbaum. Eichenbaum had not been present when Kgosie and Carol met with Longhini and Hogan the first time. He had seen the referenced family document just moments before it was shown to the reporter when Kgosie thrust the release and waiver into his hands, saying, "This is what Hogan came for." The press secretary had been tilting with phantoms for eight days.

Eichenbaum, who was nothing if not nimble, took this time—while the rest of us waited—to talk with Carol about how she needed to not be defensive but rather to be as aggressive and as forthcoming as possible on questions dealing with Medicaid.

In Rockford, she did just that. Of course, the next day, the *Trib* devoted one paragraph to Braun's "nine-point economic plan," which writer Rick Pearson said was "designed to divert attention from the Medicaid flap." So much for getting the message out. The subhead on the Pearson story was "Braun threatens to go on attack after foe's 'character assassinations.'"

And that she did. Many times during the campaign, Carol had thought about attacking Williamson, whose whole campaign seemed to be about attacking her, but with an overwhelming lead in the polls, that would have been folly. Now, circumstances had changed, and what had been an expression of frustration in Rockford would soon become campaign policy.

Meanwhile, two members of our small band were very happy when we took off from Rockford on time and headed back to Chicago. Today was Yom Kippur, the "Day of Atonement," and Dayna Bender and David Eichenbaum wanted to be back in time for services. The rest of us asked if they would take our sins, please, since we all felt the need for spiritual relief. Dayna said that "at $500 a ticket for services," she figured she could handle a few extra sins. (Jeez, and I thought the Bulls courtside was the highest ticket in town.)

Then Carol, a superb joke-teller with an impressive repertoire, laid a classic on us. Using dialect and gestures, she said, "Lil 'ole black lady is sittin' in her rockin' chair, dippin' snuff. She says, 'Jews are smart. They only ask for forgiveness one time a year—and look how good they do in this world! We negroes, we just throwin' up our hands every day, wailin' Lawd have mercy! Lawd have mercy! The Lawd, he git tired a hearin' all that gas!'"

"Lord, have mercy." It seemed a fitting prayer to end the day.

"Not so fast," sayeth the Lord.

Gus met us at the airport and while David, Dayna, and I headed into our personal lives, Anita, Des, and Carol went on to a fundraiser in the Korean community. Shortly before ten o'clock, Edna Moseley was admitted to Rush-Presbyterian-St. Luke's Medical Center after complaining of chest pains. Still wearing the ceremonial costume she'd been given by her Korean supporters, Carol left the party in Chicago's northern neighborhood of Lincolnwood and sped to the Near South Side hospital. Edna was hospitalized for two days, suffering from angina. Carol would blame "the Medicaid thing."

Thursday, October 8, late morning

I was in the press office, culling file clips from the primary election cycle, when David Eichenbaum got a call from Paul Hogan. After the customary greetings, there followed a long silence, then David said: "Let me get this straight. You have another letter, allegedly written by Carol, and you want a response?" The anticipated second hit, the letter that network correspondent Bob Kur had unsuccessfully presented on the evening of October 5, had surfaced again. This time, the campaign might not be so lucky.

It was a small office, and although I was burning with curiosity, I had never been comfortable with eavesdropping, so I left for the copying machine.

I returned a few minutes later, in time to see David striding down the hallway, looking for Matthews and Jerry Austin. Indeed, for the rest of the day, there was a kind of furtive scurrying about the campaign offices. Interestingly, with a crisis clearly in progress, only the men seemed to be involved. Even the guy who'd worked for Carol's primary opponent, media consultant David Axelrod, showed up, closeting himself with Matthews, Eichenbaum, and (rival) media consultant Austin. Carol was out on the campaign trail.

Then I got lucky. I ran into Kgosie's lovely assistant, Roxanne Volkmann, awkwardly attempting to deliver drinks and food to the campaign manager's office. I offered to help. As Rox kicked the door open, I instinctively announced, "So here we are again, the girls delivering food to the boys! Enough of this!" I got a smile out of the K Man as Axelrod got up and announced he was leaving.

I walked out with David. "So what's this about Hogan and another letter?" I asked, picking up on a fragment of information.

Axelrod looked surprised. "Walk with me," he said. "The letter says—remember, this is Carol to her mom—something like, 'I'm handling this money for you, and I hope you will launder it in accordance with state regulations.'"

"Oh, God," I cried. "We're dead!"

"Yeah. It's bad. I think she'll go on live with Hogan, face up to it, challenge him. At least that's what I suggested."

"Do they listen to you?"

"I hope so," said the man who one day would be instrumental in electing the first African American president of the United States.

David Eichenbaum walked back into the office at about 6, went straight to his chair in the corner, and hunkered down in a way that suggested both exhaustion and relief.

"Will you tell me what's going on?" I asked, not letting on that I already knew part of the story.

The press secretary looked at me evenly and said: "Remember this day. We could have lost the election today. It could have been gone. I will remember this day for the rest of my life."

Thursday, October 8, had been a long and journalistically tortuous day for Paul Hogan and for Doug Longhini as well.

At this point, they still only had a portion of the letter containing the damning word *launder* that NBC News correspondent Bob Kur had presented to Carol the night of her fall fundraiser. Significantly, during the course of the original interview Hogan had done with Carol on September 28, the following exchange had taken place:

> CAROL: It is my belief that we did everything according to the law and regulations. We certainly worked as a family to make certain that everything was appropriately done as we always have.
>
> HOGAN: You did not do anything that attempted to hide or keep away from or launder that money so that Medicaid could not know about it?
>
> CAROL: No, no, of course not, of course not. No, we've always—the idea of laundering is just stunning

to me—no, absolutely not. I was aware, and I am
aware, that there are a thousand different rules and
regulations having to do with the receipt of money
by someone who is in a nursing home. My mother received a windfall, one-time money falling out
of the sky. We have chipped in and supported my
mother and paid for all of her expenses for years.
Since 1970—whenever the first stroke was.

HOGAN: '78.

However casual it seemed, Hogan had deliberately used the
killer buzzword, *launder*.

The author of the damning paragraph might as easily have written,
"Look, I'll keep this money in my account, but we need to settle
this quick. So, if you don't want it to go to the state, let's just get our
shit together and do a legal disbursement." Most of the electorate
would have accepted that. But "launder" in order to "not run afoul
of state regulations"? Not likely.

Hogan and Longhini's problem was that they had no idea
whether or not Carol had actually written this paragraph with its
startling sentence. Although they were assured by their source
of its existence, they did not have the complete letter. What they
had was a typewritten fragment with neither salutation nor signature. But they also had confidence in the veracity of their source.
So, once again, the Bob Kur ploy having been unsuccessful, Paul
Hogan went fishing.

"That Friday, the campaign was sure we were going to go with it,"
remembered Longhini. But then, two things happened. The first
was that Carol's representatives said that if WMAQ went with the
story, then they wanted the candidate to be in the studio live to
deal with the charges.

"We said, 'We'll decide that; it certainly is a possibility,' said
Longhini. "'What does she want to say?' Well, they wouldn't tell
us." And the fact was that Hogan had an unsigned, typescript

paragraph with absolutely no way to prove Carol had written it. While WMAQ thought Carol would be taking a foolish risk to go on live, this also had the effect of calling their bluff. This time, the candidate hadn't taken the bait. Axelrod's advice had prevailed.

Then Jerry Austin had a conversation with Paul Hogan. Jerry and Paul were old acquaintances from the political beat in Ohio and shared many of the same views. Austin, Longhini, and Eichenbaum—who heard Jerry's end of the conversation—all agreed on the gist: Paul was a good liberal; how could he hand the election to a guy like Rich Williamson? The campaign members who were privy to the drama of October 8, Medicaid II, as it were, all gave Austin credit for saving the day.

And so did Carol, who called Austin that afternoon to say thank you.

But the fact was, whatever Hogan's politics, he and Longhini were good journalists. Without confirmation, they had no story.

There are two addenda to the Medicaid thing. The first is that, according to Eichenbaum, Carol herself found a copy of a letter to her mother very similar to the one Hogan had been given, and it contained no reference to money laundering.

The second is that WMAQ's source subsequently turned over a copy of the entire "launder" letter (still without signature or salutation), and Hogan and Longhini had this new document and the release and waiver that Carol had acknowledged both analyzed by a forensic expert. Although to the naked eye there was no difference in the typeface, the analyst confirmed without a doubt that the letters had been produced by different printers.

"We were really knocked out on that last day by Jerry Austin," Longhini admitted. "It's just that we were so confused about what to do with this story. We were convinced it was true. But then later, when we got the analysis, well, we were really glad we hadn't pursued it."

Longhini wanted to say one more thing. "I believe the dynamics of what she [Carol] was trying to describe in that press conference were honest. It was her mother's fault, but she took responsibility. Clearly, she had a stormy relationship with her mother. I know she's a sworn member of the bar, but at the same time she's a daughter and a mother and in a family setting. Nobody else was watching; she wasn't running for anything. It was just her and her family. I didn't leave the story thinking less of her."

Nevertheless, there was now a perceptible atmospheric change. Like a sailplane, Carol had been held aloft, bouncing from one updraft to another. The Medicaid thing would not send her into a dive but rather a long glide. The question was whether there would be enough lift to bring Carol Moseley Braun home safely on November 3.

During the first two weeks of October, the headlines that had for so long been propelling Carol forward were now sending her in the other direction. Perhaps the most wrenching piece done during this period was written by a woman and a sympathizer.

Columnist Mary Schmich had been a member of the *Chicago Tribune* editorial board that had met with Carol four days after the Medicaid hit, the meeting Eichenbaum had described to me as "terrible." Knowing his candidate was exhausted and upset, the press secretary later blamed himself for not postponing this very important session. But Eichenbaum was also to blame Schmich for what he believed was a violation of journalistic ethics. Editorial board meetings were off-the-record forums, designed to inform newspaper staffers for purposes of making a determination regarding endorsement, not for creating news.

Yet now, on October 7, five days after the meeting took place, Schmich felt compelled to tell what had happened that afternoon when Carol, accompanied by Kgosie Matthews and David Eichenbaum, sat around a conference table with the most important editorial decision makers at the newspaper. Wrote Schmich:

> In every love affair there arrives the first awful moment of truth. The beloved, once bathed in the fuzzy, flattering light found in department store dressing rooms, suddenly stands under a fluorescent glare, every line and ounce and pore exposed. Having seen

the flaws, you're forced to ask yourself: Is this who I really want?

So it is with Carol Moseley Braun.

Schmich then went on to describe the foregoing months of the campaign, during which "Queen Carol became the delegate to the future."

> She was earthy, witty, charming. With her luminous smile, she could make an audience feel they were cruising in a new Cadillac down a freshly paved road. What a smooth, reassuring ride toward the new world.
>
> And so it is hard to say what follows.
>
> Braun has skated through on charm, and her supporters—of which I hesitantly remain one—have been complicit in her failure to grow beyond charm.
>
> On Friday afternoon, Braun came to the *Tribune* to meet with the editorial board. There in the high-ceilinged, paneled boardroom, she had her chance to win the paper's endorsement. It was a painful show.

Although Schmich didn't say so in her column, for the first 20 minutes, board members questioned Carol exclusively about the Medicaid situation, unknowingly stirring the emotional turmoil she had been stonewalling around the clock for days. So when the conversation got to specific issues—entitlement cuts, farm subsidies, NAFTA—Carol, according to Schmich, "batted away questions with a smile, as if what she didn't know didn't matter. Until the very end. It had been a hard week and a hard hour. She cried."

As Carol recalled:

The Tribune editorial board session was a disaster, an absolute disaster. Of course I could speak about all the subjects they brought up. I'd been doing it for months. But it was as if my emotions disengaged my mind—not that that is an excuse. My mother was in the hospital with an as-yet-undiagnosed heart problem, and I felt guilty about what I had caused Edna to go through, this public approbation. And at the same time, I was angry at her for what she had caused me to go through. But I couldn't talk about it, not the pain and ugliness of it. Yet that's what these people kept asking me, these journalists, these judges. It was so hostile.

I think a male politician in my position would have strategized the situation much more coolly, would have undoubtedly had a wife to handle the family and the emotional side of things, maybe even to absorb some of the heat. Every member of my family had been involved in this, but now, once again, it was my problem, and they looked to me to solve it.

But perhaps there is a legitimate political question intrinsic in my ordeal: Would you rather have someone who didn't feel anything? Who'd never had to deal with the health care system because he or other members of his family were so well insured or had the money to pay for whatever came up?

Years ago, my mother never would have survived that last set of strokes. Because of medical advances, she did, but not in such a way that we could take care of her at home.

So now those of us in what is called "the sandwich generation" have parents requiring very expensive medical care—and children requiring very expensive educations. This is not a poor people's problem; this is virtually everybody's problem.

But in October of 1992, all the difficulties, all the pain and poison that had beset so many parts of my life, found new form in my campaign for the United States Senate. Somebody had dropped a dime on me, somebody who didn't need a dime to call my number, somebody who could not deal with my perceived success. And now I know who that person was—but you will not.

PART III

It's Airplane! *The campaign movie!*

—DAVID AXELROD

CHAPTER 12

The Debate

U NDER THE HEADLINE "Politicians Are People Too, We Find," *St. Louis Post-Dispatch* columnist Pat Gauen listed a number of high-profile political candidates, then detailed the personal failings the 1992 election process had revealed in each. Carol's Medicaid transgressions were among those described. In conclusion, Gauen said:

> We say we want to be represented in government by people just like us. But we fail to examine our own pasts and to imagine the kind of mudballs that could be slung our way if we were the ones on the stump.
>
> Candidacy in 1992 is an act of bravery, not so much for being subjected to those mudballs as for being subjected to a lot of voters who won't take the trouble to decide which mud sticks and which doesn't.
>
> I have learned too much from my own mistakes to want to elect someone for any office who never made one.

Gauen's wisdom was briefly comforting to the Braun camp, but by this time, both the campaign and the press were focused on an upcoming opportunity for redemption.

As the October 12 date of the first televised debate with Rich Williamson approached, Carol's numbers were falling—and the pressure on her was building. Illinois House speaker Mike Madigan, worried about the other candidates Carol had been expected to pull along, told the *Sun-Times'* Basil Talbott, "This [Medicaid] could hurt us. It won't cause her to lose, but she'd better get her act together."

Bill Daley,[23] the mayor's brother and Bill Clinton's man in Illinois, thought the Braun candidacy would survive the Medicaid story, "but," he said, "Carol will have to perform at the debate."

Just before the debate, Matthews invited me to what would be my first senior staff meeting. "I'm buying lunch, and we're just going to air things out," he told me. Finding a seat was no problem as Kgosie had dismissed his last secretary, and there was an empty desk that would remain so for the rest of the campaign. Roxanne Volkmann, the young woman who handled travel arrangements for the campaign and was an established Matthews confidante, had now taken over whatever secretarial functions he required.

I entered Matthews's office to find him relaxed and gregarious, his staff ranged around him. Once again, I marveled at the racial/gender balance in this campaign. Among the mid-level and senior staffers present were five black women, four white women, three black men, and three white men. Kgosie Matthews was in control.

As I walked in, Matthews was saying, "I don't believe this place. I read in Lynn Sweet's column today that David Axelrod was playing Rich Williamson in debate prep. Who leaked that?"

Press secretary David Eichenbaum's hand shot up. "I told her," he said. "She asked me." Matthews looked disgusted but said nothing further on the subject.

Issues papers were the next on the agenda. Reported Ira Cohen: "They're ready. They can go out tonight." And that's when the campaign manager commented that he was uncomfortable with issues papers because they would have to be defended.

---

23   Bill Daley subsequently served as Bill Clinton's secretary of commerce and, for a time, as President Barack Obama's chief of staff.

At one point in the meeting, Carol walked in. She sat in a chair, hands folded in her lap, ankles crossed, a pleasant but somehow distant look on her face. I was reminded of childhood lessons in female decorum. Carol spoke very little, deferring to Kgosie's authority.

Ira Cohen broached the subject of debate preparation. "Debate prep" had been on the schedule since October 7, and so far, none of the issues people had spent time with Carol. The candidate, forced by headlines to confront a cascade of personal and political realities, still seemed to be in shock.

While all manner of campaign trivia was being discussed around me, I couldn't help thinking about the emotional conflicts that semisweet look on Carol's face must be concealing: betrayed at a vulnerable moment by someone close, someone who should have supported her; people depending upon her success to advance their political agendas, not to mention their careers; a public losing faith in her; a feminist who liked to be in control and who should be—at minimum—cochairing this meeting. But all I thought I saw behind that tiny smile was a scared girl. Who was going to hurt her next?

When I arrived at Meigs Field at 10 a.m. for another trip to Rockford, David Eichenbaum, issues diva Dayna Bender (whom Carol called "my little genius"), and Officer Anita Ashton were already there. David was worried about debate prep—another session was scheduled upon our return this afternoon. Anita was still laughing about something I'd told her the day before: that Matthews had referred to her as "the copper." Anita, in turn, frequently referred to Kgosie as "that little fucker." She was free to call Matthews whatever she wanted, she said, because her boss was the Chicago police commander who had assigned her to be Carol's bodyguard.

When it became clear to Anita that she was on the campaign manager's shit list, she'd gone to her commander and asked him to back her up should Kgosie try to get her reassigned. Anita's superior officer had given his word that Anita would be with Carol unless and until the candidate herself asked that she be removed. Despite pressure from Kgosie, that never happened. Carol liked and trusted Anita—for good reason: she was a consummately conscientious and professional "copper." Also, Anita cared for Carol and believed in her. "When she has to chose between the Senate and 'him,'" Anita maintained, "Carol will dump that little fucker."

As the small plane took off, paralleling the brilliant Chicago skyline before heading northwest out of the city, Carol slumped in her seat, saying, "My body just aches all over." She said her phone had begun ringing at 6:30 in the morning. "That's when people can be sure I'm home." I'd given up asking why she didn't just turn the damn thing off. The way she internalized it, as Heather Booth had described, the campaign was the punishment Carol had to take in order to gain the reward she sought. When her energy was down, Carol clearly felt more like a victim than a leader.

On the plane, David tentatively broached the subject of the cover story just out in October's *Chicago* magazine. He said, "I've had several people tell me 'great article,' but I don't think they read the second half."

"You mean the stuff about Kgosie and me being an item?" Carol asked David, indicating with a dismissive gesture that she thought the information—in print for the first time—was of no consequence. "The story was hard on Kgosie, but what's new?" Carol was not allowing herself to understand that what was hard on Kgosie was hard on her because she then became his defender, his front person. Said *Chicago,* after reiterating the usual complaints about Matthews: "He, clearly, is some kind of lodestar for her. (The irony of the 'women's candidate' seeming at times so dependent on a man is not lost on many of those who have commented on the two.)"

The true irony was that in the other important part of Carol's base, the African American community, this stand-by-your-man ethic *was* understood, although not always approved, given the guy in question and the stakes involved. Carol was a black feminist—ahead of the cultural curve politically, behind it personally. To a few who were close enough to see her bleed, the battle for the US Senate was nothing compared with the conflict going on inside Carol Moseley Braun.

But on the plane to Rockford, we were about to witness another demonstration of this dichotomy. It started when Carol told us that Kgosie had "reduced Darlene Mackey to tears the other day." Carol loved her "cousin" Darlene, and clearly the incident had bothered her. Carol said that when she chastised Kgosie for the pain he had caused, he professed surprise that Darlene had been hurt.

"But," she said, switching to defense, "you've got to understand Kgosie. He's a combination of three different cultures: British, American, and African—specifically, Zulu."

"Zulu is the mean part," Carol continued. "If you could see him when he speaks Zulu, his face freezes in that fierce expression we all know so well."

"You're saying that Kgosie's stern countenance is the face of manhood in the Zulu culture?" I asked.

"Exactly," responded Carol.

I'd seen that look all too often. To me it was a shield, brought out to mask insecurity and confusion. (But then, what else is the face of manhood?)

"Kgosie got his formal bearing from living in England," Carol went on. "He complains about my manners. He's constantly correcting me," she laughed.

"And from America," said Carol, "Kgosie draws many of his cultural tastes. For example, he loves Michael Jackson. I have no idea why, but he just loves Michael Jackson. On the other hand," she added, "he's very straight. Like his grandfather, who was educated by missionaries, Kgosie is a believing Christian. He doesn't smoke; he doesn't drink. He doesn't even want alcohol in the house. He says grace before meals."

Captive in a tiny airplane, we listened respectfully, the others probably doing as I was, bouncing this information off our own experience with the man. But while I may have been smiling on the outside, on the inside, I was aching for Carol and trying to remember a passage about the end of painful love from Zora Neale Hurston's *Their Eyes Were Watching God.* I knew I had marked it because I had lived it myself, and when I returned home, I found it:

> Janie stood where he left her for unmeasured time
> and thought. She stood there until something fell
> off the shelf inside her. Then she went inside there
> to see what it was. It was her image of Jody tumbled
> down and shattered. But looking at it she saw that it

never was the flesh and blood figure of her dreams.
Just something she had grabbed up to shape her
dreams over.

Would that Carol could find her inner Zora.

Monday, October 12, 1992

I met David Eichenbaum and Desiree Tate outside the campaign
office at 7:30 a.m. for the drive to Peoria for the debate. Anita Ashton and Kgosie would fly with Carol. The remaining seats on the
plane were reserved for the issues people, including Bob Borosage
of the Institute for Policy Studies in Washington. Borosage was a
policy wonk who'd met Kgosie in the '88 Jackson campaign. Matthews had called Borosage in to help shape Carol's message for the
final weeks and, specifically, to prepare for the two crucial live television debates.[24]

When we got to the Pere Marquette Hotel in Peoria, Carol
was in her suite being briefed by Borosage and issues director Ira
Cohen. The session broke up about 12:30. Carol had an editorial
board meeting with the Peoria *Journal Star*, so Des, Ira, and I headed for lunch. Kgosie had "suggested" that Anita's protective services were not needed at the newspaper meeting, so Anita joined
us, reluctantly leaving her room, where she was enjoying a good
book. The atmosphere was growing tense between the copper and
the campaign manager. Anita said she had made arrangements to
get back to Chicago with friends, "Just in case Kgosie kicks me off
of the plane." (He did.)

At lunch, Ira announced that the issues papers had all, finally,
been approved, 22 days before the election. He said he believed
Carol would win the election, "but not because of anything we've
done. We've done everything wrong." Ira was a 15-hour-a-day volunteer and a true believer. He believed strongly that despite the
crazy campaign, Carol would be a good and effective senator. Ira's
big regret was that if the campaign had been "done right," a lasting

---

24   Robert Borosage is now with the think tank Campaign for America's
      Future.

movement might have grown out of it, a reshaping of the Harold
Washington coalition and spirit.

The Dingledine was a lovely, small auditorium, originally a church,
but now primarily used for musical events at Bradley University.
It was also a perfect size for the debate audience, although all of
the television technology had to be imported, and there were unadorned cables everywhere. We arrived to find the streets clogged
with TV trucks, their satellite dishes aimed skyward.

I was outside the holding room assigned to Carol when she
arrived. The candidate looked tense, her smile forced. In the best of
circumstances, Carol was not a person who relished hand-to-hand
combat, and current circumstances were not good; they were even
worse than I knew at the time. Carol requested that someone fetch
her old friend and spiritual counselor, the Reverend Addie Wyatt.

Good, I thought, she'll pray. Perhaps that will help to settle her
emotions and clear her mind.

Sitting on a folding chair between Jerry Austin and David
Axelrod, I watched the debate on a television monitor in the press
area (or, more accurately, the "spin room") below the auditorium.
The two men, both Democratic media consultants, were actually
business competitors, and while their relationship was cordial, it
was definitely strained. When I asked Axelrod what he was doing
in Peoria, he said he wasn't sure: "Spin, I guess." He'd been called
from his vacation home in Michigan at the last minute. "I sure as
hell never played Rich Williamson in debate prep," said Axelrod,
who wasn't any happier than Kgosie was about the recent column
item. There had, in fact, been almost no debate prep, Carol resisting every time it had been scheduled. But I didn't tell David that.

Just before airtime, Kgosie walked into the pressroom and
thrust Carol's lucky pearls into my hand. "Will you keep these?"
he asked. "They were clicking against the microphone." Uh-oh, I
thought. Some women feel naked without jewelry. I hoped Carol
wasn't one of them.

The fact is, nowhere is a candidate more naked than in a live
television debate, and moderator John Callaway went immediately
for Carol's rawest exposure, Medicaid. Then Williamson took up

the cudgel, questioning Carol's honesty, "Can you believe today what she said yesterday?"

Carol was nervous at first, but she hit her stride when she turned the ethics question back on Williamson, saying he ran "the most sleazy campaign in Illinois history." She called him the "Freddy Krueger of Illinois politics," referring to the slasher from the *Nightmare on Elm Street* movies.

He said she was a tax-and-spend, old-time liberal politician. *She* said he wrote the book on "the New Federalism" that transferred responsibility to state and local governments. *She* repeatedly connected him to Reagan and Bush. *He* invoked the names of Ross Perot, Mayor Daley, and Bill Clinton. *He* said she was against the death penalty. *She* said the same people who were for the death penalty had done nothing to stop the flow of drugs into the country. *She* said that while hardworking people lost jobs, he bailed out of a short stint with Beatrice Foods on a golden parachute. *He* said he'd have her know that he paid $700,000 in taxes that year. (Now there was a vote-getter!)

Most experts declared the debate a draw. Certainly there was no knockout, although some thought Carol won on points.

Under the banner "The Media & The Message," two *Sun-Times* columnists offered these conclusions:

> Richard Roeper said, "The problem for Rich Williamson is that no matter what he says, he reminds you of your high school principal, while Carol Braun is the counselor who takes a special interest in you and makes you feel good about the future." [*Feelings!*]

> Vernon Jarrett said, "Fortunately for Braun, the most talented fighter, they have a return match scheduled before Nov. 3."

When I offered Carol her pearls, she reached for them gratefully. "I wondered where they'd gone," she said. Carol was glowing, not so much in triumph but with relief.

Williamson entered the spin room and, spotting David Axel-rod, said, "Hey, thanks for playing me in the debate practice!" David, swallowing a mite of puke, answered, "No problem." An accurate statement, of course, as neither he nor anyone else had been required to fill that role.

When Kgosie Matthews stopped in, he did not join the others in complimenting Carol's performance. Rather, his demeanor suggested that the campaign manager was not at all happy.

It was an exhausted crew that crawled into a rented minivan for the long drive back to Chicago—David Eichenbaum, Bob Borosage, Ira Cohen, Jerry Austin, and myself. Just as we were pulling away, Des came running out. "I'm not getting on that plane with them fighting," she said, referring to Carol and Kgosie. Borosage jumped at the chance to trade transport with Des; he had an early flight out of Chicago to Washington in the morning.[25]

"Why," I asked Desiree, "would you trade a half-hour flight for a three-hour drive, no matter how poisonous the atmosphere?"

"I just couldn't handle it anymore," said the candidate's thoroughly stressed-out traveling aide.

It seemed that moments before Carol was to leave the Pere Marquette for the debate at Bradley University, Kgosie had burst into her room demanding that she get rid of Anita. Apparently, he'd gone to check out of the hotel and found that Anita had charged her room to his account, and that had sent him into a rage. Knowing he couldn't fire Anita, Kgosie wanted Carol to commit to dismissing her bodyguard—*now*!

---

25   Borosage joined us from time to time, and once, when I was the only person staffing Carol during a day of speeches, he turned to me when the candidate was out of earshot and asked: "Do you have a safety pin?" "No, why?" "Carol is showing too much cleavage. You need to get her to fix that." My journal records my mental reaction: "Fuck no!" Like many of our white Jackson alums, Bob was attuned to stereotypes, and he didn't want Carol looking "Jezebel," the term used to describe the false (but historically useful to white men) stereotype that black women were overly sexual and promiscuous. But in my perhaps less-informed opinion, Borosage overreacted. I thought Carol looked great.

Carol, already at her wit's end, trying to calm herself for the debate, asked, "Kgosie, how can you be doing this to me at this time? Anita is fine. I like her. Can we talk about this tomorrow?"

"*No.* Now!"

And so, at a time when she was especially vulnerable, Carol came under attack by the one person upon whom she most wanted to depend.

Months later, discussing her debate performance, Carol was still asking, "Why did he pick a fight with me at that time?"

As for the rest of us beginning our long trek back from southern Illinois to Chicago, we were starving. Jerry Austin spotted a place that looked good to him, "Nothing like burgers and beer in a road-side saloon!" So Ira, David, Jerry, Des, and I sat down among a scattering of good old boys, the stale air heavy with grease, cigarettes, alcohol, and thrice-worn shirts. Once we settled the question of whether Carol had played well in Peoria (the conclusion: well enough), Jerry Austin launched into what I came to think of as a vagina monologue. He just ripped on Carol for sacrificing herself to her sexual needs. "They say guys have dicks for brains, well, this woman is being led around by her fuckin' vagina!"

Ira shook his head, looking disgusted; this wasn't his kind of issue. David just seemed exhausted. Des looked miserable. Having spent my career to this point shuffling between newsrooms and locker rooms, nothing about Jerry Austin or his opinions surprised me, but I knew Carol's dependency was much more complicated than her sexual needs, and I said so. For all Jerry's lifelong devotion to liberal causes, for all the excellent work he had done for Carol so far, Jerry Austin was a total jock when it came to women. He knew some of what tormented Carol, but he thought she should just "get over it."

I was sitting by Des, who was staring into her plate of fries. "Don't let Jerry bother you," I smiled, trying to lighten the moment. Des looked up at me, her thoughts clearly somewhere else. "I'm the only black person in this place," she said. "This doesn't feel good. Didn't you notice?"

I had not noticed. But I *had* noted the lack of women. Perspective. It comes from deep inside, shaped and filtered by so many experiences—not to mention cultural forces and inherited attitudes. How many press boxes had I been shut out of in the early days? How many rooms full of sportswriters had fallen silent when I walked in? I was now accustomed to being the only woman, but I should have realized that this was a new kind of room for Des. We were all clearly outsiders in this mini environment, but Des was *feeling* it. No, I hadn't noticed. Jerry Austin was not the only insensitive person at the table.

On October 13, the Braun campaign began to air its first negative ad. When asked why they'd waited so long, media consultant Jerry Austin said, "We had to wait until people knew who Williamson was before we could attack him."

The "Golden Parachute" ad, as it was called, reiterated some of the points Carol had signaled in the debate: that Rich Williamson had been running one of the most negative campaigns in Illinois history, that the policies he'd helped develop for Republican administrations punished Illinois families, and that he'd bailed out of a junk-bond merger on a million-dollar golden parachute.

Reacting to the ad, Williamson's press secretary, David Loveday, borrowed the word David Eichenbaum had used numerous times to describe the Republican's negative campaign tactics: Braun, he said, was "desperate."

With just over two weeks until the election, "desperation" was not the most accurate word to describe the Braun campaign; "anxious" was more like it. Thus, when WLS political reporter Andy Shaw broke a story (planted weeks before by the Braun campaign) revealing that Williamson was a member of an exclusive North Shore country club, Steve Cobble sought to break the tension by circulating an explanatory top 10 list.

TEN REASONS WHY RICH WILLIAMSON JOINED AN EXCLUSIVE COUNTRY CLUB (NO AFRICAN-AMERICANS, NO LATINOS, NO JEWISH MEMBERS, ONLY A "FEW" CATHOLICS):

(10) He didn't know discrimination is a character issue.

(9) He thinks character issues only apply to Black women.

(8) He thinks "diversity" means having members from both Kenilworth and Wilmette.

(7) Some of his best friends are "non-members."

(6) He opposes quotas, in this case, a quota of one.

(5) He thought Calvin Peete and Lee Trevino were the only minorities who liked to play golf.

(4) He thought "WASP" was the state bird of Illinois.

(3) He did not want to be the "special representative" of Blacks, Hispanics, Jews and Catholics.

(2) After all his years in the "culturally diverse" Ronald Reagan and George Bush administrations, he was tired of being around so many top black executives.

(1) He was practicing up for the U.S. Senate (which is made up of 97 males, no Blacks, no Latinos and lots of millionaire lawyers).

Despite the anxiety inside the campaign, outside, virtually every day now, endorsements were being printed and broadcast, and while these were inevitably tempered with reservations, most supported Braun.

The fact that the opposition chose this week to air a television ad in which Chicago Bears coach Mike Ditka endorsed Richard Williamson provided further comic relief. Said Ditka, "I'm conservative. I'm ultraconservative. I'm voting Republican." At a Williamson fundraiser, Ditka, never one to understate his opinion, declared, "If the Clinton-Gore team was ever elected, it would be the biggest step backward this country has taken in its 200 years of existence."

On October 13, the Associated Press reported that Lake County clerk Linda Hess said Ditka had not voted in 14 of the last 17 primary or general elections. In addition, since moving to a new home, Ditka had failed to re-register to vote. When his credibility was challenged on these points at a football press con-ference, Ditka shot from the lip, as usual: "I can endorse anybody I want," he said. "Now, do you want to know about my religion? I'm for Jesus Christ."

I had known Mike since he joined the Chicago Bears right out of college, and as a reporter, I had covered him for another couple of decades. I treasured Mike; he was the best copy in football. To borrow one of his own favorite expressions, Ditka was "a piece of work." Chicago loved Mike but also knew him. So this particular endorsement would have no effect.

On October 16, the *Chicago Tribune* reported results of another of its periodic polls. Under the headline, "Braun's Support Appears to Be Weathering Storm," Tom Hardy wrote:

> With the most combative two weeks of the cam-paign thus far and an argumentative first debate now behind them, Braun has halted the slippage of her support and Williamson has raised his name identity into a range competitive with hers, the poll found.

Carol was ahead 49 percent to 29 percent with 20 percent un-decided. She was down from her September peak (58 to 24 per-cent), but, according to the *Tribune*, her numbers had stabilized.

So much for the numbers. But something else was going on. On the evening of October 14, I joined Officer Anita Ashton and Leti-tia DeWith-Anderson—who was still, as far as I knew, surviving as Carol's scheduler—for cocktails at Oscar's, a lawyers' bar at LaSalle and Wells.

Letitia took one sip of her screwdriver and announced to us that Kgosie had fired her. You'll recall that Letitia was on loan from Springfield, where her husband and children still resided, and was working for Carol to fulfill a promise made to her father on his deathbed. But, Letitia added, she wasn't going to stay fired because she'd told Kgosie that if he fired her, she was going to call a press conference and "tell everything."[26] Letitia had powerful friends in the state capitol. She was bluffing, but it worked. Letitia said that after their confrontation, she broke down crying and Kgosie walked off giggling. Letitia said she was "this close" to attacking him physically.

"Don't worry about it, Letitia," Anita interjected. "I'm gonna get his Zulu ass. He's on a green card, and he is not going to make it to Washington with Carol." (What we didn't know then was that Washington was only one of the world's capitals that interested Kgosie Matthews).

It's hard to describe the ecstasy Letitia seemed to feel as Anita assured her that Kgosie was, in Anita's words, history. Anita was sure Carol was just biding her time and would dump "the little fucker" soon, so Letitia should stick it out. Carol would win, go to Washington, and be a great senator. It would all be worth it.

Anita shared Letitia's faith in Carol's future, as did I. But I wasn't as sure that Kgosie was a goner. Carol, I believed, was in love with this brilliant but difficult man, a man, in ways, not unlike her own father. Regarding Kgosie's sexual behavior, the candidate was clearly in willful denial.

Whatever. We ordered another round of drinks.

After repeated assurances that Kgosie Matthews had indeed suggested him as a good source on campaign strategy, Steve Cobble finally agreed to an interview. On a crisp October evening in a restaurant overlooking a Chicago river sparkling with city lights, we discussed the fascinating, compelling endeavor in which we were both totally—if quite differently—immersed.

Defending Matthews, Steve disputed the oft-repeated quote that Kgosie had been Jackson's "valet," explaining: "Kgosie traveled with Jackson for three years. He was his advance guy, and part of

---

26   Among the damning anecdotes Letitia had filed away was a time when she was alone with Kgosie in his office and he'd complained about a female writer's negative coverage, then "made like he was swinging his penis around and said, 'She's just pissed because she wants some of this big Zulu dick.'" Shocked as she was, Letitia said, "I think he really believed that!"

his job was to say no to all of the people who thought they were hot stuff and wanted to be around Jesse. Somebody had to be a jerk, and it wasn't going to be Jesse Jackson.

"When Kgosie first went to work for Carol," said Steve, "he asked Jerry Austin, 'What's the first rule of being a campaign manager?' And Jerry said, 'Tell people no.' Kgosie liked that; he was good at it. Combine that with his contempt for the press, and it's a wonder he hasn't had more trouble.

"But Carol counters that effectively. When she wants something, she's the best I've ever seen. She makes people feel good about themselves. Obviously, she's emotionally conflicted right now but...." Steve paused for a moment, then continued. "Carol is a woman with poetry in her soul. People feel that. She's already a skilled legislator and, personally, I think she can be a great senator."

"Ironically, some of the things about Carol that give us trouble are the things I like about her," Steve went on. "I mean she's no windup doll. You cannot tell her, 'Carol, we're gonna go here, then there, and you're gonna smile at this point. No. Come hell or high water, she's her own person. She gets pissed when people who should be her friends don't behave that way, like the AFL-CIO because they supported Alan Dixon in the primary despite Carol's 90 percent labor record. And she tells those guys about it every time they get together! It's not the most politic thing, but it's human."

Having said all that, Steve admitted that things weren't rosy within the campaign. "I don't think she trusts us," he sighed. "And she's about to get rid of Jerry Austin."

Jerry and Steve were good friends. Steve said, "Someone called Jerry Austin 'a junkyard dog with a heart of gold,' and that describes him perfectly. He'll take on candidates, like he did with Carol in the primary, who have no money and almost no chance to win because he believes in them. On Jesse's campaign, he was always taking care of the kids—somebody's car would break down, they couldn't pay for an apartment because they were making virtually no money, somebody would need to fly home for a family emergency. Jerry would just pay for it. Jerry believes that it is important to nurture these well-educated, idealistically motivated young people who are drawn to campaigns. But Jerry Austin is too outspoken for his own good."

Everybody knew Carol was not fond of her media consultant—and then there was the obvious fact that, as Steve put it, she had been "playing footsie with David Axelrod." But most expected Jerry to stick through the election. According to Steve, Kgosie had saved Jerry's job more than once already, telling Carol, "If he goes, I go."

Carol and Jerry Austin had disliked and distrusted one another almost from the beginning. She thought he operated too independently. He thought she was a "control freak." Then there was the fact that Jerry and Kgosie were old friends; they had a male bonding thing going on that excluded Carol.

Eventually, Carol explained:

It was Kgosie who kept Jerry [Austin] in the mix. Jerry and I never set sail, never hit it off. I thought Jerry was crass, even crude.

The final incident was triggered when I was talking to [my sister] Marsha, who worked for a cable TV company at the time. We were discussing personal matters and she said, "Oh, by the way, we have the TV ads Jerry Austin sent us to go statewide. They go on the air this afternoon." Well, I didn't know what was in this ad, hadn't seen the final copy! So I got Kgosie on the phone, and we called Jerry. I said, "What's this business about an ad going statewide today?"

He said, "Well, it was important that we get on the air right away because with the Medicaid thing, you're dropping so fast in the polls, and if we don't get this up, you're going to have a problem."

I said, "Nobody could be more concerned about my position and my actions than me, but at the same time, we've been around this tree before, Jerry. I can't believe you're still doing this."

And Jerry replied, "Well, as disorganized as this campaign is, I felt I had to take some initiative here."

Wrong. That's when I decided I'd had enough.

The campaign dynamic was this: Kgosie and I made virtually all the decisions together. We would battle it out on scheduling matters—there was definitely consternation between us about where I should and should not appear—but on everything else, there was not a decision made that I didn't sign off on. Not one. Outside the campaign, the perception was he hid behind me; inside, I hid behind him.

And this gets to the race/gender thing. Feminists would be thrilled to know I was running the show. Conservative blacks, on the other hand, would be just as happy to think a man was calling the shots. These were the extremes of our base constituency. These were people who needed to be comfortable with my candidacy—along with a vast number of mostly white, middle-thinking people. My record reflects a fidelity to issues important in the African American community, just as it does to women's issues. Socially, economically, I am a middle-class American. In reality, my record and I both reflected what the people of Illinois were looking for in 1992.

This business of reality versus perception is something I continually grapple with. Campaigns are dedicated to strategizing so that voters with disparate priorities can all be brought comfortably under the same tent. And even though this is central to the democratic process, and even though it is the nature of politics, I am personally discomfited by the pressure to be a sort of chameleon. And believe me when I tell you, that pressure is real.

CHAPTER 13

An Anonymous Letter Threatens Disaster

ON OCTOBER 21, Bill Clinton came to town.

Crowd guesstimators said there hadn't been that many people in Daley Plaza since the Bears won the Super Bowl in January 1986. The weather wasn't much better than it had been on that January day either. But as cold and blustery as it was, nothing would dampen the spirits of the Democrats. As people danced around Chicago's Pablo Picasso landmark sculpture to R.E.M.'s "Shiny Happy People," the spirit was more like a victory party than the long-planned get-out-the-vote rally it was designed to be.

I had a VIP ticket that was to get me near the platform placed at the intersection of Washington and Clark, facing diagonally onto the plaza. But when I got to the Clark Street exit of the county building, I couldn't get out the door; Daley Plaza was that packed. So I jumped on an elevator and went up to the headquarters of the Cook County recorder of deeds.

Carol's large office was the corner room just above the heads of the celebrities who were beginning to crowd the 15-foot, two-tiered platform below. On both the Clark Street and Washington Street sides, the windows were lettered with the words, "Carol Moseley Braun, Cook County Recorder of Deeds." One county worker rejoiced, "Clinton will be sure to notice!"

Carol's longtime assistant, Sue Bass, was running what had developed into gallery seating for the hottest show in Chicago. She allowed a limited number into the room, all people who worked in the recorder's office and knew Carol well. We had a marvelous (and warm) view of the proceedings as virtually every Democrat of note jostled for position below us. Only Bill and Hillary Clinton, Al and Tipper Gore, Mayor Daley, and a few entertainers, like singer Michael Bolton and diehard Chicagoan Jim Belushi, would be allowed on the top tier of the platform. Said Belushi when his turn came, "I've voted for Mayor Daley since I was six years old!"

"Yeah! And you'll still be voting for him when you're 130!" shouted a fan who knew his Chicago lore.

Since the county workers, all Democrats, could identify virtually every politico in view, the running commentary in Carol's office was more fun than the show below, which by this time was at least a half hour late getting started.

But it didn't matter to the recorder's office staffers, who were content to entertain one another.

"There's David Orr. I wish he would be our next mayor."

"Look at that sign across the way, 'Hi Slick Willie!' Very funny."

"There's Kgosie. Carol can't be far behind."

"Where?"

"Across Washington Street in that doorway, in the brown overcoat, talking on his little phone. He's always on the phone."

"Here they come! There's Hillary! There's Tipper. Al is so good-looking."

"Too good-looking."

"There's Carol. Look everybody! She's waving at us! Carol! Carol!"

They were all up on the platform now, the Clintons, the Gores, Mayor Daley, and Carol. Gore spoke, the sound of his voice bouncing off the high-rise buildings that surround the plaza. Tipper, clearly not listening (none of that "gazing up at my hero" stuff for these Democratic wives), was busily clicking pictures with her 35-mm camera.

"Look. Carol is whispering to Clinton. Look! They're turning around. She's showing him the offices. *They're waving at us!* Hi, Carol! Hi, Bill!"

Gore had the crowd really warmed up now. "We cannot let down! Two weeks is a long time, and four years is an even longer time. We have got to keep our eyes on the ball and keep our energies focused on the 14 days that are remaining in this campaign!"

Then Carol got to the mic, "Chicago, you are beautiful!" she declared, and the Chicago multitude roared back with pride. Hillary spoke, then Bill. And then Michael Bolton sang a rousing, "When I'm Back on My Feet Again." During the ovation that followed the singer's performance, Bolton shook hands all around. But on that very narrow platform, Carol's access to the singer was blocked by the Clintons and the Gores.

Sue Bass had been predicting every move Carol made. Now she warned us, "Watch Carol. Watch her. She's going to get to Bolton. There she goes! She's pushing Clinton aside. *Look!* She's gonna kiss Michael Bolton!"

But Carol did not kiss Bolton, just spoke into his ear as they held one another's hands. The rock music was pounding, Daley Plaza was swaying, and folks were still encircling the Picasso, like full moon at Stonehenge.

"What's Carol doing with Daley? My God! Carol is dancing with Richie Daley! What a party."

After the speeches, the Clintons and Gores dove into the crowd and began shaking hands, the four of them instinctively staking out separate areas. The Secret Service people, many of whom we had identified from our perch, had their heads on swivels. After 15 minutes or so of this activity, Clinton led the way back to the platform.

"Carol won't be far behind," said Sue. Hillary Clinton and Tipper Gore were standing off to the side as Carol moved between their two husbands. Then the presidential and vice presidential candidates grasped Carol's hands and held them aloft. The flashes popped.

"That's the picture!" said Sue.

Ten minutes later, Carol walked into the office, kicked off her shoes, lit a cigarette, and said to her lingering friends, "Great day. Let's order lunch."

The photographs adorning front pages across Illinois on October 21 were all essentially the same: Carol in the center, Al Gore holding up her left hand, Bill Clinton raising her right—and $3 million in smiles lighting up the scene.

But walking through the campaign offices back at Lake and Wells, one would never guess that Carol Moseley Braun still held, as the *Tribune* would report on October 23, an 18-point lead over her opponent. Carol had survived the Medicaid hit; all should have been right with the world. But in the small space behind the looking glass, nothing seemed right.

Something strange was going on. Some staffers seemed almost sick with anxiety. When I asked Eichenbaum what all the whispering was about, he replied, "I can't tell you. And I hope you never find out." Thus challenged, I began to look for clues. Life on the Braun campaign became curiouser and curiouser.

"Hey, David!" said Steve Cobble, poking his head into the press office. "You seem to be the only one they're still talking to."

For a week or so, an intern named Chris (Letitia had been removed) was in charge of Carol's schedule. Then one day, Chris disappeared, and, with just days to go, Liz Nicholson moved from the quietest seat in the campaign (outside Carol's almost always empty office) to the hottest seat, that of campaign scheduler. Now the desks in front of both the campaign manager's and the candidate's adjoining offices were empty.

Julie Gantz, one of Ira Cohen's "issues kids," revealed that Matthews had called Ira in and told him that he was "not to be trusted" and would no longer have access to the computers. Ira, the resident computer genius, had helped set up the system that was the repository of all campaign information, including donor lists and financial operations. Since Ira was a man of unquestioned integrity, Julie was not only mystified by the Matthews action but also distressed to see her boss hurt by an unwarranted insult.

David Eichenbaum had been walking on eggshells since August when he'd been put on notice by the campaign manager.

MEMORANDUM:

FROM: Kgosie Matthews

TO: David Eichenbaum

DATE: August 19, 1992

SUBJECT: Circumventing Campaign Manager

I am concerned about the continuing tendency you exhibit by acting as a "freelance" member of the staff deriving your authority only from the Candidate particularly as in regards to by-passing me as the Campaign Manager and not consulting with me on critical issues relating to the campaign. There have been several instances where this has happened.

This memorandum serves as notice to you that I do not expect this trend to persist. I assure you that I will no longer ignore deliberate acts of not communicating or providing me full disclosure of sensitive information on time. I hope that I will not have to draw your attention to this matter again.

On another matter, whoever travels with the candidate is expected to be in continuous contact with the office and myself. That includes you.

Eichenbaum had never been clear on the specific offense that led to the memo, but he now suspected that it might have had something to do with the fact that he and Carol were enjoying a cordial relationship "and she seemed to trust me." Though he was concerned throughout August and September that he might be fired, by October, Eichenbaum had decided he would be allowed to complete the job he had signed on to do.

Now, two weeks out from the election, without consulting his press secretary, Matthews added a new person to Eichenbaum's staff. Steve Brown, a Springfield public relations man, was loaned to the campaign by Illinois House speaker Mike Madigan. Brown was a pleasant fellow, and Eichenbaum accepted the addition good-naturedly. "Hey," he said. "Steve can go with Carol, and I can work the phones. Now I don't have to be two places at once."

What senior staff members were soon to find out was that on October 15, an anonymous letter, clearly written by a campaign staff member, had been received at the recorder's office by Sue Bass. Sue, understanding the threat the letter represented to Carol, gave it to the woman whom she believed Carol trusted the most, her old pal from statehouse days, Ethel Alexander. The letter accused Kgosie Matthews of sexual harassment and named four senior staffers who, the writer said, would confirm this information for the candidate.

Had the actions—and attitudes—triggered by this letter happened earlier in the campaign, it would almost surely have meant disaster for Carol's candidacy. As it was, where it mattered most, outside the Chicago headquarters, strategies were in place and the so-called Coordinated Campaign that united Clinton and Braun funds and forces was proving a great success. But at Lake and Wells, where Carol's diverse and dedicated staff had labored long hours together for six long months, it was emotional rock 'n' roll time. Kgosie Matthews, who had, with Carol, so carefully assembled a staff balanced by race and gender, in the end was not fit to nurture the required harmony. In the end, all many people would remember about late October was sound and fury, a dissonance grown out of the very issues of race and gender that the Carol Moseley Braun campaign had been born to overcome.

Yet, because he would not or could not express himself on these matters, it was not until the spring of 1993 that most campaign members finally fully understood the construction Kgosie had put on the events of October 1992, when, for the first time, Matthews spoke about the campaign in an interview with the magazine *Emerge.*

Asked by the interviewer, "What was the most serious attempt to get you out of the campaign?," Matthews cited post-primary suggestions that he be replaced, brought up his conflict with Alton Miller, and then, himself introducing the subject of sexual harassment, said: "But there was never anything as insidious as the issue that developed near the end of the (general) election."

> EMERGE: You're talking about the anonymous sexu-
> al harassment charges by two women whose names

still haven't been published so far as I know. What do
you think was the motive behind those allegations?

MATTHEWS: Two things: jealousy and envy. The
timing was set to force Braun to remove me from the
campaign before any kind of public scandal could
do damage to it. Those people must have wanted to
damage her candidacy to have done something so
insidious and calculated.

I recommended that it be investigated and that
an attorney be brought in to interview the people
who were named in the anonymous letter. That
was done. And we made sure that we would keep
campaigning right up until the last minute until the
election and not let ourselves be distracted by this. It
was a distraction.

Now, during the final days of the campaign—and with the exception of his chief of staff and director of operations, Marlene
Johnson—Matthews kept his contact with staffers to a minimum.
Always capricious when it came to granting his charm—or venting
his anger—Kgosie virtually disappeared. At one point, Marlene
called everyone together, acknowledged the gossip corroding the
headquarters staff, but told the mostly young people they had no
idea what was really going on and they should "put a lid on it."

"It was the right thing to do," Steve Cobble said later. "The
place was out of control."

The sexual harassment charges became the interior focus of
the campaign's tiny world and its inhabitants. But Marlene Johnson had been slightly off the mark when she had cautioned that
nobody really knew anything. A more accurate statement might
have been, "nobody knew everything." Each of the people involved
had a different perspective.

The candidate, still haunted by the family problems implicit in the
Medicaid thing, was now plunged into another personal, emotional conflagration and one with huge political implications should it
get out. The irony that a charge of sexual harassment was what led

to her Senate race in the first place was not lost on Carol Moseley Braun. Had the Williamson campaign planted this letter? Or was her most trusted adviser, her lover, a sexual harasser? Carol did not really know or, more likely, would not allow herself to know.

The campaign manager, apparently deciding to represent himself to Carol as the victim of a conspiracy rigged by his senior staff, set about convincing her that this was the genesis of baseless charges.

As dismayed as they were by Matthews's behavior, of the senior staffers named in the letter—Heather Booth, Ira Cohen, David Eichenbaum, and Steve Cobble—none knew they were suspected of plotting to get rid of him. Astonishingly, considering the pressure, the turmoil, and the numbers of fingers in the dike, nothing leaked. Or, more accurately, nothing was printed or broadcast.

Dreading every phone call, Eichenbaum felt like a shortstop at line drive practice. The press secretary told each reporter who called what he or she already knew: that "in the final week of a major campaign with national implications, you can't go with an anonymous letter that would potentially destroy it." Still, there was always the possibility of the blind column item and the questions it would raise: "Could it be true that Kgosie Matthews, campaign manager/companion of Senate hopeful Carol Moseley Braun sexually harassed several young women on his staff?"

"I was terrified," said David Eichenbaum. "I thought there was about a 50-50 chance it would come out and that it would be a real challenge to keep that from happening. At one point, Channel 7 sent a camera crew over and asked to speak to Letitia. Marlene and I asked Letitia if she wanted to talk to them, and she said no. I sent them away."

The fact was no member of Carol Moseley Braun's campaign staff, regardless of how she or he might have felt about Kgosie Matthews, would corroborate rumors of sexual harassment. And no member of Chicago's journalism community would print—or even hint at—unsubstantiated charges holding such destructive potential. Nor would any of the rumors flying about ever be mentioned by Carol's opponent, Richard Williamson.

On October 20, five days after Carol had received the anonymous letter charging her campaign manager with sexual harassment, Ira Cohen agreed to meet with me privately for the first time. Surprised, because Ira had always been friendly but reticent in my presence, I soon found out that while he did not wish to be interviewed about the campaign, Ira did have a mission: He asked me to consider changing my mind about writing a book. He said it couldn't be done honestly without hurting the larger cause, implying that people would not accept Carol's imperfections. For all his own altruism, Ira is fairly cynical about humanity in general, and he particularly believes in the palpable evil of racial prejudice. Yet, said Ira, despite all the campaign's problems, he still believed Carol would win and that she would be a fine senator. That was what was important. That was all that was important.

After my talk with Ira, I headed north across the Michigan Avenue Bridge, walking briskly in the cold night air, hoping to clear my head. This, I found, was not possible. There was too much: it was too complicated. I wondered if all political campaigns suffered this painful duality. The bottom line was that Kgosie Matthews, whatever he was, didn't matter. Only Carol mattered, and while she was a woman with weaknesses shared by many, she was also a person with a bundle of skills that made her an extraordinary legislator and politician. Yet what Ira had been telling me was that the public would not accept Carol's reality. She was black, she was a woman, she had to be perfect.

Despite the emotional chaos and confusion inside the campaign, like Ira, others plodded on with their work. Field director Heather Booth, with assistance from experienced people like Alice Tregay and Janice Bell, worked the state, coordinating hundreds of volunteers dedicated to getting out the vote a few days hence. Velma Wilson, committed from the very beginning, was still raising money. Darlene Mackey prepared a last round of church appearances for the candidate. Steve Cobble stayed in communication with pollster Celinda Lake as well as with media strategists Jerry (soon-to-be-fired) Austin and David Axelrod, all the while—wearing his hat as finance coordinator—wondering where the hell to get the money to pursue any strategy at all. Desiree Tate, always at the side of the increasingly exhausted and distracted candidate, coordinated the zillions of details that connect the traveling entourage to the campaign.

And David Eichenbaum continued to massage the press.

When the chicken-and-egg fertilization process between campaign press office and the media is in full form, it culminates in something like what transpired on October 22, the day of the second debate between Carol and Richard Williamson, when information that had been planted months earlier bloomed in a timely way, acing the final in Campaign Strategy 101.

The campaign had employed Ace Smith of San Francisco to do its opposition research, and from the beginning, a large bound book of negative material regarding Richard Williamson lay fallow in the files while the Braun campaign pursued a positive strategy. Nevertheless, it was important to get certain information out there in order that it might be exploited when circumstances dictated. Therefore, during her keynote address to the Democratic State Convention in Springfield back on August 20, a speech that centered on a proposal for ethics legislation, Carol dropped in the information that Williamson had lobbied for Swiss company Nestlé in a way that was counter to the interests of the people of Illinois. She was able to do this by quoting from a column written by the *Chicago Sun-Times'* Steve Neal just days before the Springfield meeting.

"We had given the information to a couple of reporters. It was just a question of when they were going to use it, and we were in no rush," said Eichenbaum. "But as it turned out, we were thrilled with the timing when Neal did that column. It was a perfect jump-off to attack him [Williamson] on the foreign agent thing. Carol's speech got some coverage, but who's watching? We're talking August here."

Dropping this negative information about her opponent into a speech that emphasized positive approaches to guaranteeing ethics in government was not as high-profile a hit as, for example, calling a press conference to levy such a charge might have been. But the expectation was that another newspaper would then take up the story and add its own information. This happened, and in October, it allowed the campaign to deliver a second blast, with the added cachet of the *Chicago Tribune*'s authority. David Eichenbaum was also able to find some Ross Perot quotes that dovetailed nicely with the *Tribune*'s material. The following release was then circulated to every media outlet in Illinois. With luck, other news organizations would take up the case, re-fertilizing the process once again.

For Immediate Release Contact: David Eichenbaum
October 22, 1992

WILLIAMSON'S LOBBYING AS A FOREIGN AGENT
GOT TAX BREAKS FOR FOREIGN COUNTRY

Chicago—The *Chicago Tribune*, in a profile of Richard Williamson today, said that the Republican Senate nominee, within six months of leaving the State Department, took a $300 an hour job lobbying for tax breaks in this country for Nestlé, the Swiss food company.

The Tribune states: "... Williamson tried to influence tax regulations affecting international companies. His efforts helped modify a rule that according to Nestlé required firms to keep duplicative financial records, but according to the Internal Revenue Service helped ensure that foreign companies with U.S. subsidiaries would pay taxes."

On October 6, Ross Perot said on CBS that the "core cause of the problem ... is coming to Washington, to cash in, and then go get a several hundred thousand dollar job as a foreign lobbyist, and use your influence on the White House and Congress to shift, not only jobs overseas, whole industries overseas."

Perot continues: "Between 1980 and 1985, 76 former federal officials left office to become registered foreign agents ... This is like a general switching armies in the middle of a war. They should come to serve and go home, and not cash in ... As far as I'm concerned [this is] economic treason."

"Rich Williamson's entire career has been defined by the revolving door, influence peddling ethic that prevailed throughout the 1980's," said Democratic Senate nominee Carol Moseley Braun. Mr. Williamson denies he lobbied for tax breaks for foreign companies, yet the *Tribune* story says he clearly did. It makes you wonder whose side this guy is on."

On October 22, Senate Debate II was staged in Chicago at the ABC affiliate television station, WLS, located at the corner of State and Lake Streets, a short walk east from Braun campaign headquarters.

Once again I watched the debate on pressroom monitors, this time sitting beside Ira Cohen. Standing behind us were the "four tops"—David Axelrod, David Eichenbaum, Bob Borosage, and Jerry Austin—waiting to spin. Actually, Austin said his main function was to walk into the room and piss Carol off. Carol, he said, was one of those women who *really was* beautiful when she was angry.

But Carol didn't need Austin or anybody else on this night. She was ready.

In a change from the previous, more formally structured debate, now there were three audiences posing questions to the candidates, one in the studio where the debate took place and two from remote locations. Deftly managed by the moderator, WLS anchor Mary Ann Childers, Carol and Williamson were able to stake out their starkly different positions on many issues. Carol got in one of her best hits when the crime problem came up. In recent days, Chicago had been reeling from the death of seven-year-old Dantrell Davis, the third child shot at a single elementary school on the North Side and a dramatic example of the street violence besetting the city.

When Williamson criticized Carol for being soft on crime because she favored decriminalization of marijuana possession and opposed the death penalty, Ira gave me a little poke and whispered, "Here it comes!"

Said Carol, turning to Williamson: "On the day that little boy was shot to death, you had a party hosted by the National Rifle Association! We have to have real gun control that will get the guns off the streets that are killing our youngsters, that are victimizing people."

Carol favored the Brady bill, Williamson did not. Carol supported a universal health care system. Williamson felt the present system was pretty much OK. Carol wanted to downsize the defense establishment, shifting funds to infrastructure improvement and education. Williamson thought tuition vouchers would solve the education problem. The debate was neither neat nor sweet, but the people of Illinois were presented with a very clear choice.

However, at every opportunity, Williamson employed one rather peculiar tactic. Once again ignoring his roots in the Reagan and Bush administrations, the Republican repeatedly cited as authority Bill Clinton, Mayor Daley, Ross Perot—even former Democratic mayor of Chicago Jane Byrne! These names came up so often that at one point, the pressroom burst into laughter.

It was the wrong way to amuse.

Following the debate, Carol, who had one of the sharpest funny bones in the business of politics, walked up to the podium and began her press conference by smiling graciously and saying, "I'd like to welcome my opponent to the Democratic Party." The press erupted in an appreciative guffaw. The four tops could relax; Carol would spin for herself.

CHAPTER 14

Hold On: Less Than Two Weeks to Election Day

C AROL SCORED WELL IN THE DEBATE, and outside indica-
tions were that she was holding her own. Poll numbers were
dropping but not precipitously. Inside the campaign, it was a different story entirely.

The anonymous letter had arrived on a Thursday. Sue Bass had
passed it on to Carol's pal and mentor, Ethel Alexander, who had
prayed over it for three days.

*I'm not making this up! She prayed that I would be able to deal with
this letter in a way that was not personally painful to me. And she
knew—as I did when I saw it—that it was a political bombshell.*

*Ethel lived just a couple of blocks from me, and so on Monday
morning, she called and said she'd like to pick me up and drive me
downtown. I said fine; but Kgosie was there, so she didn't say anything, and we all rode downtown together. On Tuesday, Ethel called
again, and she went through this whole cloak-and-dagger thing. She
said, "I've really got to talk to you. Can we meet somewhere and not
in your office?" So we agreed to meet at Marshall Field's. It was ten
o'clock on a Tuesday morning when she showed me the letter. Ethel
was very distressed, and so was I when I read it; but I was also furious at Sue and Ethel for the way they'd handled it.*

249

I called an attorney friend, Joyce Moran, that same day, Tuesday, the 20th. I just knew this was something out of the Williamson campaign, a setup, an October surprise. I wanted more than anything else not to be accused of covering up anything. I wanted to act as an executive getting to the bottom of a messy story. I did not consult Kgosie; nobody advised me. In fact, Kgosie was not very happy with my decision to initiate an impartial investigation. He was angry about the whole thing, but I thought it was the right thing to do.[27]

Joyce Moran is a solid and methodical lawyer, as steady as they come. But she didn't feel qualified to handle what was essentially a question of labor law, and so she called in labor specialists from the firm of Vedder Price. There were four lawyers who interviewed the four senior staff members. And to this day, I don't know who the lawyers were who actually conducted the interviews and did the analysis.

But before they went over, I called in Heather, David, Ira, and Steve, and I said to them, "Look, I want you to talk to these people, the lawyers, and I want you to be honest and candid with them because," I said, "quite frankly, if a person that I'm involved with would disrespect me so much that he would fool around in my office, I want to know that."

Steve Cobble, David Eichenbaum, Heather Booth, and Ira Cohen all agree that Carol *did not* call them in before they met with the lawyers but rather sent them each a note, which they were asked to read and return. The note said essentially what Carol thought she had told them in person: that the four staffers should disclose to the Vedder Price representatives everything they knew about charges of sexual harassment against Kgosie Matthews.

Staffers guessed that the conversation Carol remembered where she told her people she genuinely wanted to get to the truth about Kgosie's actions took place after the lawyers' interviews, which happened on October 21, had been completed. That would have been Sunday, October 25, the day when the simmering tensions between Carol and Kgosie and certain other members of the staff, broke into the open. October 25 came to be known as "Foley Day."

---

27   Matthews later claimed that he had instituted the investigation.

Don Foley was the political director of the Democratic Senatorial Campaign Committee (DSCC), based in Washington, DC. On Sunday, October 25, Foley arrived at Braun headquarters for a scheduled meeting with Kgosie Matthews, but since Matthews had not yet arrived, Eichenbaum greeted Foley, and the two men went to find Steve Cobble. Cobble was very happy to see Don Foley because Foley had access to real money and Cobble wanted some of it—$100,000, to be specific. The fact was the Braun campaign was broke.

In his original media plan, Jerry Austin had recommended "buying time from Election Day backwards." Estimating that "a statewide buy for a general election in Illinois would cost between $400,000 and 500,000 per week," Austin explained that all candidates would be competing for airtime and that while commercial space couldn't be reserved, "We own it when we pay for it." He suggested that by shortly after Labor Day, the campaign should have purchased "the last week to 10 days before November 3."

But while campaign coffers were bulging in late August and early September, so were Carol's numbers, and the decision was made to limit the advance buy to $130,000.

"I'd called a bunch of people at the Democratic National Committee—Ron Brown, who was an old friend from the Jackson campaign, Bill Morton, Steve Rosenthal, Harold Ickes," said Cobble, "and when I told Ickes we were broke, he said, 'You people have raised $6 million. How can you sit there and tell me you need money?' I said 'Harold, you know me. I'm telling you the truth; we have spent it all.'"

Each senatorial candidate has access to funds under what is known as 441(a.d.) authority. The "tally," as it is called, is proportionate to the population of each state. Carol's share under this formula was some $930,000, of which only $400,000 to $500,000 had been paid out. During a presidential year, these funds are generally administered and distributed by the national Democratic (or Republican) Senatorial Campaign Committee.

Carol had been one of the more successful fundraisers for the national party, but because the DSCC felt she was a sure winner in Illinois, she had not received her full tally, and on Sunday, October 25, Cobble was after another portion of that money.

Don Foley told Eichenbaum that since he had to wait for Kgosie, one thing he'd like to do was get to know Heather Booth. He'd never met the woman who was a legend in political organizing, and Eichenbaum was happy to make the introduction. Celinda Lake was also in from Washington and shared the latest poll numbers, about which she was very concerned. Celinda thought Carol had become vulnerable.

Since Matthews was still among the missing, the group moved into Carol's spacious office, where most meetings with dignitaries were held. When everyone was settled, Cobble decided to hit Foley with his best shot.

"I told Foley that if Carol lost, there would be all kinds of fall-out, and a lot of it would be racial. People who had nothing to do with the campaign would stand up and say, 'Lynn Yeakel got more money even though Carol Moseley Braun raised more for the Democratic National Committee and the DSCC, and Carol lost because you sold her out!' 'Now,' I said, 'you can stand up and say we ran a lousy campaign and we're a bunch of idiots, but it isn't going to help you any. Because as far as you're concerned, you're a white guy, and she's going to lose by a point, and you were asked to turn over $100,000—but you decided to send it to Pennsylvania or New York or someplace else!'"

"I said," Cobble continued, "'from your point of view, Don, and from Ron Brown's, this should be your number one race. And even if you think we're 15 points ahead, you'd better cover yourself. That's my political judgment; that's my cover-your-ass judgment. And it's not based upon how you can end up with the most seats in the US Senate next year; it's based upon how you can defend yourself if you lose the one race you should have won!'"

Asked later if his pitch to Foley had been appropriate, Cobble said that whether it was appropriate or not was moot. Kgosie Matthews, apparently less concerned, only asked for (and received) $25,000 from the DSCC during the last days of the campaign.

"Carol and Kgosie walked in," said Eichenbaum, "and Kgosie took one look, nodded to Don Foley, and stormed into his office through the adjoining door. Carol sat down at her desk and glared. I got up and left, but as I got to my office, my buzzer was ringing; Carol wanted me back."

In the meantime, Kgosie had invited Foley into his office.

"Basically, Carol wanted to know, 'What is going on here?'" said Cobble, who kept notes on the conversation that ensued. "Why were we having this meeting with an official of the Democratic Senatorial Campaign Committee without her knowledge or approval? David explained how it all came about, but it was obvious that Carol wasn't buying his explanation."

Cobble said, "Finally, I just felt we had to be clear on all of this. 'I think this discussion is about trust,' I said, 'and Carol, it is clear that you do not trust us. In no campaign in America would it be considered strange for the political director of the Democratic Senatorial Campaign Committee to meet with the political director of a Democratic senatorial campaign. With 10 days to go in this election, it is perfectly reasonable for me to be meeting with Don Foley.'

"'Well,' she said, 'I didn't say it wasn't reasonable.'

"'Yes, you did, Carol. You're sitting here asking us why we were meeting with him as if we were doing something unfaithful, disloyal.' And then I said, 'For God's sake, Carol, at least give us some credit. If we were planning a coup, don't you think we'd be smart enough not to do it in your office?'

"I think Heather blanched at the word 'coup.'"

Cobble was angry and sarcastic, reflecting the raw nerves being exposed by the campaign's double life. But he had no idea that Matthews had led Carol to believe that there were no other women in his life and that the people sitting before her on this Sunday afternoon in late October were coconspirators in a plot to get rid of him. Yet in succeeding remarks, Carol revealed the true basis of her personal anguish—and Cobble didn't let her off the hook.

"She said," continued Cobble, "'It's just that so much is going on right now, the lawyers' investigation, the rumors flying around about Kgosie, and I just want to know what's going on.'

"'Are they just rumors?'

"'Well,' she said, 'I've talked to two of the young women myself, and they both assured me that there was nothing to this stuff.'"

Cobble knew about one of the conversations Carol referred to because the young woman in question had come to him to say that she'd been put on the spot and lied because she didn't want to hurt Carol.

Cobble continued, "So I said—I'll admit, in a real disgusted tone—'Carol, you can't ask a young woman, off the cuff, in your office, without any warning if anything's wrong and expect her to give you a full description of her problems with your boyfriend. You're not going to get an accurate reflection of the truth.'

"David looked at me—I was in the middle—Heather looked at me, and across her desk, Carol just took this deep drag on her cigarette and didn't say anything. I remember thinking: This is like a movie. But I believe that's when she clicked me into 'reject.'"

However, the conversation didn't end with Cobble's challenging remark. In fact, it went on for some 45 minutes, and for the very first time, Carol openly admitted her involvement with Kgosie to this particular group of people.

Cobble continued, "When I said she couldn't expect a young woman to give her an honest answer in these circumstances, Carol said, 'Well, I know that. And that's why I asked the lawyers to come in.' Then she said, 'Don't you think I want to get to the bottom of this considering my relationship with him? Don't you think I want to know the truth?'

"And that's when I said, 'I don't know, Carol. I guess we'll see.'"

Cobble recalled, "The conversation was steering dangerously close to an explosion, and Heather could feel it. She interrupted me and tried to turn us into a more productive direction. But I just said, 'I'm not sure I want to give this up. The bottom line is Carol came in here, and I think she's saying she feels that she can't trust us anymore, and that's why this conversation has been about trust. And I'm not trying to get you guys fired, but maybe she should just send me home.'

"Carol said, 'It's not that we don't trust you. It's that Kgosie feels like you let him down, that you haven't been supportive of him in recent weeks.' And I said, 'Well, on his terms, I probably haven't.'

"It was interesting the way she said it. She knew we were doing our jobs; she trusted us to do our jobs. The craziness was: here was a campaign where loyalty to the candidate meant standing up for her boyfriend even if it cost her the election!"

What Cobble didn't tell Carol was that DNC chairman Ron Brown had been in touch to say he was going to call Carol and tell her she should replace Kgosie.

Cobble said, "I told him it couldn't be done. Because of Carol, I'd done everything I could to promote Kgosie's interests: win— and keep him in a position to take credit for it. Some coup!"

The four senior staff members named in the anonymous letter had done as they had been asked: appeared before a panel of lawyers and answered the questions put to them. But apparently, Matthews, at least, had not expected them to fully respond to Carol's request. Even though they had nothing to do with the accusations of sexual harassment, had in fact—knowing that it would be the candidate who suffered, not the campaign manager—tried to quell the gossip, speaking frankly to the lawyers was now characterized as an act of disloyalty.

"At one point, where Carol said she'd brought in the lawyers because she wanted to get at the truth," Cobble continued, "she said that she couldn't believe that with all this gossip, the sexual harassment thing hadn't been brought up before. I said, 'Have you asked Kgosie if this has been brought up before?' Because, of course, I, myself, had discussed sexual harassment issues with him way back in early September."

Cobble recalled, "It was soon after Kgosie fired Jeremy Karpatkin. He'd called me into his office on another matter, and we just got to talking, and I said, to him that nobody really understood why he'd fired Jeremy, although we'd been told Jeremy was a 'leak.' But Jeremy aside, I said, 'You're 20 points and $2 million ahead with 60 days to go, why not just let it ride? Ignore the papers, ignore the gossip, keep Carol focused, keep raising money, don't fire anybody else—just do your stuff and in the end you can say, "I elected the first African American woman to the United States Senate." They can call you any name they want and you can say, "Yeah, but I won." Because in America, once you win, nobody cares about that other stuff.'

"Well, that was the gist of it, but it was a long conversation, almost an hour. I thought Kgosie ought to know about the tensions around the office. I mean, this was not a happy campaign. I said, 'There are black and white tensions back there and male and female tensions.'

"He said, 'What do you mean, male-female tensions?' I was surprised that he didn't seem to know what I was talking about. I now think that in some fundamental way, Kgosie didn't understand what sexual harassment was and that after he became a figure of authority, he continued a pattern of behavior that was normal for him but inappropriate. Women were prey. You know, if a guy in a bar comes on to a woman, she can ignore him. With your boss, it's another matter. Now maybe I'm being too generous, but there was an element of that, I think.

"He wanted to know, 'Who?' I said there'd been complaints from four or five women. I mentioned Jan Hensley because she was already gone. And Roxanne. 'Everybody notices when you go away for parts of the day.' He grinned and said, 'Poor Roxanne.'

"Then he complained about Carol, about putting up with her moods. I had a clear sense that he felt trapped by this whole arrangement, almost like it was a business deal.

"I said, 'Just let it go for 60 days. You're on the verge of vindication. If people make you mad, that's petty stuff. Winning this election is big stuff.'

"I know the sexual harassment part of our conversation got to Kgosie because he called Jerry Austin right away. I think Kgosie felt comfortable airing it out with Jerry. Jerry told me later that Kgosie wanted to know if he could get in trouble over this sexual harassment thing."

Cobble concluded, "I felt pretty good about that September conversation. It was serious, a little tense, but not hostile. And I left Kgosie's office thinking the campaign was in good shape—and we were winning big—at least until Medicaid."[28]

At Braun headquarters, the sun had yet to set on Foley Day. Before October 25 ended, a player who had been sitting in for a hand now

---

28   My favorite Steve Cobble-ism? "Sometimes I wish I was a regular political hack, just, you know, what is the expedient thing to do? Life would be so much easier without principles and ethics."

and then was invited to pull a chair up to the table for the remainder of the campaign. With eight days to go, David Axelrod was invited to replace Jerry Austin.

Axelrod had been called in by Carol and Kgosie that Sunday and met briefly with Don Foley and Celinda Lake. "Celinda's numbers were sobering," Axelrod said. "It was 10 days before the election, and it seemed to me that Carol was on a pretty steady decline. The favorable-unfavorables were shifting unfavorably.

"We talked this through, then Kgosie and Carol left the meeting," continued Axelrod. "Shortly after that, I was told I had a call and was taken into [campaign treasurer and close Matthews confident] Earl Hopewell's office, where Carol and Kgosie were on the speaker phone from the car. And Kgosie said, 'We want you to take over the media the rest of the way.'

"And I said 'OK....'

"'And we want you to do the buy.'[29]

"And I said, 'I think Jerry's already placed a lot of the buy. Maybe we can work out our own deal.'

"'No,' they said. 'We don't want that. That's not what we want.'

"Jerry had already made a television buy, but there were no television spots to run," said Axelrod. "Apparently, Jerry had done one but they didn't like it. So they had no spot. So in the next 18 hours, I produced three."

With his caustic sense of humor and deep pockets, Jerry Austin had been well liked by staffers who got to know him, but Axelrod was popular, too. Both men were creative and competitive; the rumpled Axelrod was just a gentler, zanier version of his predecessor. Meeting a group of his colleagues in the hallway during this final, frenzied period, Axelrod opined that the staff deserved a Purple Heart, then came up with the perfect metaphor for the Braun campaign.

"Have you ever seen the movie *Airplane!*?" Axelrod asked, sticking his arms out to imitate the aircraft. "I mean, that's this campaign [*the media consultant's arms started to wobble.*] He

---

29 The "buy" refers to placing a print or television ad. Media consultants generally get a 15 percent fee on each buy.

continued, "At this point, nobody's worried about how soft a landing to make; everyone's just trying to get this baby on the ground.

"You got one engine on fire [*sputtering sounds*], one wing's
fallen off [*left arm down*], the pilot and the copilot are fighting up
in the cockpit, all the passengers have food poisoning, the wind is
bouncing the plane from side to side [*bounce, bounce*], there's rain
coming down, and snow and sleet, the storms are horrible, no one's
in charge, the control tower is yelling instructions over the radio but
no one's listening, the landing gear won't go down, the runway lights
are out, people are screaming and crying in the back, the plane is in
total chaos—and a few of the passengers are taking turns trying to
fly the damn thing, just trying to bring it in without crashing!

"It's *Airplane!*" Axelrod concluded. "The campaign movie! All
that's missing is Leslie Nielsen!"

Tears were rolling down faces in the hallway audience. Already
on the verge of breakdown, for Braun campaign staffers crying
came as easily as laughing. Who needed Nielsen when you had
Axelrod on board, now charged with helping to maintain sufficient
altitude for the next eight days?

On October 26, Steve Cobble noted in his diary: "Jerry Austin
cut off."

Daily now, media outlets were covering the issues that divided Braun
and Williamson—and the divide could hardly have been wider. By
November 1, virtually every major newspaper in Illinois and the *St.
Louis Post-Dispatch* had endorsed Carol Moseley Braun—with one
interesting exception. The conservative *Chicago Tribune*, while giving George Bush the nod for president, declined to endorse either
candidate for the US Senate. Although not necessarily a plus for
Carol, this was a huge slap in the face to Richard Williamson, who,
the *Trib* said, had indulged in a racially divisive campaign.

But perhaps the real bellwether came from the even more conservative Kankakee *Daily Journal*. Calling Carol a "beacon of hope
to minorities," the *Daily Journal* forgave her for Medicaid, saying,
"Even mistakes serve a purpose if a person learns from them. Each
person also has potential, the possibility to grow, to serve some
larger purpose."

On Friday, October 30, following a bargaining session during which many of Edna Moseley's expenses against her $28,750 inheritance were disallowed, Carol turned over a check to the Illinois Department of Public Aid. Carol's siblings did not contribute to the payment. "The client has voluntarily paid the department $15,239.92," said spokesman Dean Schott. "Receipt of that payment concludes the administrative review by this department." "Case closed," said all parties save Richard Williamson, who had three more days to hammer Carol on the Medicaid thing.

On November 2, Steve Cobble ran some figures based on Celinda Lake's latest polling. After setting out various options, Cobble chose the one that had Richard Williamson getting 90 percent of the undecideds and Carol winning by 0.87 percent, or about 40,000 votes. Cobble was about to get a pleasant surprise.

The weather was awful on Election Day, and I was shivering as I waited in line to vote. Radio stations reported that despite rain and 40-degree temperatures, turnout appeared to be good. After voting, I stopped at campaign headquarters to take the indoor temperature and was surprised at the lack of anticipatory excitement.

I spotted the campaign manager in the corridor and said, "So, Mr. Matthews, how are you spending Election Day?" Inviting me into his office he replied, "Keeping in touch with the world!" He seemed elated. As I entered, he was unwrapping a brown box that he said had just been delivered. As the layers of wrapping came off, Kgosie revealed two lovely soft cloths from which he withdrew a pair of elegant Ferragamo shoes. "Nice," I said. "Thank you," he said. I then asked him if I could "spend some time with Carol today." "No," he said. That was more like it.

As she left her home early on November 3 to vote, then join her close friends for her traditional Election Day breakfast at Lou Mitchell's, Carol laughed and threw a little punch at a needlepoint pillow a fan had sent her. The pillow's inscription read: "A Woman's Place is In the House ... and In the Senate."

So I breakfasted with my small group of friends, then I went to the beauty parlor and, really, just lolled around, had everything done, even a pedicure. Des [Tate] was with me, and as we were driving home with Gus [Fordham] in the afternoon, she wanted to turn the car radio on, but I wouldn't let her, (I know. I'm as superstitious as any athlete before a big game.) But then Kgosie called. And in this tight, tight voice, very formal, he said: "It appears you have won this election." It was funny. He's so formal, so British sometimes—and African and American, a strange amalgam. "It appears you have won this election," in this droll, dry voice. And I knew he must have been as crazed as I was.

Election night on the Braun campaign reminded me of some weddings: countless hours to put the thing together, huge emotional buildup, but when the great day arrives, there are these little hurts everybody is feeling, and the climax is a letdown.

So it was with November 3.

Carol's longtime assistant at the recorder's office Sue Bass was hurt because she had offered to orchestrate the celebration "and make it the most wonderful party anybody had ever seen," and nobody had wanted her help.

Major contributors Christie Hefner and Lucy Lehman were bewildered because there was no VIP suite where they could express their support and excitement to the candidate.

Joey Moseley was angry because Marlene Johnson, on Matthews's instructions, had hired a virtual security army from a private firm, and Joey's loyal troop of off-duty Chicago cops, who had protected Carol from Carbondale to Crystal Lake (not to mention from totally impossible candidate to US senator), were being pushed around by a bunch of uniformed guys with guns that nobody knew.[30]

Broadcasting live all evening, hungry for video and with reporters vamping, the local TV guys were pissed because nobody would tell them when or through which door the candidate would arrive.

---

30   Officer Anita Ashton later told me that the private security firm had been hired because Kgosie had heard that Joey and his men wanted to beat the shit out of him. "And it's true!" Anita added. "They—well, *we*—fantasized about it all the time!"

Darlene Mackey was frustrated because she'd been assigned to take care of Edna Moseley, who was unhappy because she had no opportunity to be with her daughter before the triumphant moment when Carol would take the stage. Edna and other family members were isolated in a suite on the 23rd floor at the opposite end of the hallway where Edna thought Kgosie and Carol would be celebrating.

Comptroller Dawn Clark Netsch, Attorney General Roland Burris, and Illinois Democratic Party chairman Gary LaPaille had been asked to be present. They approached the stage to await Carol's entrance and were pushed back by Marlene's husky boys from DB Security. "Attorney general ejected by a private army!" Burris laughed. LaPaille wasn't amused. "I'm outta here," he said, and left.

But some weddings are like that.

The polls closed at 7 p.m. At 6:55, Chicago's NBC affiliate, WMAQ, declared Carol the winner.

At 7:05 p.m., Bryant Gumbel, anchoring the NBC network coverage, announced that Carol Moseley Braun of Illinois would be the first African American woman to serve in the US Senate.

At 7:08 p.m., Dan Rather expanded on CBS's declaration of victory for Carol by adding that exit polls indicated that she had won with an estimated 59 percent of the women's vote and 52 percent of suburbanites' votes.

At 7:10 p.m., Larry Shapiro, watching television in suite 2102, literally jumped for joy as he shouted, "Who will be the first woman president of the United States?"

At 8:40 p.m., Carol arrived at the McCormick Center Hotel and was whisked straight up to suite 2300.

A dozen TV cameras were lined up on a platform across from the stage in the grand ballroom, and reporters with Minicams roamed looking for people to interview. This was a big story, but where were the principals? The word was that Carol was already in the hotel and would be down at 9 p.m. CNN was prepared to go live worldwide with the first African American woman elected to serve in the US Senate. But where was she?

Press chief David Eichenbaum had not been told when Carol would arrive or what suite the campaign was holding for her, and the hotel had been instructed to keep her suite number confidential. But finally, at about 9:30, Eichenbaum coerced the information from Marlene Johnson and was able to reach Kgosie Matthews. "Kgosie," he said, "George Bush is scheduled to go on live at 10 p.m. Carol has got to get down here in time to do her speech before Bush concedes or she won't get on live TV."

"Fine," said Matthews. "Don't call up here again."

As Carol entered the ballroom to deliver her acceptance speech, it was as if some hidden stage manager whispered into his headset: "OK, the senator-elect has reached the microphone, cue the president," because just as Carol started speaking, the face of George H. W. Bush appeared on television monitors scattered about the room, and people were immediately drawn to watch. However thrilled these Democrats might be about Carol's victory, George Bush's concession signaling a Clinton presidency was just as delicious.

Dressed all in white, with 15-year-old Matthew Braun her only companion, Carol came on stage. As I recorded much later that night, "It was a great picture for America, one millions of women, millions of African Americans, could rejoice in: single mother, handsome son, obvious love between them. Change. But it was for our eyes and hearts only."

> Thank you. Thank you so much. Praise the Lord! It's a new day in America! ... I just heard from Mr. Williamson, who conceded this race. And you, you, you have made history ... you are showing the way for our entire country to the future. ... We put together a campaign; one that they said couldn't be done. Well, we did it. ... I want to start off by thanking my family for all that they've gone through, and they stood by. To my family and to the wonderful staff that made this happen. Raise your hand! ... And to the campaign manager, who is my knight in shining armor, Kgosie Matthews. ... In closing, I would like to quote from another Illinoisan, our great 16th

president, Abraham Lincoln: "Let us have faith that right makes might and that in faith, let us, to the end, dare to do our duty as we understand it." I'm going to work hard to be the best senator Illinois ever had. Thank you.

A month later, in a December 6 *Chicago Tribune Magazine* feature titled, "Welcome to the Club: Carol Moseley Braun's Campaign for the Senate Was Her Own Excellent Adventure," Frank James, who had been the *Trib*'s beat reporter for most of the campaign, raised the question that dominated election night:

> Here was the first African-American woman and first black Democrat elected to the U.S. Senate, a body that for its 203-year history has managed to remain, like corporate boards and polka bands, a white male bastion.
>
> Unfortunately for local and national TV audiences, they didn't get to see her speech live, though some networks had hoped to carry it. As Braun started to talk shortly past 10 p.m. to a room packed with adoring supporters, the TV monitors in the room filled with the head of President Bush conceding the election.
>
> In a quintessential campaign blunder, the senator-elect had gone on almost exactly when the president did, ruining a unique opportunity for coast-to-coast coverage. It caused much consternation among reporters and supporters alike. Was this Braun arrogance? Or was it another example of the Braun campaign as, despite all its remarkable success, the gang that couldn't shoot straight?

And then James brought up the second mystifying scene of the evening.

> [Braun's] speech's untraditional election-night staging also raised eyebrows. Unlike every other candidate that evening, Braun didn't appear on stage with her family and political buddies. Instead, there was

the odd, somewhat existential sight of Braun standing before the camera lights with only her 15-year-
old son, Matthew, a student at a Chicago Catholic
high school.

*Of course I should have come on before Bush gave his concession
speech—or after he finished. I was not aware of the timing. I was not
watching television. I was just nervously waiting for Williamson to
call me. And he called sometime between 9:30 and 10. Then we had
to find Matt, who was running from party to party with his friends.*

*Having just Matt and me on the stage was Kgosie's decision,
and he was criticized for it, but in the final analysis, I think it was
best. People draw conclusions and inferences from a picture, from
who is up there and who is not. So, based on these considerations,
Kgosie made the decision that only the candidate and her son would
be on the stage.*

*And everybody from my mother to the attorney general of the
state of Illinois was pissed off.*

Carol was the first among many for whom the evening of November 3, 1992, was a surreal, conflicted experience.

One Braun close friend and loyalist who'd been on board since
the campaign was just a motley band of poor but happy strivers on
a mission to democratize the US Senate felt a wrenching sense of
isolation as she watched Carol deliver her speech.

"If it had been me, having accomplished this incredible thing, I
would have wanted everyone who had even lifted a pencil up there
around me. I would have wanted the closeness, the warmth, the
cocooning that this kind of thing generates.

"I was way in the back of the room. And as I looked around,
there were a lot of people who were truly intimate with the campaign way, way in the back. Such a contrast to primary night when
we all felt joined at the hip, basking in warmth.

"It was an eerie scene, Carol in white, with just Matt beside her,
such a sense of isolation. There was just this transparent wall. And
those who truly loved Carol, who were so happy and relieved, who

knew how tough it had been—it was like a big hand had pushed us back.

"She thanked God. 'Yeah!' we all cheered. She thanked her family. 'Yeah!' And then she thanked her 'knight in shining armor'— and there was nothing. That silence—that said it all."

Without exception, the campaign insiders were exhausted—and some were hurt. Following the election the *Chicago Sun-Times* ran a picture of US senator-elect Carol Moseley Braun in full color, arms outstretched, embracing the world, while the headline read, "Floating on Air."

Carol's victory astonished some political veterans and undoubtedly struck fear in the hearts of others, but above all, it sent a message of hope across the land. If Illinois was, indeed, a political microcosm of America, the word was that democracy had reached a new level of maturity. Carol put it best herself when she said, "We are writing a new chapter in our politics. This shows we can come together as Americans without regard to the things that have divided us in the past."

The final margin of Carol's victory was 10 points. Exit polls indicated that Carol, as expected, won 95 percent of the African American vote, but she also took 58 percent of the women's vote, 58 percent of the independent vote, and 18 percent of the Republican vote. Said the *Chicago Tribune*:

> An example of how Braun's candidacy transcended the racial politics of past elections is found in the returns from white ethnic Chicago wards, where Mayor Washington, even at the height of his popularity, was never able to secure more than a fifth of the vote.
>
> Yet in Mayor Richard Daley's 11th ward on the Southwest Side, for example, Braun received nearly 63 percent of the vote.

Grayson Mitchell, a former aide to Harold Washington and a consultant to the Braun campaign, nailed a significant factor when he told the *Trib* that Braun was a member "of a 'new generation' of black politicians, compared with the preceding generation whose emphasis on civil rights issues limited their appeal largely to their black base." Translation: Braun was less threatening.

On the South Side, young Barack Obama was a studied observer of the electoral profile of Carol Moseley Braun.

The sturdy partnership of the Clinton and Braun campaigns had also paid off for both candidates: Bill Clinton won Illinois by 49 percent to George Bush's 34 percent and Ross Perot's 18.9 percent.[31] Thus, Illinois retained its "paradigm" title, once again predicting the presidential winner.

The secondary story of the election, but perhaps most important in the long run, was that across America, women and minorities made historic gains. The Senate tripled its female representation from two to six with Barbara Boxer and Dianne Feinstein winning in California and Patty Murray in Washington, and the House almost doubled its contingent of women, going from 28 to 48. Before the 1992 elections, there were 28 African Americans in the House of Representatives; after, there were 40.

Regarding the women victors, Carol's pollster, Celinda Lake, offered an op-ed analysis in the *New York Times* a few days after the election. "Female candidates," Lake wrote, "were seen as populist outsiders who could make government work for ordinary people—a powerful profile in today's political environment."

Lake's polling also indicated that women had a significant advantage when it came to character issues. Speaking of aggressive campaigns around such issues against both Boxer in California and Braun in Illinois, Lake said:

> While these charges took longer to stick to female candidates, the women fell more sharply in the polls when voters began to question whether these candidates were not living up to the higher standards they had assumed. In the end, voters were harsher

---

31 Perot dropped out of the presidential race during the Democratic National Convention on July 16 but re-entered on October 1. Spending more than $12 million of his own money, he ended his campaign with 18.9% of the national vote.

in their judgments of women than of men who fell
off the pedestal.

Beware the Pedestal should be a warning posted in all political
campaigns. The pedestal may appear, but do not climb up on it.
Nor should one let oneself be boosted, for a pedestal is a flimsy
thing, thin and vulnerable to the smallest blows. Carol Moseley
Braun had spent most of her candidacy secure above the crowd,
perched on what felt like solid marble. That slender structure tee-
tered in October but held through the November election.

In December, Carol Moseley Braun's pedestal would shatter,
sending the newly elected senator tumbling.

PART IV

What a scene that must have been inside the campaign.

—TOM HARDY
Chicago Tribune, December 20, 1992

CHAPTER 15

Lawyers Called in on Sexual Harassment

I T WAS DECEMBER by the time it all hit the fan, but the seed of what grew into a political crisis was planted in October by two women whom Carol, had she known them, would have embraced as "true believers."

Far out on the west end, jammed into the northernmost corner of the chaotic slab of planet Earth that for a blink in time was Carol Moseley Braun's campaign headquarters, sat the issues office. Teetering stacks of files, reference books, and papers occupied every available space, and under Ira Cohen's supervision, the "issues kids" had to wait turns for computer time.

Except for Dayna Bender, who began to accompany Carol on the road in September, the issues staff had little personal contact with the candidate. Yet, with the exception of the schedulers, more than any other campaign workers, the issues kids' efforts interfaced with Carol daily. Every campaign appearance had its briefing paper, and every briefing paper represented not only a body of research but also some young person's vision of the candidate standing before a group—be it a labor union, a student organization, or an intimate gathering of CEOs—as well as that person's careful anticipation of questions that might be asked of the candidate and the preparation for the responses that would certainly be required.

My first contact with the issues office came prior to one such appearance when a young woman approached, introduced herself, and said she'd heard I was accompanying the candidate to a town meeting that evening. Would I read the briefing paper she'd written and report back to her about what Carol used and what she ignored? "I just want do to a better job of serving her needs," she said.

I asked why she didn't go along and see for herself. "I don't have time," the young woman answered. "Too busy writing the next one." The issues kids, like countless others in the campaign, put in long, long hours, ate gawdawful food, breathed stale air—and thrived.

If Kgosie Matthews knew these folks existed, it was only as an irritation. Their work, usually represented to him through senior staffers Cohen and Karpatkin (and later, Shapiro), was not (as noted) particularly necessary to Carol's victory. The campaign manager spent very little time in the west end of campaign headquarters.

Because of its youth and mission—not to mention its leader, Ira Cohen—the issues office represented the idealistic heart of the campaign. Among these were two ardent young feminists, who, energized by Professor Anita Hill and seeing Carol's star rise over Illinois, had come to Chicago to change the face of American politics.

In Carol Moseley Braun the two women, Elizabeth Loeb and Julie Gantz, saw spotless feminist credentials and a woman who, although African American herself, had spoken out early and courageously against the confirmation of Judge Clarence Thomas. They idolized Carol Moseley Braun and everything they felt she stood for.

But they didn't know her. And by the time Letitia Dewith-Anderson's story of Kgosie Matthews's sexual harassment reached them, confirming previous allegations by other young women, Julie and Liz felt compelled to do something about it. If Carol knew, they thought, she would dispose of this cancer that was eating at the very foundation upon which the campaign was built.

"Our number one goal was to get him out of there," one of the women later said. "We were all idealists about Carol. We believed that once she was informed of this, she would dump him." There were victims here, included among them Carol Moseley Braun, and Loeb and Gantz were advocates—and writers.

And so, the soon-to-be-infamous "anonymous letter" was crafted.

October 14, 1992

Dear Carol:

We represent several of your staff, from different departments, different ages and different backgrounds. We are writing this letter because we are disillusioned and upset about what has been going on in the campaign office. As you well know, up to now there have been many problems involving Kgosie. However, as you may or may not know (and we will give you the benefit of the doubt) some of those problems have involved sexual harassment.

We know you will be shocked to see this in writing; we hope that you will be shocked to hear this at all. But we also know that in your heart, even in light of your own personal relationship with him, you will believe us. Kgosie has had sexual relations with several staff members. That in itself is inappropriate, if not bordering on harassment. However, he has propositioned others and has fired or demoted women who would not comply with his sexual demands. We are not talking about humorous flirtation; there have been incidents that are as outrageous as those revealed in the Anita Hill hearings. We know that you are at least generally aware of Wednesday's incident and that you were not interested in knowing the details. We hope this is because you were busy, under stress and unaware of what was really going on. We implore you to ask now.

We cannot stand by silently and allow this to go on. If there is anything the Anita Hill hearings have taught us it is that women must take action to protect themselves. We are women and individuals who joined your campaign out of anger with the Anita Hill hearings and with the hope that if you had been with those white men on the Judiciary Committee things would have gone differently. We simply could not live with ourselves if we now did nothing.

Members of your senior staff are aware of these incidents; just ask them if you are in doubt. However, there is a feeling among your staff that you should not be told about them because of the pressure and strain the election is already putting on you. We have faith that this is not what you would want and that you want to know about things like this occurring on your campaign. We also think that at some point the coddling of a candidate must stop. This is that point. All we ask is that you immediately investigate the allegations in this letter, talk to your senior staff—Heather, Ira, Steve, David—and ask them to be honest with you. We think that they will be.

We realize that at this point in the campaign you cannot publically fire Kgosie. However, you can demand that he absent himself from the office, develop a flu lasting about three weeks or otherwise concoct a way to de facto remove him from operations. He is the master of lies and covers, he can surely think of something.

It is an ultimate irony that this campaign is now tainted by the very egregious behavior that was the fuel to its fire—sexual harassment. We are deeply disillusioned. But before we could condemn you as a hypocrite we must be sure that you are aware of what is going on. We deeply believe in you and that you will do something to stop this and will immediately send a message some way to your staff that you are dealing with it. We have no intention of going public with this; we still feel that the cause you represent is so important as to force us to keep our mouths shut until November 3. But you can be assured that after the election if nothing is done we will not remain silent.

One further note as to why we are anonymously sending you this letter rather than speaking up and identifying ourselves. The explanation is very simple; we are frightened of Kgosie, of the lies he generates to ruin people's reputations, and also, if this should come out, of becoming targets for the press. We also feel that our names would not add much as you don't know us.

We hope that you will take this letter as seriously as you have represented you take sexual harassment and abusive behavior. We still have trust in you and believe in you. Please do not let us down.

On October 20, 1992, ensconced in her office high in the Sears Tower, attorney Joyce Moran was enjoying a fairly ordinary Tuesday as she pursued her duties as senior corporate counsel for the Chicago-based retail giant Sears, Roebuck & Company. Then the phone rang. It was her friend of more than two decades, Carol Moseley Braun.

Moran kept detailed notes of what followed.

"Carol told me that she'd received an anonymous letter charging Kgosie Matthews with sexual harassment. She said the letter had just come to her from Ethel Alexander, who'd had it on her mantel praying over it the past weekend," continued Moran. "She said it was a two-page letter and that it named four senior staffers who might have knowledge of these charges. She asked me to investigate."

Joyce Moran made it clear to Carol that, although she would like to help her, she was not qualified in labor law, the specialty under which sexual harassment allegations would be covered. Moran suggested that she call in her friend Wayne Robinson, an attorney with the firm of Vedder, Price, Kaufman & Kammholz. Carol approved this strategy, and Moran called Robinson, who, in turn, recruited two more Vedder Price partners to help with the investigation.

The lawyers understood their mission to be limited to investigating the validity of charges of sexual harassment. They were not asked to reach a specific conclusion nor were they asked to seek out the source of the anonymous letter. On October 21, Robinson and Moran sent a memo to Carol that outlined the method by which the four attorneys wished to proceed.

"We recommended immediate interviews with those senior staffers named in the letter, followed by other staffers who might be identified who would have information, then an interview with Kgosie Matthews, after which we would write our final report," said Moran. "If the press was to become involved, we suggested the campaign office handle that aspect."

Carol then sent identical notes to Ira Cohen, Heather Booth, David Eichenbaum, and Steve Cobble. Each was instructed to read the note and return it to her. The note said that the staffers should meet with the lawyers and tell them everything they knew that might relate to charges of sexual harassment against Kgosie Matthews.

"I don't think she [Carol] thought there was a case because I don't think she believed any of it," attorney Wayne Robinson said later.

Two and a half months after the investigation, in a press conference where Carol for the first time addressed the harassment issue publicly, she said to the assembled reporters, "The day I got the letter, the first thing I did was call into my office the staffers who were named in it. I asked them about this. None of them had any evidence of anything approaching sexual harassment. None of them."

The fact that no such meeting took place was an example of then senator-elect Carol Moseley Braun putting herself at political risk, slipping through the looking glass to guard fragile Carol, a woman compelled to protect the man who, according to her construction, was devoted to "protecting" her.

When Steve Cobble got the note directing him to talk to the lawyers, he took it straight to Marlene Johnson, the campaign's remaining viable link to Matthews and the candidate. "Does she mean this? Does she really expect us to tell these guys the truth?" asked Cobble.

"Yes," Marlene answered. "Tell them everything you know." Marlene had been designated by Carol to set up the interviews for the lawyers.

"It was made very clear to Carol," said Wayne Robinson, "that we would not do a one-sided investigation, that it would be thorough, and that we were not going to allow ourselves to be compromised. Along with two of my other partners, four of us did a series of interviews, took copious notes, and the report does not misstate any of the comments that were made."

Carol had called Joyce Moran on October 20. By four o'clock that afternoon Moran, Robinson, and two other attorneys from Vedder Price, all of whom were volunteering their time for this task, began to interview the four named senior staffers. On October 22, Moran sent to Carol a five-page report on the lawyers' preliminary findings. It was recommended that the investigators interview five female campaign workers identified by the senior staffers and "any other staff witnesses whom you believe have knowledge of the facts and that we should interview."

According to Moran and Robinson, although they were satisfied with their effort given the circumstances, there were some troubling aspects to the investigation.

Of the four senior staffers, Heather Booth declined to be interviewed saying she had no direct knowledge of the allegations against Matthews and that her time in these last critical days was better spent serving her unshakable commitment to the election of Carol Moseley Braun. Although she had no respect for Matthews and had herself been mistreated by the campaign manager, Heather was convinced that once Carol got through the travail of campaigning, which Heather understood to be uniquely difficult for this particular candidate, she would dump Matthews and become the productive senator the people of Illinois hoped for. "Heather gave up absolutely no information," said Robinson.

A few days passed as the four lawyers consolidated the material they had received from the senior staff and prepared for their second round of interviews. In the meantime, said Moran, "we were asked by Carol for more details on what the senior staffers had said, and we wrote another memo on the 27th that gave those details." Moran concluded this memo by telling Carol that she'd contacted Marlene and that the lawyers were now "awaiting her [Marlene's] return call with the schedule of people we needed to talk to."

Moran and Robinson reported other frustrations. Moran was sure that Carol decided to call her and initiate the investigation without consulting anyone else. But almost immediately, campaign lawyers Ed Coxum and Lou Vitullo entered the picture. Vitullo was "being extremely protective," Robinson said, adding that this troubled him because Carol was the client and there was a question of privilege. Vitullo and Coxum created "a wall between us and Carol." Carol did not show up for a meeting scheduled on the evening of October 28. The lawyers had to settle for a late-night conference call. They had been effectively separated from their client. "We never had an opportunity to sit down and talk with her about it [the investigation]," said Joyce Moran with regret.

Wayne Robinson thought that not only were Vitullo and Coxum interfering with lawyer/client privilege but his own integrity was also compromised by a fact he learned from those very same attorneys: Kgosie Matthews was reading all of the communications that passed from Moran and the Vedder Price lawyers to Carol, their client.

"I learned that she was sending Kgosie copies of all the reports we had done," Robinson said. "That really irritated me because I felt a sense of responsibility to the women we interviewed. And if it was not sexual harassment, I didn't want there to be any retribution coming forward."

The interviews with senior staffers produced the names of five women who were or had been members of the general-election campaign who had complained of being harassed by Matthews. Of these five, one (Jan Hensley) had left the state and was now working for senatorial candidate Barbara Boxer in California, a second (Kathleen Murray) refused to cooperate because Marlene Johnson could not assure her that Kgosie Matthews would not see her testimony, and a third (Letitia DeWith-Anderson) canceled her appointment with the lawyers on advice of counsel.

This left Elizabeth Nicholson and Mandy Gittler. Mandy was a volunteer assigned to help Liz with the candidate's mail. The daughter of Hyde Parkers and longtime friends of Carol, Mandy had left the campaign after a few weeks and a number of "embarrassing" encounters with Matthews. As for Liz, she was sustained throughout several distasteful incidents by her interest in seeing Carol elected—and her "Irish." "Why should I quit? I didn't do anything wrong. Besides," Liz said months later, "I didn't have another job. Why should I sit at home being pissed off when I could be pissed off in the office—and collecting a paycheck?" Also, despite her problems with Matthews, Liz Nicholson thought she had served Carol well and was still hoping for a job in Washington.

In addition to Nicholson and Gittler, Marlene Johnson sent several other female campaign staff members over to Vedder Price to be interviewed. Robinson, who is African American, was mystified by this. All of the additional women were black. "There were some inklings that it was a race thing," he said, indicating that this move might have been an attempt to make the hostility aimed at Matthews appear to be race-based. If so, the plan backfired. "None of these women had been harassed," said Robinson, "but it was clear from them that they all thought Kgosie was an ass and thought he was not a good person. There was not a woman there, save Roxanne Volkmann, who supported Kgosie."

"But even Volkmann thought he was an ass," added Moran. "She just felt she knew how to handle him."

Before each meeting, the person being interviewed was advised of the Equal Employment Opportunity Commission's guidelines defining sexual harassment in the workplace. Robinson, Moran, and their colleagues concluded, based upon their interviews with the people provided by the campaign, that there was no "legal, actionable sexual harassment under the EEOC guidelines." Therefore, the final part of the investigation agenda was never implemented, and Matthews was not interviewed about the allegations.

On November 2, 1992, Election Day eve, Carol received the investigators' final 24-page report. Under section III, "Findings," the report stated:

> There is no evidence that Kgosie Matthews harassed women employed by the campaign. The facts do not support a finding of either quid pro quo (Category 1) or hostile environment (Category 2) sexual harassment. However, three women named by investigation witnesses as possible targets of sexual harassment were not interviewed, two because they would not consent to be interviewed and the third because she could not be located.

While no evidence of actionable sexual harassment was presented to the investigators, there was ample evidence of problems. The report concluded:

> We do find that Mr. Matthews' autocratic manage-
> ment style and condescension toward staff members
> created an unsatisfactory working environment. All
> the witnesses commented, in one form or anoth-
> er, regarding Mr. Matthews' often times rude and
> intolerant behavior. The witnesses concurred that
> he was generally nondiscriminatory in dispensing
> same. While such behavior is not legally actionable,
> we recommend that the Committee further examine
> and discuss with Mr. Matthews his management
> style which has had a negative effect on the work
> campaign environment.

I first heard about the Moran-Robinson investigation on November
6, three days after Carol was elected to the US Senate. That morning,
I'd received a call from David Eichenbaum's assistant, Kim Braxton.
Kim, who was as sweet as she was hardworking, had seen to it that
I'd gotten a copy of the daily news clips, and now she was alerting me
to what, for me, could be a potential disaster.

"You'd better get down here, Jeannie, if you haven't copied all
the backfiles. We've been ordered to seal everything up and be out
by tonight." I had been told, as had been the staff, that November
15 was the headquarters shutdown date. Since I hadn't completed
copying the press files, which went back as far as Carol's stint as
recorder of deeds, I hightailed it down to Lake and Wells.

"It was not a happy place," I later wrote in my journal. "There
was a double sadness: the sour feelings about the campaign, the
campaign manager, the lack of connection to the candidate—and
fear and concern for Carol's future. Because most staffers still love
Carol and believe she can be a great senator—if only. But only she
can fill in the blanks, perhaps, in herself. Nobody believes she will
get rid of Kgosie."

Feeling the need to talk, Desiree Tate summoned me to the wom-
en's room. She said she thought marriage was imminent. She said,
"Carol is in love like a 14-year-old girl. She is blind and dependent."
Des told me how stressful it had been to stay near Carol because

of the constant need to appease Kgosie. "If you cross him, he'll cut you off." Remembering Eichenbaum's view of his "kgosing," I thought: Or if you get too close to the candidate, if she trusts you, he'll cut you off as well.

It was then, in the bathroom of the campaign headquarters on November 6, that I first heard about the lawyers' report, which is certainly a credit to the discretion of the staff since I'd been around every day as some 12 people had stolen over to Vedder Price to be interviewed. Des had not read the report, she said, "but Carol thinks it's inconclusive. When the rumors first started, Carol asked Liz outright if Kgosie had made a pass at her, and Liz lied and said no. That's what Carol wants to believe."

Liz Nicholson remained one of the few people in the campaign who had been told, albeit early on, that she would follow the senator to Washington. She was still clinging to that promise, even though she knew she was allowing herself to be co-opted on the sexual harassment issue. And now, with the campaign ended, Liz was being told to move over to the Recorder of Deeds Office, where she would be employed and could continue to do Carol's secretarial work "during the transition." This was uncomfortable for her because the recorder's office was also in transition, Jesse White[32] having been chosen as Carol's successor in the recent election. Besides, Liz was not interested in spending the rest of her career in a county office. In an attempt to clarify her status, she'd placed several calls to Carol, whom she finally reached on November 30. "Carol, I really want to work for you," said Liz. She was answered by silence.

Like others interviewed, to the lawyers, Liz had not characterized her problems with Kgosie as sexual harassment, but she felt that was exactly what she had suffered and that this was the conclusion the investigators would reach after hearing her testimony. At this point, Liz didn't know what the report said, only that now it didn't matter because Carol was a senator and Kgosie Matthews, she hoped and prayed, would soon fade into the obscurity she felt he so richly deserved.

---

32   Jesse White is now the Illinois secretary of state.

Liz Nicholson occupied a unique role in the campaign: she was not a decision maker, but for much of the time, especially during the early months when she functioned as Matthews's assistant, she sat at the desk outside the campaign manager's east end office, geographically positioned at the center of most of the action. But beyond that, I find Liz's testimony significant because, like so many drawn to Carol Moseley Braun, she was young and politically inexperienced but also smart and motivated. And, like the senator herself, Liz is an ardent feminist interiorly beset by the classic female weaknesses: inadequate self-esteem and the need for male approval, qualities that are a magnet for men like Kgosie Matthews.

For these reasons, and because, in her own exuberant, if sometimes self-deprecating fashion, Liz offered a classic tale of the manipulative boss and the malleable young woman who sought only to please, I here include—with only a few edits and comments for continuity—a healthy portion of an interview I did with Liz shortly after Carol Moseley Braun was elected to the US Senate.

"It seemed that every ethnic group and every walk of life was on that campaign, and that made it very exciting. I've never met such an array of people and made friends with them. And everyone was idealistic about Carol's victory, but everyone also felt that it was a victory for ourselves as well.

"I think the biggest problem was that despite the fact that there were a lot of talented, competent people on the staff, they were stifled because of Kgosie Matthews. He was a dictator who had a problem with delegating authority. And if you put yourself between Carol and him, you were immediately put down and made to feel that you were worthless. The saddest thing about it was that she trusted him, and for that reason, you couldn't stand up to him because you'd lose either way. With him, you'd definitely lose and with her, you'd lose in the long run.

"After the campaign, I found out that people were a lot more discouraged than they let on. They were working for one reason: Carol. And here were Carol and Kgosie thinking people were out to get them. Carol by herself is not hard to work with; she's good-natured, she's not paranoid, and she's certainly not racist. Without him there, persuading her that everyone was against her, she would have respected people like David and Marlene and Heather and Desiree and Steve and myself. If we had been able to express ourselves, to flourish, it would have been the most beautiful campaign ever.

"But I understand the dynamic between them because Kgosie can be a very charming man. I liked him a lot at first. I enjoyed the work and felt good about the way he seemed to trust me. He took me out to dinner, and we talked about our personal lives. I was having problems with a guy I was dating, and he was giving me advice. I'd heard the rumors about him and Carol, but he never mentioned that to me, and I respected him for that.

"Then he started making very nice, more personal comments to me like, 'You look very pretty today.' I was embarrassed, thinking, I hope he doesn't like me in that way. And then he started asking me out. Sometimes, on the phone, we'd be going over things business-wise, and he'd start to get more personal, warmer, and he'd ask, 'How's your boyfriend?' And I'd say, 'OK.' And then he'd say, 'When are you and I going to go out?' And I don't know if you'd call this leading him on, but I was embarrassed and I'd say, 'Oh, we'll talk about it when you get back to the office.'

"Then it started getting to the point where we'd be in his office and the door would be closed, and he'd start to get personal, lean back in his chair, drop work for a minute, and say, 'So how are you doing?' He was always asking me, 'Are you happy here?' And I'd say, 'Oh I love it,' because I really did love it and was really into my work.

"Then one time, he said, 'I really like you.' I said, 'Thank you. I like you, too.' 'No,' he said, 'I really like you.' Oh no, I thought, here it comes. In his office, at least four or five times, he asked me out. 'Would you go out with me? Do you think we could start going out?' I'd say, 'What do you mean?' He'd say, 'I want to go on a date. We could go to dinner.'

"And finally I said, 'Kgosie, I can't. I know your relationship is with Carol.' He got a little angry with me, and he totally denied it. He said, 'I don't know why everyone thinks just because a woman and a man are together and they're friends that they're sleeping together.' I said, 'Well, Kgosie, to tell you the truth, that's all I hear, and you can't blame me for what I'm hearing. And I'd never do that to her. And I'd never do it anyway because you're my boss.'

"And he would say: 'No one has to know.'

"He knew I was embarrassed, and one time he said, 'I'm probably more embarrassed than you are.' I said, 'I don't think so. Otherwise you wouldn't have asked me.' I shot him down, but I tried to keep it light. Once, on the way out of the office, he said, 'I hope you don't think I'm a pig for doing this.' I said, 'Oh no. But I think this is how sexual harassment starts.' We were laughing about it.

"This was all before we went to the convention in New York in July. He was very nice to me, so nice it was pathetic, considering how mean he was to everyone else. He treated me with a certain respect.

"Then one day, he was mean to me. The girls in scheduling can attest to this. He was on the road with Carol. He called and I was going over things with him on the phone, and I think I said Heather wanted to talk to him about something. He couldn't stand Heather. She drove him nuts. So he just yelled, 'I don't care!' Then he went crazy, swearing at me. So I hung up on him. I was angry and crying. I ran into the scheduling office, and I said, 'He's so mean sometimes!' But this was before I knew how mean he could get.

"He called back, and Des said, 'He wants to talk to you.' I couldn't stop crying but I got on the phone, and you would have thought we were lovers the way he was so upset that he'd upset me. He said how he cared about me so much, and he'd never do anything to hurt me. And I'm such a sucker. I thought: Oh, he's so nice. He really does like me.

"Then, on a Saturday in the campaign office, just before going to New York, he said to Carol in front of me, 'Carol, Liz is going to be working for you from now on.' Carol seemed very ambivalent about that idea, and I was embarrassed.

"So we went to New York, which was very exciting, very busy, and he was with Carol all the time. But I remember at one point, we were at a fundraiser and he sat down on a couch beside me and said, 'You know, I really miss you. We should spend a day together. I'll take you to Harlem.' At this point, I still liked him, but I felt sorry for him. It was pathetic. He and Carol were an item. He was, I knew, screwing around with other women and still coming on to me.

"Then we came back to Chicago, and all hell broke loose. You know how the office was arranged. Carol's office was the nicest on the far east end and adjoined Kgosie's. There were desks in front of each of their offices, but a partition divided the reception areas. While there was plenty of activity on Kgosie's side of the partition because the scheduling office and Steve Cobble's and Jill Zwick's and Heather Booth's offices all came out of that same area, the other side of the wall, in front of Carol's office, was isolated, really out of the mainstream because Carol was always out campaigning. Well, when we came back from New York, I was still sitting at the desk in front of Kgosie's office but doing both jobs.

"Carol suddenly became uncharacteristically demanding. Literally, she'd be calling me on one line, and I'd have the other line ringing, and it would be him. And they both hated being put on hold, especially him. Or if I didn't answer the phone, he'd say, 'Where have you been? Will you get back to your desk?' Once I got a phone number wrong, and you would have thought I killed his mother. He went crazy.

"So I was doing both jobs, trying to catch up on thank-you notes and things that had piled up while we were in New York, and finally I went in and told Kgosie I just couldn't handle it. He acted like it was a personal affront, that I had attacked him. And the next day, he called me maybe 12 times: 'Have you moved your desk? Why haven't you moved your desk? If you can't stand working for me anymore, why don't you move over to her?'

"Well, I moved my desk, and that was the end of it. I went from sitting in front of his office to sitting in front of her office. It was no more kind words, no more apologies for his behavior. If he spoke to me, he was very rude. It was like he hated my guts."

Liz then went on to recount incidents in which Matthews humiliated her in front of others. He alternately ignored her, spoke to her with contempt, or attacked her for her alleged shortcomings. Still, Liz took it, as did several others in the campaign who, while there may not have been a sexual component, were subjected to Matthews's alternating charm and fury.

By early September, around the time Steve Cobble had his talk with Matthews about cooling campaign tensions and riding it out until November 3, Liz was in an emotional state.

She recalled: "The tension between us had been building and building. He knew exactly what he was doing to me. He acted like he didn't even know I was around, but in his head, he manipulated me, he was punishing me. Anyway, I can't remember what precipitated this particular incident, but he yelled at me, and I started crying, then I decided I'd had it. I went into his office, but I'm so emotional. I thought I was going to be strong, but I started crying again. And he sat there like the coldest bastard I've ever seen in my life. 'What's wrong with you?' And I couldn't get the words out. 'What the hell's the matter with you?'

"I said, 'I can't stand the way you treat me anymore.' I said, 'What did I do wrong? What did I do to you?'

"He said, 'Liz, I don't know what you're talking about. You are just too sensitive.' I said, 'You don't treat Roxanne like this or Desiree or Lynette [Stanton]. You laugh with them. You used to be so nice to me. Why do you do this to me now?'

"'I don't know what you're talking about,' he said. He made me feel crazy. So then I'm like, OK, maybe he's right. Maybe I am nuts. He was sitting at the table in his office, writing. He didn't even look up at me when he said, 'Do you think I'm acting this way because you wouldn't date me?' And I was too embarrassed to say that was the reason, so I said, 'No, that's not it.' And he said, 'Good. Because that's not why.' He said, 'If I didn't like you, you wouldn't be here. But lately I've been feeling like you've been talking a lot. You have a big mouth lately. Otherwise I trust you.'

"I thought, You asshole. I was so loyal to you. With some of the things I knew, I could have made your life a living hell. I'd thought he was so wonderful, and I was lucky to be getting along with him since nobody else could. When I left the office, I told him I was fine, but I was so angry I wanted to strangle him.

"He was nice for a couple of days, then went back to his old self. And I did tell a few people. Not that I needed to. It was obvious how he treated me.

"For example, one day late in the campaign, Dorsey Day was in the office. Dorsey is an old-time politician, worked for Harold Washington, and he stopped at my desk and said he wanted to see Carol. Later, I read in the paper that Kgosie had called Dorsey in to investigate who was spreading rumors about him, but at the time,

I thought he just wanted to chat with Carol. So Carol was in meetings, and by the time she'd finished, I couldn't find Dorsey. Then Carol left and Dorsey came back and asked, 'Where's Carol?' Well, apparently, it had been important to Kgosie for Dorsey to talk to Carol because the next day, I was standing in the hall talking to someone and here comes Kgosie. He's practically got Dorsey by the hair, and he's in a rage: 'When I send someone to see Carol! You fucked up yesterday. You told him no. You're not the gatekeeper for Carol Moseley Braun!' And he walked down the hall saying, 'You're not the gatekeeper!'

"Well, I lost it. I was crazy. I ran into the scheduling office. I didn't care if Roxanne was sitting there writing him love letters, I had steam coming out of my ears, I hated him. "Maybe if I'd slept with him four months ago...." I said. Letitia was there, Melissa, Lynnette along with Roxanne. Melissa closed the door and said, 'Liz, calm down.' Later, Marlene came and asked if I needed to go home for the day. I said, 'No, I'm not sick. I'm sick of him, but he's not going to drive me to go home.'

"Then, after the sexual harassment letter came, and, as I found out, after the senior staffers had talked to the lawyers, he started being very nice to me, very professional. He'd gotten rid of Letitia, Des was on the road with Carol, and he'd asked me to go in and straighten out the scheduling office. He knew I had to be one of the women referred to in the letter, and he had to watch his back.

"It was a Saturday, and I was alone in the scheduling office. Kgosie and I hadn't had a real conversation in two months, and here he comes—and he's locked out of his office. He was very nice. He said 'Liz, how are you doing?' And do you know I actually thought, Oh, he likes me again? I am such a wimp. My God, I'm a wimp, I know. But he was locked out of his office, so where does he have to sit? With me!

"I knew about the letter. He knew about the letter. And do you know who told me I would be talking to the attorneys? He told me!

"He was professional and nice, sitting right in front of me. So finally, I had to break the silence. 'Kgosie,' I said, 'you don't think I wrote that letter, do you?'

"What does he do? He gets up, closes the door, sits down. And we had it out. I was almost brought to tears again because here was this guy who used to treat me like a queen, then hated my guts, now is starting to turn around again. But I reminded myself: The only reason he's nice is his ass is on the line. He's gotta be nice to me because I hold the cards here.

"So we started talking about it, and he used names, but I'm not going to because they don't want to be involved in this. No one does. But he was completely privy to what the senior staffers told the lawyers, and there's no way he should have had that information! 'I don't understand,' he said. '[One woman] saying I touched her, [another] saying I sexually harassed her. Do you think I would ever want to fuck a woman like [the second one named]? She's so damned ugly!' So I'm thinking, OK, so I'm not that ugly and you wanted to screw me. He just didn't get it!

"He asked if I had been saying things, and, of course, he knew I had. But I said, 'Kgosie, it's obvious to everyone what you've done to me.' He was being manipulative again. He brought up two women he knew I wasn't crazy about, Jan Hensley and Letitia. This was his way, to pit women against each other, and that's the way he separated Carol from her natural allies, too. He said he knew I didn't write the letter. He said Letitia did (she didn't). 'She fucked everything up,' he said about Letitia. I might not have always gotten along with Letitia, but I knew where she was coming from on this issue, and she was right.

"He was trying to make me think we were big buds again. 'The lawyers are going to talk to you,' he said, very nice. I think he thought that if we straightened it out right there, I might not talk to the lawyers. So finally I said, 'You know Kgosie, I've been so upset. You admit that your behavior has changed since I would not go out with you.' I was pointing my finger like this, and we were like this close to each other. And he said, 'Liz, OK, my behavior did change.' Now, get what his excuse was: he said, 'You asked me for a raise.' I almost fell out of my chair. Oh, so that's why you hated my guts for months—because I asked for a raise?

"I *had* asked for a raise. When he told me, before New York, that I was going to be working for Carol—and knowing that others in the campaign who did less meaty jobs were being paid more—I'd said, 'Will this entitle me to a raise?' He'd said, 'Yes, we'll talk about it when we get back.' So after New York, when I was working for both of them and he hated me, I went in and said, 'How about that raise?' And he just about bit my head off: 'We have no money!' And that was the end of it.

"So now he's buddying up to me, saying, 'You and I were real good friends, then you're asking me for a raise. What do you think, Liz? I got you this job. I got you where you are. You're liable to go far because I....' Everything fell back on what he'd done for me. I was thinking, Hey, I'm too smart for this! Don't act like you saved me from hell! But I sort of wimped out again. I laughed it off. 'You told me you'd give me a raise, I followed up on it, and now you claim that's why you hated me? Right.'

"After I'd talked to the lawyers, he called me in and wanted to know what I'd said to them. Thank God somebody interrupted, and I managed to avoid it. Kgosie had no right to know what I'd said. Of course, he found out anyway. He was privy to all that information."

Matthews's sexual juggling act would have astonished some of the randiest athletes I'd covered during my years on the sports beat. While at the Democratic National Convention, the campaign manager was on the phone back to Chicago, sometimes several calls a day, coaxing a pretty, young campaign member with whom he'd been sleeping for several weeks.[33] Now she was slipping away. Persuaded by his passion, this woman had not believed the rumors about Kgosie and Carol but told Matthews she was breaking off their relationship because she had learned he was having sex with yet another young woman on the headquarters staff. When he finally became convinced that this woman was escaping his control, he ordered her to resign from the campaign. She refused.

While I learned about this particular affair shortly after the election, it was some months before this woman herself described the details. She had not come forward during the sexual harassment investigation, so humiliated was she by her own behavior. Months later, she was still trying to understand what about this man had charmed her so and why she had done something so out

---

33   This woman was not named by senior staff and thus never interviewed by the lawyers.

of character. I assured her that she was one of legions victimized in this way. The trick was to only let it happen to you once. She was not comforted.

The older, more experienced women in the campaign could only shake their heads at Matthews's behavior and try to protect their temporarily blind friend Carol. One pal of Carol's who knew about several of Matthews's conquests outside the campaign told me that at one point, she'd gone up to the campaign manager, squinted at a certain area of his anatomy, and asked, "How many dicks you got in there, anyway?"

CHAPTER 16

Off to Africa

B Y MID-NOVEMBER, Maureen O'Donnell of the *Chicago Sun-Times* was working the sexual harassment story with gusto, cold-calling virtually every female staff member on the recently concluded Carol Moseley Braun campaign. She had the press version of the anonymous letter, had been told about the investigation and report, and thought she knew who a couple of the women were who'd been harassed, but O'Donnell was having a helluva time confirming anything.

During the week that began with November 30, the senator-elect interviewed potential Senate staffers; met with ousted Haitian president Jean-Bertrand Aristide; hosted Senator Joe Biden, who was in town to try to convince her to join the Senate Judiciary Committee; flew downstate for a conference convened by the Archer Daniels Midland Company to discuss the North American Free Trade Agreement; and, required to leave her now sold South Shore condominium by November 27, searched for new housing. She accepted a quick fix when Evangeline and Nick Gouletas, owners of Lake Point Tower, a luxury high-rise, offered her temporary quarters in a vacant, partially furnished penthouse. Without a press person (Eichenbaum had "retired" following Election Day, and Carol had declined to replace him), there was no one to answer queries about how the senator-elect was preparing for her new job. Thus, the most positive item reported in the papers was that Carol had been spotted in Marshall Field's buying linens.

On December 1, Liz Nicholson was fired from the recorder of deeds staff and told that she would not be hired for a Senate job.

On December 2, *Chicago Sun-Times* political writer Lynn Sweet called to wish me a happy birthday, incidentally mentioning that Carol was leaving for Africa on Friday.

Africa? Although such a trip had been rumored for some time, neither Carol nor Desiree Tate, who was still assisting her, had confirmed that it was a go.

On the morning of December 4, both Chicago newspapers wrote that the Braun campaign had raised $6.4 million and had reported a debt of $447,000 to the Federal Election Commission. Although many staffers were owed money, Kgosie Matthews had been fully paid, the paper said, receiving $7,500 on November 16.

On the evening of December 4, Dennis Britton, editor of the *Chicago Sun-Times*, called Carol to inform her that reporter O'Donnell had testimony from three women who claimed to have been sexually harassed by Kgosie Matthews and that the paper was going to go with the story. Carol understood that the women had gone on the record. "If you've got it, go with it," she said to Britton.

On Saturday, December 5, Carol Moseley Braun and Kgosie Matthews left for Africa. Accompanying them was Carol's assistant, Darlene Mackey. They were due back on December 18. Back at the old headquarters, treasurer Earl Hopewell and a small staff continued to work on the campaign's finances while Jill Zwick and Desiree Tate, with help from Lynette Stanton and Roxanne Volkmann, handled countless media requests, job applications, and speaking invitations (including invitations for 300 commencements!) and began to prepare for the festivities that would surround Carol's swearing-in on January 5. Because they had been called by the *Tribune* and the *Sun-Times*, virtually all of Carol's former campaign staffers knew the sexual harassment hit was coming. "I just wanted to shake her to get her to confront this," said Desiree, "but all she would say is 'Steve Brown will handle it.'" The affable Springfield-based PR man had been called upon once again. Brown's problem was that he had no equipment with which to fight the firestorm of negative publicity that was about to break out.

It began on Sunday, December 6, at about the time Carol was preparing to spend her first evening in Africa. The tone was set in Michael Sneed's column on page two of the *Chicago Sun-Times*:

> Tips and Twaddle ...
> Huh huh huhhh: People wanna know ... If U.S. Senator-elect Carol Moseley Braun has $42,000 cash available and owes $11,000 in back staff pay ... why is she moving into a posh $3,300 a month penthouse apartment at Lake Point Tower? Questions. Questions.

And then, on the same day in the same newspaper on page three, another headline read, "Bias Flap Hits: Anonymous Letter Investigated."

Maureen O'Donnell's story told of the letter sent to Carol and a lawyer's investigation (only Joyce Moran was named). O'Donnell also quoted three anonymous women—a staffer, a volunteer, and a woman outside the campaign—regarding Matthews's unwanted attentions. Carol and Kgosie had also been questioned before leaving for Africa: "Braun said the [lawyer's] interviews turned up no allegation of sexual harassment or any other type of harassment or impropriety and called the letter 'character assassination.' Matthews said, 'Don't waste my time.'"

As is customary when breaking a big story, the *Sun-Times* added sidebars, one detailing the women's testimony to O'Donnell; another, a biographical piece on Matthews; and the third described the federal guidelines on sexual harassment in the workplace.

On December 7, both the *Tribune* and *Sun-Times* followed up with a statement Carol issued through Steve Brown. Describing the investigation she had instigated, Carol said, "The inquiry concluded there was no foundation to these anonymous allegations.

Should it prove needed, I will cooperate fully in any action concerning this matter." Carol told the *Sun-Times* she would not comment on specific accusations unless the women making the complaints divulged their identity. O'Donnell wrote: "The workers requested anonymity, citing concern about job prospects."

Then, on Tuesday, December 8, 1992, under the headline "Successor Fires Last-minute Braun Hires," the *Chicago Tribune* wrote:

> The Carol Moseley Braun era as Cook County recorder of deeds was unceremoniously swept from office Monday by her successor, Jesse White, who fired 10 patronage employees hired since Braun's U.S. Senate election....
>
> He not only canned Braun's last-minute hires, but also gently scolded his predecessor and said he dumped her chief political operative, Ethel Skyles Alexander.

The newspaper reported that among those who lost their jobs during White's first full day as recorder of deeds were Darlene Mackey and Elizabeth Nicholson.

By December 9, the editorialists and columnists began to wade into the controversy, and the negative press spun out of control. In a *Sun-Times* commentary, Steve Neal reminded Carol that her narrow victory over Alan Dixon came as a result of her spirited defense of Anita Hill, accused her of losing touch with her voters, and finally asked, "Is Braun covering up for her pal? Did Braun conduct a real investigation? Was it a whitewash? Braun has an obligation to release the lawyer's report."

On the same day, a *Tribune* editorial chastised Carol for stacking the recorder office's payroll, saying that just two of her late hires, employees who had taken leave to join her campaign, were legitimate. On the lighter side, columnist Irv Kupcinet, referring to a previous item he'd run saying that friends suspected Carol and Kgosie had gone to Africa to be married, quoted a "trans-Atlantic call" from the senator-elect: "'We did not get married—not at this time. When we do, you'll be the first to know.' (Promises, promises)," wrote Kup.

For the next 10 days, from December 10 through the weekend of December 20, when Carol was expected to return to Chicago, the dunning continued without letup—or response. There were too many questions: about the nature of the relationship between the new Illinois senator-elect and her former campaign manager, about why the campaign debt was so large when a relatively small amount (23 percent) had been spent on media, about the recorder's office hirings, and, most especially, about the sexual harassment issue. If there really were a report that exonerated Matthews, why wouldn't Braun release it? Wrote the *Trib*'s Tom Hardy on December 20, "It is unknown whether there was any report or if lawyers even bothered to interview Matthews."

The *New Yorker*'s David Remnick said it best: "It is the job of the press to put pressure on power and on pretenders to power," and it had become increasingly clear to me, beginning during the Medicaid scandal, that Carol, with a lifelong history of positive (if meager) coverage, had no clear concept of how the press works when it collectively decides a public figure deserves scrutiny. It's one thing to watch someone you don't know, say, a Clarence Thomas, come under attack, but it's quite another when you yourself become the object of what feels, to the subject, like unadulterated venom. Carol, I knew, thought of herself as essentially a good person. And I agreed with that assessment. She was a person of considerable achievement who had overcome difficult circumstances to live an adventurous and productive life in the uniquely challenging political milieu of Chicago—and Illinois. Her record reflected a normal adult share of personal and political errors. But until now, nobody had paid attention. Until now, she had been able to bat those errors aside and reach for the next rung on her ladder of success.

I tapped out a note and took it down to the now virtually deserted campaign office. I asked Desiree Tate to fax it to Carol in South Africa. Understanding that it was as much the lack of resolution as the substance of the material being generated and regenerated daily, and fishing for a simple metaphor, I suggested that the senator-elect think of the press as a pool of sharks. If you don't give them a little hamburger, they're gonna go for your arm. Carol

Moseley Braun was delicious, a still-mysterious persona, and becoming more mysterious every day as the cauldron of controversy was stirred.

Indeed, in this same period, Kup reported that *People* magazine was to name Carol one of the "25 most intriguing persons of 1992," while gossip columnist Sneed wrote, "Hellooooo, Carol … is Sen.-elect Carol Moseley Braun ever coming back from her trip to Africa with campaign aide/inamorato Kgosie Matthews?"

And the beat went on. And every day, at Carol and Kgosie's request, Roxanne Volkmann faxed the press clippings to Africa.

The campaign's out-of-towners had gone home to their families, but those who had been with Carol from the beginning, those who cared and still believed in her, were in a state of frenzied helplessness. There was talk of staging an intervention. Names were popping up who might have the strength, the influence, to persuade Carol not to marry Kgosie, everybody from her old Springfield pal Billie Paige to North Shore philanthropist Lucy Lehman to Democratic strategist Ann Lewis in Washington. They wanted to shake her: "Get rid of this guy! He's ruining you."

I was just as frenzied. Now, everybody was talking to me about everything. Everybody, that is, except Carol. So I did something I had up until now avoided. I went to see her ex-husband, attorney Michael Braun.

Despite the insistent sparkle of holiday decor, December 15 was cold and gloomy, reflecting my mood exactly. I had expected Mike Braun to be hesitant about talking to me, but he agreed immediately and was as relaxed and forthcoming as everyone, including Carol, had described him. Braun's comfortable corner suite featured big windows that looked across Daley Plaza past a glittering Christmas tree and straight into the office of the Cook County recorder of deeds. I couldn't help commenting on the proximity. "Lynn Sweet made the same observation," he laughed. "You journalists!" When I started by apologizing for getting him involved, he said, "Can't help it. I am involved."

Most of our conversation was confirming rather than revealing. Mike talked about Carol's overwhelming charm and charisma, "When we lived together, our house was like a sitcom, with people wandering in and out. And she always had someone who was her aide, a sort of all-service person, a role that Sue Purrington served for a time."

My mind wandered back to Sydney Faye-Petrizzi, who, despite Carol's many female friends, was the last person I knew of to serve that need. As hard as she tried to force Kgosie Matthews into that emotional caretaker role, his narcissism and his ego (and, I thought, his fundamental contempt for women) would never handle it.

Switching topics, I told Mike how much I enjoyed his son, Matt. I asked him if Matt's mom's candidacy and all that went with it had been hard on the kid. On the contrary, Mike said, "He revels in it." Mike seemed resigned to the circumstances, yet worried, too, about how all of this—especially the negative stuff—might affect his son.

The phone rang. It was Carol calling from Africa. I rose to step out, but Mike gestured for me to remain. When he hung up, he shook his head, sighed, and said, "She's going to stay for Christmas. She wants me to get Matt's passport, shots, pack, whatever, and get him over there." Mike said he had really been looking forward to Matt's spending Christmas with him but said, "I can't deprive him of this opportunity."

Michael Braun was thinking about the welfare of his son, but this news was another bombshell. Carol was supposed to be back in three days. A few blocks from where we were sitting, a handful of Carol's loyalists were juggling countless tasks, yet there was no one to make decisions. I was speechless.

Mike, on the other hand, did not even seem surprised. "She said to me once, 'I would sacrifice years off my life to be in the history books.' Well, in her mind, she's accomplished that already. Carol has reached her goal."

There was a depressing finality to what Mike was saying, to what it implied. "But won't she want to make substantial history by the influence she can have in the Senate?"

Carol Moseley Braun's ex-husband leaned back in his chair and smiled. "Well," he said, "we'll see."

That dark day, as I left Michael Braun's office, I felt like I'd been kicked in the gut. It wasn't even about the potential book and my work. Mike was a good man—a liberal, probably a feminist even—and he knew Carol as well or better than anyone. *He* had fallen in love with her, too. But maybe we'd both been seduced by the packaging—the brains, the charm, the sharp political instincts that matched our own needs. Maybe she wasn't the flesh-and-blood figure of our dreams. Maybe she was just someone we had grabbed up to shape our dreams over.

On December 23, I opened my *Sun-Times* to Kup's column and read the following item:

> SENATOR-ELECT Carol Moseley Braun on the long-distance horn from Cape Town, South Africa, where she is vacationing with her steady, Kgosie Matthews: "I'm calling to give you a report of what I'm doing here. First of all, I'm meeting all Kgosie's relatives here, and he has hundreds of them. I also have been privileged to hobnob with the country's leaders like Nelson Mandela, Walter Sisulu, Archbishop Desmond Tutu and Zulu Chief Mangosuthu Buthelezi.
>
> "AND I FOUND many blacks and whites who feel they can live together, which is most encouraging. On a personal note, Kgosie and I will be back in Chicago right after Christmas. No, we're not married, but I repeat, you'll be the first to know."

It was a classic case of too little, too late—and much too exclusive. Rather than a general release detailing the countries she had visited, the leaders she had met, and what she had learned that might stand her well in the US Senate, Carol sent an item to Kup, the well-respected, soft-core gossip columnist who was a Chicago institution. Predictably, rather than placate the press, this action simply pissed them off, particularly prickly Tom Hardy, the *Trib*'s top political guy. On December 27, after ripping Carol for 19 column inches and under the subhead, "Carol to Kup," Hardy reprinted the entire item from the rival *Sun-Times*, then wrote:

> Earth to Carol: The party is over. Hobnob with
> some Illinoisans for a change, Sen. Incommunicado.
> It's time to buckle down and go to work. Welcome
> home, and Happy New Year.

Interestingly, nobody seemed curious, as I was, about the nature of this so-called vacation. Obviously, these meetings with top
South African leaders had to have been arranged well in advance by
Matthews, who, I was pretty sure—even with the help of his family—could not have accomplished such a feat without the celebrity
he was escorting, that is, the first African American woman ever
elected to the US Senate. And in her note to Kup, Carol had also
neglected to mention the couple's visit to Nigeria to meet with that
country's military leaders, including the notorious kleptocrat Sani
Abacha, who was to become president (dictator) a few months later.

Kgosie Matthews never intended to go to Washington, except,
perhaps, as a lobbyist. He was looking to do business in Africa.
What was it a very elated Matthews had said when I asked him
about how he was spending Election Day? "Keeping in touch with
the world," he'd answered. The picture was coming into focus.

On December 30, delaying her scheduled return by 12 days and
less than a week before she was to be sworn into the US Senate,
Carol, Kgosie, and Matt arrived back in Chicago. Darlene Mackey
had returned earlier at Matthews's request.

I got a call from a friend at the *Tribune*. Carol was holding a
press conference. When? "Now, at Lake and Wells," I was told. I
arrived moments before Carol and Kgosie walked in, both looking fresh and cheerful, having come directly from Midway, where
they'd arrived from New York on a private jet. I was frightened
for Carol. I'd stopped by the press area on the way up to the ninth
floor offices. At least seven cameras and perhaps 50 reporters and
technicians were jammed in an overheated room that was bursting
not only with people but also with anticipation. The sharks were
circling, hungry. "Are you ready for this?" I asked Carol. "Oh sure,"
she said. "I want to get it over with." It seemed to me that the senator-elect had no idea what was awaiting her.

As for Matthews, he hid upstairs as Carol descended one floor to meet the assembled reporters. Former press aide Don Rashid, whose expertise was in radio, had returned to set up the required equipment, but Rashid had no experience in controlling a press conference (and in any event, was not called on to do so). I noticed that Steve Brown arrived late, stood in the back, and left the minute the press conference was over. As had too often been the case, Carol was without support and was winging it on her own.

The following day, December 31, the *Sun-Times* featured a front-page color photo of a very pretty but distressed senator-elect sitting behind an impressive bank of microphones. In one of five articles on two full pages of the newspaper, reporter Fran Spielman accurately referred to the press conference as "a 47 minute inquest.... The questions were fired at Braun from all sides by a media horde that had waited 27 days to ask. Braun responded coolly, with flashes of humor and defiance."

Carol said her trip to Africa, her return from London to New York on the Concorde, and her flight to Chicago that morning in a private jet had been paid for out of "private resources," and she defended her right to privacy on these matters. She declined to discuss the details of her African adventure, saying she had promised an "exclusive" to a friend. Carol said the Lake Point Tower apartment, at $3,300 per month, was admittedly expensive, but she was unaware that it was a discounted rental price (the newspapers had reported the going rate to be over $4,000). She said Matthews, at $15,000 per month, had not been overpaid, and Carol produced salary figures of other campaign managers to buttress that assertion. She said that when she signed off on the hires at the recorder's office, she'd been on "automatic pilot," and she apologized for not giving the matter proper attention.

But the majority of questions asked were about the charges of sexual harassment, the reported lawyers' investigation, and Carol and Kgosie's relationship, which, for the first time publicly, Carol admitted was a romantic one.

Carol had lively responses to all of the questions but few satisfactory answers. The problem was that there were two realities alive in that room, and they were working mightily against one another.

Carol characterized the charges of sexual harassment by anonymous sources as "McCarthyism." Yet, while insisting that the investigation exonerated Matthews, she refused to release the lawyers' report. At the same time, there were a substantial number of reporters in the room who had talked to many campaign workers, including those interviewed by the lawyers, who had asserted, albeit off the record, that Kgosie was indeed a sexual harasser. The press had no way of knowing that of the several women complainants rumored, only two had come forward to the lawyers. So in the minds of reporters, there was a clear choice: either the investigation was a whitewash or Carol was lying about the report's conclusions.

Carol's reality was this: the lawyer's investigation had concluded that there was no legal basis for a charge of sexual harassment, even though the report unquestionably portrayed Matthews as a bad manager. Based on the fact that the primary allegation was unfounded, that staffers had spoken to lawyers with an assurance of confidentiality, and that Carol's instinct was to protect Kgosie from having his employment record saddled with this unsavory document, the senator-elect felt herself on firm legal as well as moral ground in not releasing the report. But, perhaps more significant, in Carol's reality, Kgosie was a personally fastidious, well-mannered, sophisticated man who said he loved her and wanted to marry her. She could not imagine him making a low-life pass at anybody. As attorney Wayne Robinson had said, Carol simply did not believe the charges.

As I listened to the exchanges between Carol and the reporters, I thought: We are caught in the looking glass again. Carol is stating what she consciously believes to be the truth, but the image being reflected back is a virtual opposite.

Outside the room in which the press conference was held on December 30, 1992, there was a third view of the issue, one held by the lawyers who had done the sexual harassment investigation. Wayne

Robinson and Joyce Moran saw no reason why, with the names ex-
cised to protect confidentiality, their report could not be released
to the public. Both felt that it was in Carol's interest to do so. Said
Moran, "The report speaks for itself, and I have no problems with
it being released, and we certainly have urged her [Carol] to do that
whenever there has been an opportunity."

In politics, it is said that perception is nine-tenths of reality.
Carol's problem was—and continued to be for some time—that
she insisted upon her one-tenth, refusing to internalize, even consider, issues that would disrupt the personal dream she had constructed. Thus, as 1992 drew to an end, the bottom-line political
reality for Carol Moseley Braun was that after 27 days of questions,
followed by 47 minutes that offered too few definitive answers, the
senator-elect had suffered a serious blow to her credibility.

Said Carol to the assembled press: "If I've learned anything at
all from this exercise, it's that you guys have the power to build
somebody up, and you have the power to make them look like idiots as well. You can take any situation and make it ugly." True,
indeed. The Illinois press had helped shaped Carol's star-studded
image and was now questioning the perceptions it had created. But
neither the ascent nor the descent was accomplished without assistance from Carol Moseley Braun.

In the end, Carol said this to the gathered press regarding the
sexual harassment situation:

> If somebody has information that I don't have, I
> would be more than willing to look at it, to open the
> door and invite everybody in this room to sit in judg-
> ment. We can have Anita Hill revisited. If anything,
> I would absolutely want to know the truth because,
> quite frankly, I've been fighting for women, fighting
> to end discrimination in the workplace for the 15
> years of my public life. My record is very clear. And
> to think that at this stage of my public life, the idea
> that something like this would happen on my home
> front and I not know about it is stunning to me—and
> so I would want to know the facts.
>
> But the point is, with respected lawyers looking
> at the issue, the bottom line is there is no evidence

anywhere. And if the media, if you guys have something, please share it with me. The reason we all
respected Anita Hill so much, and we respected her
courage, is that she came forward and made a statement. I have to ask what kind of courage is involved
with an employee that won't go to the employer but
goes to the media and still won't come forward?

If Carol had been dissembling about these matters, this was a
risky (and totally unnecessary) challenge. But the senator-elect was
expressing her conscious truth, her own reality.

Carol's two base constituencies, the African American and feminist communities, both national in scope, were understandably
confused. The *Chicago Tribune* reported the reaction of Lu Palmer,
longtime activist and chairman of the Black Independent Political
Organization: "Many African Americans he has talked to about
Braun recently are 'baffled and disgusted' by her actions since
the election. Though he believes she will be a 'good' legislator, 'it
reduces her effectiveness when her image is tarnished, and I am
convinced it is tarnished today. She blew it during the transition
period. The only question is, will she understand she has blown it
and try to make amends?'"

The most heartfelt feminist reaction came two months later, in
the March/April edition of *Ms.* magazine: In a commentary titled
"Sexual Harassment: Is There a Feminist Double Standard?," *Ms.*
first described the events in the Braun campaign, then asked,

What to do? The Fund for the Feminist Majority and
the National Organization for Women issued no formal statements. To the press, feminist leaders said
"Perhaps it will take a little time for her to adjust."
Patricia Ireland said that "Carol Moseley-Braun has
not been accused of harassing anyone." True. But
Braun was the employer. We are not asking her to
repudiate Matthews, who is not on her Senate staff,
but surely we can ask for some candor—some sign
that charges were taken seriously. Can we demand
anything less from her? Otherwise, don't we abandon

our leaders to the principle-eroding pressure of their power and positions?

Many feminists say that the women must come forward to substantiate the charges. Well, the women may not be named, but they are not ghostly apparitions, either. They have been interviewed by the *Chicago Sun-Times* and the *Chicago Tribune*. (And would you want your name on charges that could embarrass the first African American woman senator?)

Many a woman has said she would like to awaken Senator Braun from her romantic reverie. It's wishful thinking—and a private act. Public protest demanding full accountability is the only way to lay all such charges to rest, and let a genuinely new politic begin.

CHAPTER 17

Carol Moseley Braun, United States Senator

O N JANUARY 5, Carol Moseley Braun was sworn in as a member of the US Senate.[34] For three days, beginning on January 3, hundreds of Illinoisans celebrated in Washington, DC. They were exhilarated by the fact that the Democrats had elected their first president in 12 years and that the entire 103rd Congress, including 17 new African American representatives (bringing the Black Caucus to 40 members) and 48 women would be seated that week. But what mattered was that Carol Moseley Braun's election would be sealed in history, and a vast number of individuals felt the call and, indeed, deserved to be a part of that event.

It was a time of joy and chaos. Carol, who had barely had time to unpack from Africa and repack for Washington, appeared to be under severe stress, her tension increased by the fact that Matthews, while he stayed nearby, remained practically invisible. Why would the man who had led this historic campaign to victory and was now Carol's acknowledged romantic companion and natural escort wish to hide? Carol's loyalists who had lived through the

---

34 Not long after she joined the Senate, Carol began to hyphenate her last name. That meant, rather than being "Braun" and high in the roll call, as "Moseley," she would answer comfortably closer to the center. For consistency, I've chosen not to hyphenate unless quoting another source.

campaign were frequently asked to explain. But it was impossible. Too long a story—and too complicated.

When Carol got up on the morning of Tuesday, January 5, the day she would be sworn in to the US Senate, she was slapped with tortuous headlines. "Ill. Gives Braun 'Wake up' Call" shouted *USA Today*. And perhaps more painfully (because not a soul in the Washington establishment would miss it), the *Washington Post* followed its headline, "Spotlight's Glare Shines Harshly on Braun," with a four-column rehash of every issue that had been flogged to death in the Chicago papers for the past month. For the hundreds invited to the party that afternoon to watch the reenactment of Carol's swearing-in, it was like being handed a litany of the bride's past affairs as you prepared to attend the wedding.

The official swearing-in had taken place on the morning of the 5th when Vice President Dan Quayle administered the oath to Carol and the other new senators in the Old Senate Chamber. But for the 500 or so invited guests in a large room on the ground floor of the Dirksen Senate Office Building, this was the real party. Nobody was to be disappointed.

In the beginning, there appeared to be an agenda. Illinois politician Neil Hartigan shared MC duties with Sherry Bronfman, a New York socialite and Braun supporter. Carol's friend and pastor, the Reverend Addie Wyatt, asked that we all join hands for the invocation. Standing just to the left of the VIP seats, with my head bowed, my eyes roamed the row of celebrities: Carol's beautiful, slender hand was grasped by the Reverend Jesse L. Jackson, who, in turn, was holding hands with Senator Ted Kennedy, on whose left was the fiery Reverend Willie Barrow from Chicago's Operation PUSH. I thought: Would that real communication could flow through those hands. Politicians and preachers have a lot in common; Reverend Jackson, of course, was the ultimate synthesis of both.

Jackson had, for understandable reasons, been the invisible man throughout Carol's campaign, yet this was to be the reverend's third speech at a Braun celebratory function in as many days. Washington, DC, was Jackson's current bailiwick, but, although a son of South Carolina, Jackson had a long and volatile history in

Chicago, and many in this largely African American audience were likely to be less than awed by anything he had to say.

But for this milestone event in the painful progress of African Americans toward full equality, Jackson had the right message. Each of his three presentations had contained two cautionary elements, the first demanding responsibility from Carol's constituency, specifically the African American community. For example, on Sunday, preaching at Washington's Metropolitan Baptist Church, Jackson had said to Carol and the congregation, "My fear is that we who celebrate you here today are willing to assign you to the fire and not even stand close enough to throw water or even spit ... we must not subject our senator to foolish expectations, where we become judges and not participants."

Yet, on each occasion, Jackson had reserved most of his considerable rhetorical passion for Carol herself. Over and over again, he reminded her of who got her where she was—and at what price. On Sunday, he'd said, "When you stand in the Senate ... the bloated body of Emmett Till takes on new meaning. When you stand ... the bullet in Dr. King's neck takes on different meaning. And so, this is for us a holy experience. You stand between us and hurt and harm and danger."

I had been sitting in a back pew at the Metropolitan Baptist Church with Carol's good friend Barbara Samuels, and as our eyes met, I thought I read in hers the full impact of what I was feeling: There are 30 million African Americans in this country and now, politically at least, Carol is first among them. It was an incomprehensible responsibility.

On this day in the public culmination of a three-day celebration, Jackson found an audience overwrought with anticipation— as well as a certain unease. Almost every speaker was to refer in some way to Carol's recent troubles, so generously outlined in the newspapers that morning. Illinois poet laureate Gwendolyn Brooks established the theme when she finished the poem she'd written for the occasion with a salute: "Bravo, Senator Carol. And hold on!" Then, when Neil Hartigan introduced Jackson, the emotional tempo for the day was set.

With his customary cadence, Jackson started out slowly and quietly speaking for this audience of Chicago's heroes: Ralph

Metcalfe, Jesse Owens, Ida B. Wells, Harold Washington. When he reminded us of Dr. Martin Luther King's march in Marquette Park, I wondered if Jackson was aware that young Carol Moseley had been alongside Dr. King that day in 1966, that it had been an epiphanous moment for her, the day she chose the political path that led her to this day. Very soon, warming to his purpose, Jackson addressed Carol directly:

> You are blood of our blood, flesh of our flesh, spirit of our spirit. When you hurt, we share the pain. When you succeed, we rejoice together.
>
> The laws of sacrifice lead to greatness; the laws of convenience lead to collapse. Retain a spirit of resilience, get better and never bitter.
>
> "Why me?" you must ask in your lonely moments. "But I'm normal!" Well, not really. "But I'm innocent!" Well, so was Jesus. It is by the blood of innocence that we are saved. So you stand in that tradition of suffering service.
>
> We've been beautiful for a long time. Your beauty radiates because you stand on the shoulders of many. So many African women have been beautiful, but, looking at themselves in dirty dishwater, they thought themselves to be ugly. They were not ugly! The water was dirty!

By this time, the audience was captured and was laughing, applauding, and responding in kind to Jackson's flourishes:

> So we've had giants standing in holes. They appeared to be midgets. They were not midgets; the holes were deep! We've seen midgets standing on the shoulders of other people. They were not giants; those were the shoulders of the unthanked, who never got the credit!

Following thunderous applause, Jackson launched into a tale about one of his own achievements, the day he brought downed flier Robert Goodman out of Syrian captivity. The reverend's purpose in this became clear when he spoke of meeting the press upon his return. Did reporters ask how long the negotiation was? What Hafez al-Assad was like? Jackson quipped, "No. They said, 'Now that you are back, who paid the hotel bill?'" The audience's laughter led Jackson back to Carol:

> So when you leave this place and the hounds of hell follow you, tell them this: Meet. Me. In. Englewood.
> Meet me in Englewood for our children are dying!
> Cover that!
> Meet me on the West Side, on vacant lots and abandoned buildings!
> Meet me on an Illinois farm, where farmers have been forsaken!
> Meet me in East St. Louis, the poorest city in America today.
> Meet me in Cook County Jail, where young, strong men languish.
> Meet me!
> Suffering breeds character.
> Character breeds faith.
> In the end, faith will prevail.
> Keep your eyes on the prize!
> It's healing time.
> It's bridge-building time.
> Keep hope alive!
> You do not stand alone. God bless you.

The audience's response was deafening. Neil Hartigan looked around, scanning the VIPs ranged behind the podium. "Do I have any volunteers who might wish to follow Reverend Jackson?" he twinkled. Kennedy had left, pleading another appointment, and it was hard to guess who might have been scheduled next on the program. Then an old man emerged from the crowd behind Hartigan and wobbled up to the platform.

It was the notorious segregationist senator Strom Thurmond! The audience gasped. Hartigan, adjusting quickly, gracefully introduced the 90-year-old senator from South Carolina, who said he had come to welcome a new colleague. The crowd, moments before in a revivalist mood, didn't know how to react. Polite applause was sprinkled with boos. Then, in a show of goodwill, Darlene Mackey and Velma Wilson, two women who had been with Carol from the very beginning—and I can only imagine what they must have been thinking—stood up, clapped, and cheered. When other Braun staffers followed Darlene and Velma's example, the audience joined in. Yet people were laughing, too, and buzzing: "What's *this* guy doing here?"[35]

In his best country politician style, Thurmond launched his remarks. "I just came by to pay my respects to the new senator here," said the man who had been the political archenemy of this crowd for more than two generations. But they cheered him anyway, all the while talking and laughing. This, in the flesh, was the old geezer with the bad hair whose twang had become so familiar during the Clarence Thomas hearings! "And I don't object to seein' mo' ladies in the Senate!" shouted Thurmond.

"He's lying," said the man standing next to me.

Thurmond continued:

> Shortly after I became gov'na of South Carolina, I was invited to speak to the inmates of the state prison. Not thinkin' just for the moment about the crowd I was speakin' to, I began as I customarily did. I said, "Ladies and gentlemen, I'm glad to be here, and I'm glad to see you here." You can imagine the reception I got on that occasion. [*laughter and much nodding from the audience*]
>
> But, at any rate, I just want to say that we welcome this fine lady to the Senate. She's in a different party from what I am, but it's not the party that counts, it's the....

Applause drowned out the rest of Thurmond's thought. He waited for it to die down and continued:

---

35   When Thurmond died at age 100, the news came out that he had an African American daughter, Essie Mae Washington-Williams. Her mother had been a 16-year-old servant in the Thurmond household, and Thurmond was 22 when Essie Mae was born. Essie Mae led an extraordinary life and was honored by her own family as well as the Thurmond family when she died on February 3, 2013, at age 87.

> I've heard she's a lady that gets things done, a lady of action. That reminds me of the woman who won the lottery of a million dollars. She called up her husband and said, "I've won the lottery, a million dollars. Pack your clothes!" He said, "Summer or winter?" She said, "Both. And be out of the house by six o'clock!"

Howls of laughter rolled up to Thurmond, thus encouraging him to continue:

> Ladies and gentlemen, we have a great country. We're proud of this situation. We have more freedom, more justice, more opportunity than any other country in the world. Millions want to come here....

From the back, a deep voice yelled, "Preach, Brother!" and that was just enough. The audience basically applauded—and laughed—Strom Thurmond off the podium.

Then, without introduction, Senator Joe Biden moved to the microphone. "You all just witnessed a piece of history!" declared Biden, pointing out the obvious. "If anybody here is over the age of 40 and you can tell me you ever thought you'd see this day...." Interrupted by applause, the senator nevertheless continued, "Where there is life, there is hope, and we have a whole lot of hope pinned on this woman from Chicago." Biden then turned to Carol. "I just want you to know," he said, "that everybody who anybody takes seriously starts off in this town on a rocky road, and although I should leave the preaching to Jesse [*that got affirmative applause*], this too shall pass."

"I also want you to know," Biden continued, reaffirming his very public campaign to get Carol on the Judiciary Committee, "that a lot of people want Senator Braun on their committees. Well, I'm gonna get her! You see, I can take care of Strom Thurmond, but somebody's got to handle Orrin Hatch!"

By this time, Carol's thoroughly entertained supporters had almost forgotten what they came to Washington for: to witness the reenactment of Senator Braun's swearing-in. So far, although I had seen him backstage earlier, Kgosie Matthews had not made his presence public. Now, Carol, who wanted the man she planned to marry to witness this crowning moment of her life, sent word starting with Sherry Bronfman: "Get Kgosie out here." Since some 20 or 30 of us were packed into the area between the platform and the backstage door, Carol's request went down the line like a game of telephone: "She wants Kgosie." "Get Kgosie!" "Kgosie." "Kgosie...." And seconds later, the message came back, this time only one syllable: "No" ... "No" ... "No" ... "No."

As she heard the answer to her plea, Carol, for a brief moment, looked stricken. I stood a few feet away from her, and as I watched her face, I could see the flash of pain. Then Carol stood, smiled, and, clutching a Bible, approached the podium. It was the same Bible upon which she had been sworn into the Illinois legislature 15 years earlier. Illinois senior senator Paul Simon administered the oath:

> I, Carol Moseley Braun, do solemnly swear that I will support and defend the Constitution of the United States against all enemies, foreign and domestic; that I will bear true faith and allegiance to the same; that I take this obligation freely, without any mental reservation or purpose of evasion; and that I will well and faithfully discharge the duties of the office on which I am about to enter: So help me God.

After a lengthy standing ovation, Carol began her speech. Her voice, throaty and lyrical when she was relaxed, was metallic with strain. Carol had written a short speech, and she, as had others before her this afternoon, referred, if more obliquely, to what she considered the abuse she'd absorbed in the past few weeks.

> I hope to be given the chance to do the best job I can ... precisely because the symbolic promise of this historic moment will be lost if not matched by the substantive effort of the next six years.... I am, by definition, a different kind of senator—an African American, a woman, a product of the working class. But I will not do the job the people of Illinois have entrusted to me by being a symbol alone. The change I was elected to represent can and will only happen if I am afforded an opportunity to contribute to the maximum extent of my ability.

Carol thanked those who had made the journey to Washington to celebrate this moment with her; then she said,

> I will work to make sure the dreams I carry with me become realized dreams and alive dreams and are not somehow lost in the shuffle. There is a passage that says, "This is the day the Lord has made, let us rejoice and be glad in it" as we prepare ourselves to write a new chapter in the annals of American politics and government.

Tears filled the eyes of many of those closest to Carol—tears where a few minutes before there had been laughter. There could only be one first time, and many in that room had played a role in creating the historical moment we had just witnessed. Some cried, too, for their friend Carol and the lonely burden she would carry.

Then the Reverend Willie Barrow, director of Operation PUSH and a Chicago treasure, rose to offer the benediction:

> Shall we pray?
>
> God, our father, God of the people, we are all here together witnessing the mysteries of history. Just to connect with Strom Thurmond [*from the crowd: "Yes!"*] was a mystery in history! [*"Oh, yes!"*]. Just to be here with the first African American female elected to the United States Senate was a mystery in history. We thank you for Carol Moseley Braun. We ask your blessing on her, your guidance and direction. Lord, we pray also for Carol to take on the "Noah" principles.
>
> Noah didn't receive credit for analyzin' the rain! He received credit for building the ark! Carol got to build an ark! Health care is an ark, jobs and job training is an ark, building strong families in America is an ark. Give her the sense, the wisdom, and the understanding. Dismiss us from this place but not from your presence. Help us to be a constituency of help and not of hindrance. In the name of the Lord, our Savior, we pray.
>
> And let us all say together ...
> Amen!

"*Now* what do we do?"

I N HIS ROLE as a newly elected US Senator, Robert Redford asks this final plaintive question in the movie *The Candidate*, and the same question echoes relentlessly in my exhausted head as 1993 dawns.

Now what do we do? What does *she* do? What do *I* do?

As disappointed as I was by Carol's self-destructive behavior in the romance department, I still believed she would be a fine senator. Though I spent a few days in May following her around DC, it was not until August 1993 that Carol found time for a long-promised visit to my cabin in the Utah Rockies. Every day for three days, we sat on the warm deck, the mountains towering around us as a stream rushed below, and hummingbirds squabbled among the potted flowers. It was finally peaceful, and I was able to record most of the family history and commentary you have read. But the senator did not relish discussing the campaign and had little to say about her campaign manager, except to lament that there had been a "heated discussion" with Kgosie just as she left town.

"Why does everybody hate him?" she half asked. Of course she knew the answer, but since we did not have time for a battle of realities, I simply responded, "Because he is mean to everybody."

Carol went on to describe how Kgosie was "so controlling." Then she smiled, "But he is my protector."

Sure enough the predictable arc of this current episode in Carol and Kgosie's stormy affair came to a melodramatic conclusion when a huge bouquet of roses arrived "with a note of apology." Carol was ecstatic. She was now anxious to return to Washington and did.

Carol's first months in office were not easy. For one thing, her stunning victory caused the detritus of the campaign to hit the national fan. In April, Carol announced that she and Kgosie were engaged, and that brought up the sexual harassment issue again. "Braun, 46, and Matthews, 36," would likely be married in June, the columns reported. It didn't happen.

Shortly after Carol announced their engagement, the *Chicago Sun-Times'* Lynn Sweet reported that Matthews had joined the Washington Strategic Consulting Group, Inc. While his title was vice chairman for national affairs, Sweet noted, "The group also represents foreign governments."[36] That meant two not-good things: the senator's fiancé was now a lobbyist, and he would be hanging around Washington. Much later, we all learned that in the first four months of 1993, Carol had paid Kgosie $47,600 "to help raise money for her treasury at the same time its debts were mounting."

It's hard for anybody to be a freshman—anywhere, anytime. But think what this new senator was facing; try to be Carol for a moment. For starters, you are a 46-year-old black woman, the first ever, in the all-white, very male US Senate—a speck of chocolate in

---

36 It was later reported that from mid-May to mid-July 1994, Matthews had filed with the Justice Department as a foreign agent for the Republic of Cameroon, the government of the Federal Republic of Nigeria, and the government of Haiti. "At the time, Matthews listed his residence as the Kalorama neighborhood address in Washington where Moseley-Braun was living," reported Basil Talbott of the *Chicago Sun-Times* Washington bureau.

a chamber otherwise defined by vanilla. Expectations are sky-high. Carol's stresses were pressing from the inside and the outside.

But there was something else that hadn't quite come into focus for me until one day early in her first term. I was hanging out in Carol's Washington office, hoping for a bit of her time, when the senator walked in and announced that she had asked political commentator and columnist E. J. Dionne to join her for lunch in the Senate dining room and—surely on a whim—she invited me along.

It was no secret that Carol was at home with trappings of luxury and power, so I was not surprised at her comfort as we breezed by the Senators Only sign and were ushered to a corner table that my senator appeared, by her manner, to claim as her regular space. This elegant room with its arched windows and blue leather seating was, according to lore, the most exclusive dining area in the Capitol. While some senior staff had access, at this time of day, one could only be invited by a senator. Carol smiled and greeted a couple of her colleagues as we were seated, while I resisted scouting the room for celebrities. I was about to ask Carol why she had invited Mr. Dionne when the diminutive columnist arrived at our table.

Dionne is a sweet guy, a good liberal, and I'm sure he was delighted and yet very curious—as was I—as to why we were all sitting here together.

But Carol got right to the point. She had read one of Dionne's columns that impressed her and wanted to work on legislation related to the information Dionne's excellent reporting revealed. She asked the esteemed journalist if he would head a committee to help her study this issue and create that legislation.

I'm pretty sure *my* mouth dropped open but I *know* E. J.'s did. He stammered a bit and explained that he was pleased about her interest, but as a journalist, he could not get in the business of advising a US senator (except, of course, via his punditry).

I was surprised at Carol's naïveté. But at the same time, the incident offered insight into what her term might, and, in fact, did, become. Carol was strong, especially on domestic issues, and had been a good legislator at the state level. But in Washington, probably not unlike other rookies, in many ways, she was an innocent abroad. As smart as she was, she still needed to trust a savvy staff. And putting that together would be no easy task. There was no

question that simply *who she was*—black, female, and *the first*—
was going to put enormous constituent pressure on freshman senator Moseley Braun.

While every day that first year of her term I was hearing staffers'
tales of frustration from both Washington and Chicago, one incident, for which I had two equally appalled sources, stands out.

Carol had spoken frequently about two of her constituencies
that were polar opposites—feminists, with whom she personally
identified, and the group she always referred to as "black nationalists."[37] It was never a secret that, although they supported her politically, Carol was not a favorite among many of the male African
American leaders of Chicago, and to call them all black nationalists
was an extreme generalization. But she knew these men were important, and when she was asked to meet with a group of community leaders in mid-April 1993, at the home of former acting mayor
Gene Sawyer, it was an invitation she could not refuse. Although
he had not been invited, the senator immediately called Matthews.
It seemed this group wanted to propose that they serve as advisers,
a sort of kitchen cabinet, a role several had filled for Mayor Harold
Washington. When that proposition was finally put to Carol, she
hesitated, smiled, and said, "I don't know..." and then, turning to
Matthews, "Kgosie?"

"We were all sickened," remembered Desiree Tate, who was in
the room. These were well-respected leaders in business and community affairs speaking to a *US senator*. *"Kgosie!?"*

Kgosie, addressing the gathering, made it clear that it was a
bad idea, and that was the end of it. My journal entry for that day

---

37   Black nationalism generally refers to the movement emphasizing strong
     racial pride and the creation of separate cooperative communities. Al-
     though he had predecessors, in the early 20th century, Marcus Garvey's
     Universal Negro Improvement Association was the foundation that, to
     some degree, later expressed itself in the Nation of Islam, a huge influ-
     ence in the Chicago black community in which Carol grew up. Rather
     than a political reference, however, I think Carol's problem with black
     nationalists had more to do with their patriarchal and antifeminist ten-
     dencies and was largely the source of her sense that she was more likely
     to be discriminated against because of her gender than her color.

was, I think, correct: although they knew all about their affair, this accomplished group of men did not understand the power Kgosie had over Carol. They thought it was pretty special to be a US senator and (like many close to her) assumed that Carol would reassert herself and return to being the affable politician they had worked with before she decided to run for the Senate. They didn't know that Kgosie Matthews—certainly enabled by Carol herself—had burrowed into her mental and emotional systems. And that day I wrote, "He's eating her alive."

But I still didn't want to believe it.

It was just short of a year from the day she was elected when the *New Republic* ran a cover story: "'A Star Is Born,' Ruth Shalit on the Art of Being Carol Moseley-Braun."

Shalit had written a ballbuster—and it was stylishly snarky to boot. While she featured all the ways Carol had exerted extraordinary influence as a freshman senator, especially in terms of Illinois interests, she also rehashed every campaign scandal, from unaccounted-for campaign funds to unresolved sexual harassment charges against Matthews. Most damning, however, was Shalit's retelling of the Medicaid thing. You have to credit her reporting skills because she had been able to access the whole discomforting story, including the entire "launder" letter *and* an official transcript of that terrifying interview, never aired, in which NBC reporter Bob Kur had confronted Carol with the letter and she had *not* denied writing it.[38]

With Shalit having reopened the story and with both sources now claiming to be in possession of the complete two-page letter from Carol to her mother, WMAQ, Chicago's NBC affiliate, ran the previously sequestered Kur interview in its entirety. It was hard to watch.

Only a year had passed since virtually every newspaper in her state had endorsed Carol and most Illinois voters had empathized

---

38   To refresh your memory, the damning sentence was, "In an effort to help you 'launder' the timber proceeds and not run afoul of the state regulations, I agreed to handle your $28,750."

with the health care and family issues the Medicaid story represented and elected Carol to the US Senate. But now it was a national headline. It grew legs that were not going to quit. And it hurt.

As I watched the televised report, I knew what Carol knew: that the hard family history, the anger and frustration stirred by the betrayal at the core of the Medicaid thing would never be fully understood. Nor would it go away. Even in her reelection campaign in 1998, Carol would assert that her opponent used the "welfare cheat" stereotype to characterize her.

My journal for 1993 is so full of distress that even two decades later, it is disturbing to read. Some of the problem was mine, but mostly it was a cauldron of angst still bouncing around Carol, the old issues that were still alive and what all those close to her described as "denial." And now Edna Moseley was dying. Darlene Mackey, who had known Carol all her life, felt that Carol, shut off from those who might really understand and confiding only in Matthews, was reaching for comfort from a man who was totally incapable of giving it. Carol could not give up her fantasy, and Darlene thought that I, who had so much of the truth in writing, was the only one left who could force reality on her.

"I've tried," I told Darlene, "but she is so fragile."

"That's right, very fragile—and she's such a good actress you would never know she had problems." And there it was again: the interior battlefield that was Carol Moseley Braun.

November 3, 1993, from my journal
Carol was elected exactly one year ago—and she called me first thing this morning. She's been anguishing, she said, since the *New Republic* article stirred up Medicaid again. So in the middle of the night, she got up and wrote me a long letter positing Auntie Darrel—with the cooperation of Carol's now dying mother, Edna—as "the source." [NBC investigator Doug Longhini assured me that he'd never heard of Darrel.]

But as we talked this morning, I heard something new from Carol. At first, she spoke of "free associating," the kind of talk, she said, we'd had on the deck of my cabin in the mountains a few months before. She said that was as close she'd come to talking to a shrink. She said, "I don't want to put you in the position of being an analyst, but I've been thinking along the lines of *My Mother, My Self.*"

Carol told me that two days ago, she had been at the hospital visiting Edna when Mike, her former husband, came by. She said to him, "I'm so angry at Edna. I just wish she'd come clean with me on Medicaid. And Mike said, 'Oh, don't blame your mother.' He was convinced she didn't do it."

"My mother lied on my birth certificate," Carol said. "She told them I was white. She forged my birth certificate to get me into school when I was four years old. She always constructed her own realities, and she lied, and I never wanted to be like that. In fact, all my life, I've been afraid of being like that."

Carol repeated the childhood cautionary tale she had told me before: "Edna told us our souls were like a glass of milk, and every time we'd lie, there would be a speck in the milk. And I was scared to death of getting those specks in my milk.

"And yet, I see it in myself, this ability to create my own reality. The stuff that used to piss me off about Edna, I think I just smushed in around inside and it became a real part of my character. Like Edna, turned inside out.

"The realities I create don't allow me to see the monsters. Like that *Far Side* cartoon: 'Monsters next door? Just ignore them and they'll go away.' So I wasn't afraid to run for the Senate because I didn't see the monsters, didn't recognize the boundaries."

In that long letter she'd written to me during the night, Carol had constructed a whole scenario, including denying writing the "launder" letter, and now she was continuing this over the phone just hours later: "I'm a lawyer. I'd never use the word 'launder.'" Yet here she was confessing her dual character to me; sure, the lawyer might not use the word "launder," but the angry daughter might.

Interestingly, Carol's ability to, as she said, "go through life sort of peripherally, like I'm outside looking in, has the upside of having allowed me to do difficult things, but there's a downside too."

Indeed there is. The downside is huge; she does lie—to herself. Since I've known Carol, this skewed reality has most detrimentally focused on Kgosie—this misplaced trust—so that even when she looks right in the face of deception, her powers of *self*-deception do not allow her to register the pain. Senator Carol Moseley Braun seemed lost, lost in the extraordinary maze of herself.

But this conversation tells me she does take it in. Somewhere in her psyche, this registers. And now I allow myself to hope that the sheer mass bottled up inside Carol might—maybe—wake her up. Others, Des Tate and Velma Wilson among them, think she'll eventually break down.

January 11, 1994

Dear Carol:

My son Tim called me at 1 a.m. on Sunday morning to tell me that Kup had reported that you and Kgosie were no longer together. I've confided in Tim and he knows the anguish I have felt in reconciling the public record (and disturbing private testimony) with what I believe to be the essential, the important and the very promising person who is Carol Moseley-Braun. Although he knew he would wake me up, Tim thought I'd sleep better after hearing the news.

The fact is I haven't slept much since, trying to figure out how you can help me help you.

First, I have to tell you that I know you haven't really broken with Kgosie because feelings don't just quit, needs don't stop, thought patterns don't change overnight. Nevertheless, Kgosie is a huge problem in this task I have undertaken, and because you were such a tight team, and—due to what I assume from the evidence was his paranoia—because you increasingly separated yourselves from friends, political allies and staffers during the campaign, I'm just having a helluva time telling this story. There are a handful of people who don't criticize Kgosie because they are loyal to you. After that, forget it. Few people have anything good to say about him.

I realize Kgosie puts a racial skew on this, particularly in regard to the campaign, but I think he got it backward. His critics are equally distributed among the races, as you well know.

One of the dangerous things about being both powerful and a celebrity as you are, Carol, is that people don't always tell you the truth; they stroke you because you have influence over their lives. Well, nobody has more influence over my life than you do; in fact my professional future is at stake here. But I can't deal with anything but truth, *especially* with you, between you and me. In terms of the book, we have to tell the truth, the best truth, although not the whole truth. Your life belongs to you. Your obligation is only to address the issues that came to be a part of the public record.

With that in mind, let me give you an example of what I am struggling with: Election Day, November 3, 1992. There is no question of this day's importance for women, for African Americans, for our democracy.

That's the "outside" story. What was going on inside?

You won by a good margin; your victory was announced before the polls closed. But nobody was really happy, including you (except, according to my extensive notes, Larry Shapiro, who felt you should think about running for President after your second term). Now, how do I shape this historically important day that should have been the pinnacle of your political career? Everybody—from network producers, to brother Joey Moseley, supporters Lucy Lehman and Christie Hefner, to your oldest friends who couldn't find you, or others who knew where you were but were prevented access by an army of "security" people—*everybody was pissed off.* That's an "inside" story, but I don't want to write it; it's too petty. It doesn't match the importance of the event.

So, okay, I go (outside) to the newspapers, get all the stats, statements, your speech and so on—stuff everybody knows, dry stuff.

Back I go (inside) to my one significant post-election interview with you, looking for how you felt about that day—and it seems to me, you were pretty pissed too, at least part of the time. Or maybe exhausted, or stressed out, but in any case, not elated. Perhaps I asked you the wrong questions; but it seems to me that both on election night and later when we talked about it you were in a kind of emotional turmoil that clouded your ability to think and feel about some of these events—and that turmoil had to do with Kgosie. Do correct me if I'm wrong. Please correct me if I'm wrong.

This problem extends both back to the beginning of the general election campaign and forward to the end of the time frame of the book, which is your swearing in to the United States Senate. On issues you are great, on your personal history you are great—but whenever the campaign itself is mentioned your commentary is overlaid with Kgosie's persona. Either you are defending him as being misunderstood, explaining his cultural amalgam, or praising his charms—but never telling us what he did or why he was a good campaign manager.

I know that at some level you have a clear comprehension of the events of the past two years, but I also know that you have resisted acknowledging some realities. I understand this behavior, believe me, I do. But you are my Senator and I want you to be what I know you can be: the best.

Your story needs resolution. You need to come to terms with the past in order to move into the future. I want to help you, but I've got to ask you to help me first.

Jeannie

A week after writing this letter, I sent Carol the first draft of the manuscript.

I knew that parts of it would upset her but felt that if she would confront the truth and react to it, we might have something, and it could be very good for her. It might accomplish what Darlene felt only I was in a position to do: force Carol to face reality.

For me, Carol's weaknesses were understandable and her strengths phenomenal. How many white guys had we resurrected from much worse scandals? For God's sake, we'd just forgiven Bill Clinton for Gennifer Flowers and elected him president of the United States! Carol Moseley Braun could spawn a whole new political paradigm. Powerful people were picking up the phone when she called. She could accomplish great things.

I used the word "forgiven" in regard to Clinton's dalliance with Gennifer Flowers. But that's probably the wrong word. It was more like "acceptance."

In the same election in November of 1992 that brought Carol to the Senate, Senator Bob Packwood, Republican of Oregon, was reelected for a fifth term. As chairman of the Senate Finance Committee, Packwood was very powerful. Surely with that in mind, and showing the same restraint the Chicago press had displayed in Carol's case, the *Washington Post* delayed until after the election a story it was sitting on, in which Packwood was accused by 10 women of sexual harassment, in some instances harassment bordering on assault. Eventually, the initial accusations turned out to be the tip of an iceberg revealed by Packwood's journal, in which he proudly recorded serial conquests. A 2014 Politico story on "redemption" of "disgraced" former members of Congress (all men, now lobbyists) set the tone with this entry by Packwood about a staff member resisting his groping: "'She made this big stink about it,' Packwood wrote. 'I have one question—if she didn't want me to feather her nest, why come into the Xerox room? Sure, she used that old excuse that she had to make copies of the Brady Bill, but if you believe that, I have a room full of radical feminists you can boff.'"

It took *three years*, but in October of 1995, after more revelations of dubious conduct and being threatened by the Senate Ethics Committee with expulsion, Senator Packwood resigned.

There have been countless randy politicians throughout history—notably, all three of our iconic Kennedy brothers. But suppose that rather than Bill Clinton's Oval Office "sexual relations" with a White House intern, it had been revealed that First Lady Hillary had taken a tumble or two in the Lincoln bedroom with one of those strapping Secret Service dudes? How would the public have responded to that? Would Hillary have had a future in politics?

I'm just asking.

My correspondence with Carol in the following months indicates that we had several potential appointments but never really spoke again. It became clear that she did not want the book published, and I did not want to go ahead without her. Her success was important to me. But so was the truth.

A few months later, I was told by someone very close to Carol that she had immediately passed the manuscript on to Matthews and that he'd told her if it were ever published, she would live to regret it.

And he wasn't done with her yet.

I was surprised to read in April 1996 that Carol had sought a waiver from the Senate Ethics Committee that had do with her home in Hyde Park.

Carol and Kgosie had bought the Hyde Park penthouse together in August 1993. He stopped making payments in February 1994 when the couple broke up. But although he was currently residing in Cape Town, South Africa, Kgosie had now resumed paying his share. The condo was on the market for $525,000. They might not be together, but Kgosie and Carol remained "involved."

A few months later, on August 22, 1996, the *Chicago Tribune*'s resident curmudgeon, Mike Royko, wrote:

> When Carol Moseley-Braun beat Sen. Alan Dixon many women wept tears of joy....
>
> Boy oh boy, is the joke on them.
>
> It now appears that Moseley-Braun is that most embarrassing of female symbols—the woman who is manipulated and used by some shrewd, masculine guy.

Royko was reacting to this headline in the *Chicago Sun-Times*: "Moseley-Braun Goes to Nigeria; Top Aide Quits: Senator's Secret Trip."

On August 9, 1996, Carol once again flew to Nigeria to visit the notorious dictator (murderer, thief) Sani Abacha. The papers reported that Matthews escorted the senator. In 1994, when he was living in Washington, Matthews had been a registered agent of Nigeria, but now, as a resident of South Africa, he was under no obligation to report his lobbying activities.

When the story broke, Carol called a news conference. "Senators travel," she told the assembled reporters. "That's what senators do. Senators deal with foreign policy." But then she said she had gone to Nigeria to console Maryam Abacha, a personal friend, over the death of her son in a plane crash.

Royko again:

> In one breath she says that as a senator she is expected to make foreign trips. In the next breath, she says

she went there to express her sympathy for a death in the dictator's family.

Then she decides that, no, it was not a senatorial journey, it was strictly a vacation on her own time. That makes sense—who goes to Disneyland when there is Nigeria?

The blowback was devastating.

Carol lost her third chief of staff in as many years, Edith Wilson, who told reporters, "Absolutely nobody on the staff knew about this trip, and I have submitted my resignation."

Walter Carrington, the US ambassador to Nigeria, learned of Carol's presence in the country from the local newspapers. "The State Department was not advised of her trip, nor were we asked to brief or assist her," was the careful statement of Washington.

Human rights activist Randall Robinson was beside himself. For some time, he'd been mystified by Senator Moseley Braun's inconsistency when it came to Nigeria. Carol had been a supporter of sanctions against apartheid South Africa, so Robinson said, "I don't see how someone who can argue and fight for sanctions against South Africa can argue against sanctions against Nigeria. This is an undemocratic, mean-spirited, corrupt, and cancerous regime."

And for us, the millions of women who had supported her, under the headline "Moseley-Braun Has to Say it: Hit the Road, Kgosie," the *Chicago Tribune*'s Pulitzer prize–winning columnist Mary Schmich wrote:

> We'd rather she steal stamps. We'd rather she steal votes. We'd rather she perpetuate any of the routine sins that her male counterparts commit. None of those does as much damage to the image of women in power—or to our image of ourselves—as the sight of a U.S. Senator handing the reins of her decisions to a man and simpering, "Honey, you drive."

Finally, calling her "Abacha's chief American apologist," *Sun-Times* columnist Steve Neal—whose coverage of Carol had at times been so adoring that her ex-husband Michael Braun told me he thought the writer might be in love with her—quoted one official who expressed what most Democratic insiders were saying: "She's gone. There's no way she can win reelection."

Not so fast, responded the senator. She *would* run in 1998, and she would win: "The answer is absolutely, positively. And if you want to run me for president in the year 2000, maybe I'll do that."

And so, in 1998, Carol ran against Peter Fitzgerald, a multi-millionaire, anti-choice Republican from the tony Chicago suburb of Inverness. Fitzgerald's was a family fortune (banking), and he used a bundle of it to beat up on target-rich Carol. A six-year state senator, Fitzgerald was not especially liked by many of his fellow Republicans, who variously described him as "inflexible, unwilling to hear out the other side, an arrogant rich kid ... too big for his preppy britches, willing to do anything or to roll over anyone in a quest to quench his raging ambition."

All that and a winner, too—but only by 2.9 percent.

Carol should have defeated Fitzgerald because despite her personnel problems, she had been an effective senator. Carol had a solid record in terms of serving the interests of Illinois business and agriculture. She was, as she had historically been, fiscally moderate and socially liberal—a perfect match for Illinois. But the Nigerian fiasco of '96 had eroded her support among women and, sadly, the passionate wave that had lifted her into office six years earlier had melted into indifference. Elections are emotional affairs.

Years later, in his memoir, *Believer*, David Axelrod, who had stepped in late in '92 to help Carol win her first term, offered an empathetic take on his old client:

"Carol was the daughter of an abusive father," Axelrod wrote. "It's hard to know how much that factored into the drive that led her into a political career, or the erratic, self-destructive behavior that claimed it. In my experience, such struggles are not uncommon among men and women who are drawn to the great emotional risks and rewards of the public stage. So many are chasing ghosts—trying to live up to the legacies and demands of a parent, or compensating for one's absence."

As for Fitzgerald, he remained unpopular within his own party, accomplished little in the Senate, and declined to run for a second term. His seat was taken in 2004 by another little-known Illinois state senator, Barack Obama. Axelrod would become Obama's good friend and chief strategist.

For Carol, losing her job had its rewards: Bill Clinton, having won his second term, appointed her ambassador to New Zealand, a posting that—from all reports—Carol thoroughly enjoyed. That sweet sojourn ended when George W. Bush was elected president in 2000.

Then, in 2003, Carol started talking publicly about running for the Senate again. This did not please her fellow South Sider, Mr. Obama, who had his eyes on that particular prize. But he need not have worried because Carol Moseley Braun decided instead that she would run for president of the United States! Carol's was accurately described as "a vanity run," and her campaign was typically underfunded and disorganized, but NOW—the National Organization for Women—and the National Women's Political Caucus got behind her, and Carol acquitted herself well in the primary debates, usually at the far end of a the row of blathering white men, including John Kerry, John Edwards, Dennis Kucinich, Richard Gephardt, Wesley Clark, Joe Lieberman, and Howard Dean. Carol bowed out in January 2004, endorsing Dean. But it had felt good to see her up there, displaying her easy wit, her passion on women's issues, and, as always, the brilliant smile flashing as she challenged the boys. I thought of all the young women who would not have been aware of Carol's troubled history, and I was pleased. Pictures count.

In 2006, calling herself a "recovering politician"—and always interested in health and agriculture, going back to her ancestors' Alabama farm and throughout her term in the Senate—Carol founded Good Food Organics, a food company with what she described as "a triple bottom-line business approach." That is, company accounting considers not only financial performance but also social and environmental performance. To that end, she has located her offices in the heart of the South Side. "I try to employ as many of the folks in the neighborhood as I can," Carol says today.

Not long after her organic food business got off the ground, a reporter for *Crain's Chicago Business* asked if she would ever get back into politics. Carol responded, "Whenever I get the urge to return to politics, I lie down until it passes."

In 2011, however, Carol decided to take on Rahm Emanuel and run for mayor of Chicago, making it "clear that I can't be pushed around, period." She persuaded interested African American contenders, notably US representative Danny Davis and state senator James Meeks, to drop out. Her campaign suffered managerial and financial problems, and, in the end, Emanuel won with 55 percent of the vote, including every ward in the city that had a black majority.

Today, Carol would say that when the notion of running for mayor of Chicago came over her, she should have opted for that nap.

In the fall of 1993, I received a four-page fax from Steve Cobble, now happily back in Washington, DC, with his family. On the cover sheet, Steve had scrawled: "This is why we loved her in the first place."

It was a copy of the *Washington Spectator*, dated September 1, 1993, and the headline read, "A Black Day for Jesse Helms."

With permission, I am going to quote liberally from the *Spectator*'s account of how Carol Moseley Braun turned the Senate's most ultraconservative, white, male, southern senator's day "black."

Referring to the 1939 movie classic *Mr. Smith Goes to Washington*, starring Jimmy Stewart, in which an idealistic young senator from Wisconsin takes the Senate floor to confront the power of evil, and with the caveat that nobody in cynical Washington believed this could ever happen, the *Spectator* declares:

> Well, now it *has* happened. And this time the "Mr. Smith" not only is a woman—one of the Senate's record-setting bivouac of seven—she is a black woman, freshman Senator Carol Moseley-Braun (D-IL).
>
> Her "Mr. Smith" moment on the Senate floor— an impassioned, unrehearsed solo stand for what's right—brought an audience of Senators and bored journalists trotting in to witness her battle with

the mindless bombast that's everyday fare in the "upper chamber."

It seems that every 14 years, the Senate routinely and unanimously had been called upon to renew the "patent" on the insignia of the United Daughters of the Confederacy. This logo pictures a Confederate flag inside a laurel wreath and the numbers 61 and 65, indicating the lifetime of the Confederate States of America. These gals were, of course, free to wave their flag without the imprimatur of the US Senate, but Senator Helms (R-NC), as he had in the past, was eager to again please the constituents he referred to as "delightful gentleladies."

Here's the backstory: Helms and Carol were both on the Senate Judiciary Committee, where Helms had, according to procedure, first sought to bring the motion to approve the flag patent. At that time, Carol had quietly persuaded 12 other members to vote "nay" because this action was not only unnecessary but wrong. And that was that. She thought.

Helms, however, wasn't through. On a day he knew the Judiciary Committee was busy with hearings on the confirmation of Ruth Bader Ginsburg's nomination to the US Supreme Court, he went to the floor and got his motion amended to Clinton's national service bill, asking for "immediate consideration."

Quoting the *Spectator* again:

> But what Helms seemed to forget was that today there are thousands of desktop TV sets in the U.S. Capitol complex tuned into C-Span's "live"—if you can call it that—proceedings on the Senate and/or House floor. In the Judiciary Committee hearing room, Moseley-Braun was alerted by a note rushed in by her TV-watching office staff. She raced to the Senate floor to confront Helms again. It was beginning to be movie stuff.
>
> As the Senator from North Carolina blandly fibbed that the Judiciary Committee's rejection had been "unintended" through the door and into the Senate chamber strode Moseley-Braun. Helms had "come to the floor, attempting to undo the work of

the Judiciary Committee," she said. "The Senator has not explained, however, why the Daughters need the extraordinary Congressional action."

"The United Daughters of the Confederacy have every right to honor their ancestors and to choose the Confederate flag as their symbol if they like," Moseley-Braun began. "However, those of us whose ancestors fought on a different side in the Civil War or were held, frankly, as human chattel under the Confederate flag, are duty bound to honor our ancestors as well by asking whether such recognition by the U.S. Senate is appropriate."

Tension was mounting. Warming up, Moseley-Braun continued, ad lib:

"The fact of the matter is that emblems of the Confederacy have meaning to Americans even 100 years after the end of the Civil War. Everybody knows what the Confederacy stands for. Everybody knows what the insignia means ... Whether we are black or white, northerners or southerners, all Americans share a common history and we share a common flag.

"The flag, the stars and stripes forever is our flag whether we are from the north or the south, whether we are African-American or not—that is our flag. And to give a design patent to a symbol of the Confederacy seems to me to create the kind of divisions in our society that our counterproductive, that are not needed."

Carol then moved to table Helms's amendment, an act that, under the rules, would effectively add the full Senate's rejection to the Judiciary Committee's action. But Helms was having none of it. He called Carol's action "inflammatory," demanded a vote, and got it. And with all Republicans siding with the senator from North Carolina, Carol's motion was defeated, 52-48.

So our senator from Illinois announced she would filibuster.

"Suspense soared," reported the *Spectator*. "So did Moseley-Braun." The article goes on:

"If I have to stand here until this room freezes over," [Moseley-Braun] declared, "I'm going to do so. Because I will tell you that this is something that has no place in this body. It has no place in the Senate. It has no place in our society." The usually unspoken issue of race—and of slavery—was coming to the fore.

"All conversations will cease," Senator Barbara Boxer of California, now presiding, declared. She need not have issued that warning, however. Attention was riveted on the black woman Senator from Illinois. Moseley-Braun stood taller.

"I have to tell you this vote is about race, the subject of racism comes up in the U.S. Senate ... and how I have to, on many occasions, as the only African-American here, constrain myself to be calm, to be laid back, to talk about these issues in very intellectual, non-emotional terms. And that is what I do on a regular basis, Madam President. That is part and parcel of my daily existence ... I'm sorry Madam President. I will lower my voice ..."

As more Senators rose to praise her, announcing that they would switch their earlier votes for Helms' motion if there could be another roll call ... They began the kabuki dance required to bring on a second roll call. Its outcome was uncertain. But then came another cresting moment.

Silencing the Senate again, Senator Howell Heflin (D-AL), a rotund, 72-year-old, self-styled "country judge" now in his third six-year term ... slowly delivered the real "epiphany."

"I come from a family background that is deeply rooted in the Confederacy," he began. "My great-grandfather on my mother's side was one of the signers of the Ordinance of Secession by which the state of Alabama seceded from the Union. My grandfather on my father's side was a surgeon in the Confederate Army ..."

You could hear a pin drop.

"But we live today in a different world," Heflin said. "We live in a nation that every day is trying to heal the scars of racism that have occurred in the past

... Perhaps racism is one of the great scars and one of the most serious illnesses that we still suffer today ...

"I do not believe the organization [the Daughters] today really has racism at its heart or in its activity. But the Senator from Illinois, Senator Carol Moseley-Braun, is a descendant of those that suffered the ills of slavery. The whole matter boils down to what Senator Moseley-Braun contends—that it is an issue of symbolism. We must get racism behind us, and we must move forward.

"Therefore, I will support a reconsideration of this motion, and I do it with conflict ... We live in a country in which we believe that all men and women—as stated in the Declaration of Independence—are created equal and are endowed by their Creator with the right of life, liberty and the pursuit of happiness." The second dramatic roll call delivered a 75-25 victory for Carol Moseley-Braun, and for America. As for Senator Helms, he called the "reborn majority" "turncoats who ran for cover for political reasons."

And later in the Senate dining room *Washington Post* columnist Mary McGrory reported that Moseley-Braun's colleagues rose from their tables to hail her. And yet ...

"What probably meant as much to her was being surrounded by black waiters and waitresses," McGrory wrote. "Their usual diffidence overcome, they shook hands with her, they murmured, 'We appreciate what you did. We thank you.'"

Tears were flowing as I put down the report that Steve Cobble had shared with me. *"This was why we loved her in the first place,"* because she was right and she was courageous.

I wept then—and anguish still—with overwhelming sadness for what might have been.

One Last Note

SOMEONE ONCE SAID, "Bad decisions make good stories." *Everyone* makes bad decisions, and Carol's singular bad decision was a very human one. But in politics, the stakes are incredibly high and, as you have read here, especially for a woman and even more especially for an African American woman. Carol's personal mistakes should not overwhelm her political accomplishments. She was a good senator with a consistent record in the service of the people of Illinois and an important role model for millions of women beyond our state.

It is my hope that people will think deeply about the Carol Moseley Braun story, will realize how hard it must have been to be this woman, to go from where she began to where she went with so heavy a load, much of it heaped upon her by the personal and political culture in which she had to survive and thrive. Yet this was a woman who breached the color barrier and smashed the glass ceiling at the same time, and the significance of her place in history must not be underestimated.

I don't think the countless believers who invested in Carol, who had faith that she could be a great senator—a servant of the people, as she herself described it—were wrong. Sadly, the individual who lacked the faith to sustain that vision, to truly comprehend and exploit her own power, was Carol herself.

But she did blaze a trail. Carol Moseley Braun was the first African American woman elected to the United States Senate, and she certainly will not be the last.

Acknowledgments

For their encouragement and support, I would like to thank Dayna Bender, Steve Cobble, Holly Morris, Pam Moreland, David Eichenbaum, Chris Mitchell, Tim Mennel, Tonya Gisselberg, Betsy Crist, Doug Seibold, Kate DeVivo, and the Agate team. And finally, with love and gratitude for being a constant source of sustenance and joy: thank you, my family.

Index

A

Abacha, Maryam, 326
Abacha, Sani, 299, 326
Abortion rights, 102–105, 140
Abramson, Jill, 6–7, 8n.2, 9n.3
Abuse, 29–32, 164, 169–170, 328
AFL-CIO, 64–65, 231
African American churches, 160–166
African American community
    beauty salons in, 71
    constituent pressures from, 318
    expectations of, 307
    gender issues in, 162–165, 233,
        318n.37
    influence on Chicago media of,
        184–185
    political role models in, xii, 9–13
    post-election views of, 303
    stand-by-your-man ethic in,
        220–222
    support for Clarence Thomas in,
        11–13
African Americans, 14–15, 78, 305
African National Congress (ANC),
    33, 200
Africa trip, 294, 296, 298–301
Alexander, Ethel, xix, 71, 240, 249,
    275, 294
American Federation of, State,
    County, and Municipal
    Employees, 168

American Jewish Committee, 156
Antisemitism, accusations of, 154–156
Archer Daniels Midland Company,
    291
Aristide, Jean-Bertrand, 291
Arthur Andersen & Company, 67
Ashton, Anita, xix, 109, 171–173, 206,
    207, 219–220, 222, 225–226,
    229, 230, 260n.30
Atlanta, Georgia, 172–173
Austin, Gerald "Jerry," xix, 38, 41, 43,
    45, 197, 201, 208, 210–211,
    223, 225–227, 231, 243, 246,
    251, 256–258
Axelrod, David, xiv, xix, 21, 22, 42, 45,
    77, 78, 137, 138, 208–209, 215,
    218, 223, 225, 226, 232, 243–
    244, 246, 256–258, 328–329

B

Bailey, Lester, 109
Baldwin, James, 11, 164–165
Barrow, Willie, 306, 313
Bass, Sue, xix, 23, 98, 236, 237, 240,
    249, 260
Bay, Carolyn, xx
Beatrice Foods, 224
Bell, Janice, xx, 243
Belushi, Jim, 236
Bender, Dayna, xx, 175, 206, 207, 219,
    271

Benton, Marjorie, xx, 131, 134
Besser, James D., 156
Bethel African Methodist Episcopal
    Church, 161–162
Biden, Joseph, 6, 202, 291, 311
Black American Law Students
    Association (BALSA), 157–158
Black Caucus, 305
Black nationalists, 318
Boesky, Ivan, 157
Bolton, Michael, 236, 237
Bond issue scandal, 152–155
Booth, Heather, xx, 168–171, 220, 242,
    243, 250, 252–254, 274–277,
    283–285
Booth, Paul, 168
Bootstrapping, 7, 126, 128–129
Borges, Webber, 88
Borosage, Bob, xx, 222, 225, 246
Boxer, Barbara, xv, 89, 266, 278, 333
Bradley, Bill, 202
Branch banking, 127
Braswell, Ollie, 186
Braswell Wood Company, 183, 184,
    186
Braun, Carol Moseley. See Moseley
    Braun, Carol "Bunny"
Braun, Doris, 115–117
Braun, John, 115, 116
Braun, Matthew "Matt," xx, 19–20, 35,
    36, 39, 108, 117–120, 128, 191,
    262, 264, 297, 299
Braun, Michael, xx, 19, 36, 113–117,
    129–130, 191, 296–298, 321,
    327
Braun, Shelly, 114–116
Braun & Rivkin, 152
Braxton, Kim, 280
Britton, Dennis, 292
Bronfman, Sherry, 306
Brooke, Edward, 14
Brooks, Gwendolyn, 307
Brown, Ron, 21, 203, 251, 252, 254
Brown, Steve, xx, 239, 293, 300
Brown, Willie, 95
Bruce, Blanche K., 14
Bryant, Lovelace, 186
Burris, Roland, xxi, 21, 173, 261
Bush, George H.W., 5–7, 13, 38,
    177, 178, 224, 228, 247, 258,
    262–264, 266

Bush, George W., 329
Buthelezi, Mangosuthu Gatsha, 33,
    200, 298
Byrne, Jane, 247

C
Callaway, John, 4, 18, 223
Canaan Missionary Baptist Church,
    165–166
Candy (housekeeper), 120
Carbondale, Illinois, 68, 117–118, 120,
    122–124
Carolvan, 173, 175–179
Carrington, Walter, 327
Carter, Jimmy, 129
Carville, James, 142
Celia (press secretary), 73
Champaign, Illinois, 160–166
Chicago, Illinois, 27–29, 48–49, 64, 78,
    121, 235–238, 330
Chicago Development Council
    meeting, 153–154
Chicago Hilton and Towers
    fundraising event, 202–203,
    205–206
Chicago History Museum Research
    Center, xxvi
Chicago Jewish Star, 156
Chicago Police Department, 109
Chicago Tonight (television series),
    3–4, 12
Childers, Mary Ann, 246
Chisholm, Shirley, 15
Chris (intern), 238
Citizens to Confirm Clarence Thomas,
    7
Citizens United, xi
Clay, John, 98
Clement, Adam, xx, 21, 96, 98–99
Clement, Kay, xx–xxi, 21, 39, 50, 71,
    96–99
Clinton, Bill, 51, 84n.13, 108, 123, 131,
    133, 138, 140–142, 145, 146,
    148, 201, 218, 228, 235–238,
    240, 247, 266, 324, 325, 329
Clinton, Chelsea, 108
Clinton, Hillary, 138n.17, 140, 146,
    236, 237
Cobb, Del Marie, 110
Cobble, Steve, xxi, 134–136, 150–151,
    161, 167–168, 173, 197, 201,

205, 227–228, 230–232, 238,
241–243, 250, 251, 253–256,
258, 259, 274–276, 283, 285,
330, 334
Coffey, Ray, 42–43
Cohen, Ira, xxi, 148, 175, 218, 219,
222–223, 225, 226, 238, 242,
243, 250, 271, 272, 274–276
Collin, Dorothy, 199–200
Colvin, Helene, 21–24, 52
Continental National Bank, 183, 187
Cook County, Illinois, 74, 78
Coordinated Campaign, 240
Court of Appeals, 7
Coxum, Ed, xxi, 277–278
Cronyism, 151–155
Currie, Barbara Flynn, 50

D
Daley, Bill, 218
Daley, Richard M., 121n16, 155, 159,
236, 237, 247
Daniels, Celia, 52
Davie, "Auntie" Darrel, 32, 192, 320
Davis, Cari, 60
Davis, Danny, 330
Davis, Dantrell, 246
Day, Dorsey, 286–287
Dean, Howard, 329
Death threats, 109, 172
Debates, 65–68, 218–227, 246–247
DeLauro, Rosa, 84
Democratic National Convention
(1992), 131–145, 201, 266n.31,
289
Democratic Senatorial Campaign
Committee (DSCC), 251–253
Democratic State Convention,
244–245
Democratic Women's Caucus, 140
Denial, 230, 301, 320–322
Department of Education, 5, 8
Dewith, Bill, 174–175
Dewith-Anderson, Letitia, xxi,
173–175, 229–230, 242, 272,
278, 287, 288
Dionne, E. J., 317
Ditka, Mike, 228–229
Dixon, Alan, xi, xxi, 12–14, 16–18, 22,
23, 38, 42, 49, 54, 60, 61, 64–70,

72, 75, 77, 78, 122, 127, 141,
181, 231, 294
Domestic issues, 149–150
Douglas, Helen Gahagan, 85
Dukakis, Michael, 21
Duke, David, 157
DuPage County, Illinois, 40–41
Du Quoin, Illinois, 124–128

E
Economic policy, 92, 178, 206–207
Edgar, Jim, 125
Eichenbaum, David, xxi, 83–84,
99, 136, 141, 143–145, 176,
177, 188, 189, 195, 197, 202,
204–209, 211, 212, 218–220,
222, 225, 227, 238–239, 242,
244–246, 250–254, 262,
274–276, 281, 283, 291
Emanuel, Rahm, 330
Emerge, 240–241
EMILY's List, 20, 21, 141–142
Energy policy, 178
Englewood neighborhood, 48
Environmental policy, 127
Equal Employment Opportunity
Commission (EEOC), 5, 8, 279
Esposito, Joan, 181
Ethics legislation speech, 244–245

F
Fair Coalition, 85
Family Research Council, 7
Farrakhan, Louis, 154, 156, 157
Faye-Petrizzi, Sydney, xxiv, 18–19, 22,
24, 51–53, 57, 58, 65, 71, 74, 79,
93–96, 100, 297
Feinstein, Dianne, xv, 89, 137, 266
Female politicians, male vs., 50, 146,
266–267, 324–325
Feminists, xii, 137, 220, 233, 272,
303–304, 318
Fields, David, 91
Fitzgerald, Peter, 328–329
Fizer, Edwin "Nick," 109
Flowers, Gennifer, 138, 324
Foley, Don, xxi, 251–253, 257
"Foley Day," 250–258
Fordham, Gus, xxi, 65, 71, 94, 121,
207, 260

Foster, Gary Steven, 108
Freedom Charter, 33
Fund for the Feminist Majority, 303

G
Gage Park neighborhood, 48, 49
Gantz, Julie, xxi, 238, 272–275
Gardner, Joseph, 111
Garvey, Marcus, 318n.37
Gauen, Pat, xxi, 217–218
Gay and lesbian issues, 105–107
Gay Pride Parade, 95, 105–108
Gender issues, 7–9, 162–165, 227, 233
Ginsburg, Ruth Bader, 331
Gittler, Mandy, xxii, 278
"Golden Parachute" ad, 227
Good Food Organics, 329–330
Goodman, Robert, 308–309
Good Morning America, 72, 86
Gore, Al, 146, 228, 236–238
Gore, Tipper, 146, 236, 237
Gouletas, Evangeline, 291
Gouletas, Nick, 291
Great Recession, xi
Gumbel, Bryant, 261
Guthman, Jack, 154

H
Haiti, 316n.36
Hardy, Thomas, 13–14, 179, 205–206,
    229, 269, 295, 298–299
Harkin, Tom, 81, 140
Hartigan, Neil, 306, 309
Hatch, Orrin, 10, 311
Hawn, Goldie, 93
Head Start, 169
Heflin, Howell, 9, 18, 333–334
Hefner, Christie, 105, 260, 323
Heinlein, Robert, 119
Helms, Jesse, 330–332, 334
Hensley, Jan, xxii, 96, 97, 135, 256,
    278, 288
Hill, Anita, 4–6, 8–10, 12, 14, 18, 60,
    86, 101, 141, 163, 272, 273,
    294, 303
Hofeld, Albert, xix, xxii, 22, 42–43, 49,
    60, 61, 65–68, 77–79
Hogan, Paul, 181–186, 188–190, 193–
    194, 203, 204, 206, 208–211
Hollywood Women's Political Caucus,
    93

Holtz, Stephanie, xxii, 135, 136
Hopewell, Earl, xxii, 97, 99, 257, 292
House of Representatives, 15
Hyde Park neighborhood, xxii, 19
Hysmith, "Auntie" Otha, 29, 32

I
Ickes, Harold, 251
Illinois Center press conference, 54
Illinois Corn Growers Association,
    123–124
Illinois delegation, speech to, 132–135
Illinois Democratic Primary campaign
    (1992)
    advertising in, 42–45, 66–68
    announcement of candidacy,
        22–23
    Matt Braun on, 19–20
    chaos during, 51–53
    columnists on Alan Dixon in,
        16–17
    connection with women in, 60–61
    fundraising in, 39–42
    in mid- and downstate counties,
        64–65
    polling during, 38, 68–69
    scheduling during, 57–60
    staff for, 20–22 (*See also specific*
        staff members)
    televised debate in, 65–68
    and Clarence Thomas hearings,
        14–15
Illinois Democratic Primary election
    (1992), 69–77
Illinois Department of Public Aid, 183,
    188, 189, 193–196, 259
Illinois Housing Development
    Authority, 152
Illinois legislature, xii, 50, 105–106,
    156
Independent Insurance Agents of
    America, 87–89
Independent Voters of Illinois (IVI),
    43, 44
Ireland, Patricia, xxii, 101, 103, 303

J
Jackson, Donna Marie, 161–163, 165
Jackson, Jesse, xix, xxi, xxii, xxvi, 33–
    34, 40–41, 55, 91, 92, 100, 110,

132, 156, 184–185, 200–201,
230–231, 306–309
James, Frank, 90, 110–111, 263
Jane (counseling service), 168
Jarrett, Vernon, 224
Jewish voters, support of, 155–156
Johnson, Marlene, xxii, 172, 175–178,
194, 205, 241, 242, 260,
276–278, 283
Jones Ware & Grenard, 153
Judiciary Committee, of US Senate,
4–6, 14, 273, 291, 311, 331–332

K
Karpatkin, Jeremy, xxii–xxiii, 135, 167,
175, 203, 255, 272
Kassebaum, Nancy, 15
Kasten, Robert, 156
Katz, Marilyn, 142–143
Kenilworth, Illinois, 150
Kennedy, John F., 131, 133, 161
Kennedy, Ted, 72, 141–142, 202, 306,
309
Kern, Danice, 185
Kerrey, Bob, 146
King, Larry, 43
King, Martin Luther, Jr., xii, 41, 48–49,
307, 308
Krasnowski, Matt, 68–69
Ku Klux Klan (KKK), 109
Kupcinet, Irv "Kup," 294, 296, 298,
299, 322
Kur, Bob, 203–205, 208, 209, 319

L
Labor management issues, 127
Lake, Celinda, 151, 243, 252, 257, 259,
266
Lake County, Illinois, 59
Lake Point Tower, 291, 293, 300
LaPaille, Gary, 261
Largent, Esther, 113
League of Conservation Voters, 20
Lee, Denise, 110
Lehman, Lucy, 260, 296, 323
Leibovich, Mark, xi
Levin, Carl, 84, 202
Levinsohn, Florence Hamlish, 55
Lewis, Ann, 150, 296
Lincoln, Abraham, 263

Llewellyn, Karl, 157
Lobbyists, 151–152
Loeb, Elizabeth, xxiii, 272–275
Long, Chris, 21–23, 55
Longhini, Doug, 184–186, 188–190,
193–194, 204, 206, 209–212,
320
Loveday, David, 227
Loving v. Virginia, 106

M
Mackey, "Auntie" Catherine, 29, 32,
120
Mackey, Darlene, xxiii, 29, 119–120,
123, 124, 128, 160–162, 202,
220–221, 243, 261, 292, 294,
299, 310, 320, 324
Madigan, Mike, 218, 239
Magers, Ron, 181–182
Magnus, Betty, 24, 139
Malcolm, Ellen, 20–21
Male politicians, female vs., 50,
266–267, 324–325
Mama Liz (grandmother), 170
Mandela, Nelson, 298
Mann, Bob, 39
Marshall, Thurgood, 7, 12
Matthews, Joseph, 33
Matthews, Kgosie, xxiii
addition of, to staff, 23–25, 33–34
Africa trip of, 294, 296, 298–301
Matthew Braun on, 118–119
campaign strategy of, 64, 76
candidate's defense of, 57, 99–100,
134–135, 220–222
Chicago Tribune profile of, 90,
110–111
control of campaign by, 126, 132,
169, 176, 197, 282–283
at DNC, 142, 143
on Election Day, 259, 260, 262, 264
endorsement from, 83–85
influence of, 318–319, 322–324
on issues papers, 218, 272
and Jesse Jackson, xxii
and Medicaid fraud scandal,
199–202, 208
Carol Moseley Braun on, 24–25,
139–140, 315–316

and other staff members, 34–39,
41, 53–57, 93–99, 171–173,
219–220, 222, 225–226, 229–
230, 232, 238–239, 289–290
post-election activities of, 305,
311–312, 316, 326
at primary victory celebration, 71,
73, 74, 76
relationship with Carol Moseley
Braun, 110–111, 136–140,
160–161, 202, 212–213, 225–
226, 243, 254–255, 282–284,
296, 297, 322–324, 326–328
scheduling by, 58–59
sexual harassment allegations
against, 240–244, 249–250,
253–256, 272–290, 301–304
Matthews, Zachariah Keodirelang, 33
Mayer, Jane, 6–7, 8n.2, 9n.3
Mayer Brown & Platt, 152
McDonnell Douglas, 178
McGrory, Mary, 334
Medicaid fraud scandal, 181–214,
223–224, 258, 319–320
Meeks, James, 330
Melissa (staffer), 287
Mentschikoff, Soia, 157, 158
Metcalfe, Ralph, 307–308
Metropolitan Baptist Church, 307
Metzenbaum, Howard, 6
Midwest Academy, 168
Mikulski, Barbara, 15, 89, 146
Miller, Alton, xxiii, 37–38, 52–56, 93,
240
Miller, Mark, 92
Mitchell, Andrea, 12n.6
Mitchell, George, 203
Mitchell, Grayson, 205, 265
Moran, Joyce, xxiii, 250, 276–279,
293, 302
Moran–Robinson investigation, 250,
255, 275–281, 301–303
Morris, Celia, 137
Morton, Bill, 251
Moseley, Burton, 170
Moseley, Edna (mother), xxiii, 27–32,
47, 63–64, 75, 102, 109, 120,
133, 169–170, 182–183, 187–
196, 198, 202, 208, 211–214,

259, 261, 320, 321. *See also*
Medicaid fraud scandal
Moseley, Joey, xxiii, 28, 75, 108–110,
172, 187, 193, 260, 323
Moseley, Johnny "Brother," xxiv, 28–31,
100, 102, 130, 170, 187, 193
Moseley, Joseph (father), xxiv, 27–31,
47, 63, 114, 133, 169–170, 194
Moseley, Marsha, xxiv, 28, 120, 187,
189, 191–193, 195, 196, 232
Moseley, Toya, 191
Moseley Braun, Carol "Bunny"
on Jerry Austin, 232–233
on bond issue scandal, 153
defense of Kgosie Matthews by, 57,
99–100, 134–135, 220–222
on departure of Sydney Faye-
Petrizzi, 100
on Election Day, 259–260, 264
family and early life of, 27–33,
63–64, 169–170, 190–191
on gay marriage, 106–107
household demands on, 117–122
on Kgosie Matthews, 24–25,
139–140, 315–316
on media coverage after primary
win, 79
on Medicaid fraud scandal,
190–194, 213–214
on Alton Miller, 54–55
on negativity, 47–49
on primary debate, 66
on Primary Election Day, 70–71
on public office, 1
on race as her defining
characteristic, 156–160
on self-image, 17
on sexual harassment allegations,
249–250, 302–303
on Clarence Thomas confirmation,
3–4
on winning Illinois Democratic
Primary, 75–76, 80
on writing her speech for DNC,
134–135
Mt. Olive Baptist Church, 162–163
Murray, Kathleen, xxiv, 154, 203, 278
Murray, Patty, xv, 89, 266

N

National Black Law Students
Association, 157n.22
National Organization for Women
(NOW), 16–17, 20, 39–41,
59–60, 94–96, 100–102, 303,
329
National Rifle Association, 246
National Women's Political Caucus,
20, 89–90, 329
Nation of Islam, 318n.37
Neal, Earl, 152
Neal, Steve, 16, 61, 244, 294, 327–328
Neale, Zora, 221–222
Nestlé, 244
Netsch, Dawn Clark, 107, 261
Newhouse, Richard, 152
New Zealand ambassadorship, 329
Nicholson, Elizabeth "Liz," xxiv, 83,
135, 143, 175, 202, 205, 238,
278, 281–289, 292, 294
Nigeria, 299, 316n.36, 326–327
Nixon, Richard, 85
No-bid work, 154–155
Norton, Eleanor Holmes, 12n.5

O

Obama, Barack, xii, xiii, xix, 37n.9,
58n.11, 78, 142, 266, 329
O'Donnell, Maureen, 291–294
O'Malley, Kathy, 199–200
Operation PUSH, 185
Opposition research, 244–246
Owens, Jesse, 308

P

Packwood, Bob, 324–325
Paige, Billie, xxiv, 151–152, 296
Palmer, Lu, 303
Papa Grant (grandfather), 170
Payne, Allison, 143–145
Pearson, Rick, 207
Perot, Ross, 43, 143–144, 245, 247, 266
Peter, Paul and Mary concert, 147
Phelps, Timothy, 4
Pinstripe patronage, 152
Planned Parenthood v. Casey, 103n.14
Political action committees (PACs),
87–89, 151
Prejudice, 164–165

Presidential run (2003), 329
Purrington, Sue, xxiv, 16–17, 20, 39–
40, 50–51, 74, 77, 97–98, 297

Q

Quayle, Dan, 306

R

Race
as defining characteristic, 157–160
discussions about, 63–64, 115–117
as filter for political issues, 169
insensitivity to issues of, 226–227
as issue in US Senate campaign,
154–160
in Clarence Thomas confirmation
hearings, 7–9
Racism, 333–334
Rainbow Coalition, 33
Rashid, Don, 300
Rather, Dan, 261
Ravinia, Illinois, 147–148
Reagan, Ronald, 38, 43, 50–51, 92
Rednour, John, xxiv, 122, 124–129
Rednour, John, Jr. "Little John," 128
Rednour, Wanda, 124–126, 128, 129
Reelection campaign (1998), 320,
328–329
Remnick, David, 295
Republic of Cameroon, 316n.36
Retzler, Laura, 168
Revels, Hiram, 14
Reynolds, Gretchen, 138–139
Riehecky, Janet, 198
Rivlin, Gary, 53
Robinson, Randall, 327
Robinson, Wayne, xxiv, 275–278, 279,
301–302. *See also* Moran–
Robinson investigation
Rockefeller, Jay, 203
Rockford, Illinois, 206–207
Rock Island, Illinois, 179–180
Roeper, Richard, 224
Roe v. Wade, 102–104
Rogers, John, Jr., xxv, 97–98
Rosenthal, Steve, 251
Royko, Mike, 206, 326–327
Rush, Bobby, 37n.9
Rustin, Michael, 7

S

Saltzman, Bettylu, 132, 142
Samuels, Barbara, xxv, 21, 35–37,
    40, 74–76, 93–94, 96, 105,
    107–108, 172, 307
Samuels, Greg, 35, 108
Savage, Gus, 156–157
Savage, Lundy, 162–163
Sawyer, Gene, 318
Sayers, Linda, 9–10
Sayers, Tim, 10
Schmich, Mary, 212–213, 327
Schott, Dean, 259
Senate Ethics Committee, 326
Senator-elect, media coverage of,
    291–296
Sexual harassment, 256, 325
    allegations against Kgosie
        Matthews, 240–244, 249–250,
        253–256, 272–290, 301–304
    and Clarence Thomas
        confirmation hearings, 3–12
Shalit, Ruth, 319–320
Shapiro, Larry, xxv, 40, 75, 175, 203,
    261, 272, 323
Shaw, Andy, 227
Shea, Paige & Rogal, Inc., 151
Sidley Austin, 152, 155
Silver, Nate, 39
Simon, Paul, xxv, 16, 72, 122, 135, 176,
    203, 312
Simpson, Alan, 10, 86
Sisulu, Walter, 298
Smith, Ace, 244
Smith, Leah Myers, 104
Smith, Mary Ann, 142
Smith, Patricia, 177
Smyser, Katy, 186
Sneed, Michael, 93, 95, 200, 293, 296
South Africa, 327
Spielman, Fran, 300
Stand-by-your-man ethic, 220–222
Stanton, Lynette, xxv, 286, 287, 292
Stein, Richie, 154, 157
Steinem, Gloria, 54, 139, 140
Stoll, Tina, xxv, 86–87
Streisand, Barbara, 93
Sweet, Lynn, 16, 91–92, 99, 104,
    176–178, 218, 292, 296, 316

T

Talbott, Basil, 92, 218, 316n.36
Tate, Desiree, xxv, 58–59, 71–74,
    76, 78–79, 95, 98, 132, 135,
    136, 143, 173, 175, 206, 207,
    222, 225, 226–227, 244, 260,
    280–281, 283, 284, 286, 287,
    292–293, 295, 318, 322
Tate-Gilmore, Ashley, 58n.11
Tatum. B. J., 165–166
Taylor, Bill, 21, 23–24
Terrell, Albert, 152
Thomas, Clarence, 3–15, 18, 163
Thompson, Jim, 92
Thurmond, Strom, 309–311
Till, Emmett, 307
Tillman, Dorothy, 71
Tillman, Ethel, 71
Totenberg, Nina, 4
Traditional Values Coalition, 7
Travers, Mary, 147
Tregay, Alice, xxv, 243
Tsongas, Paul, xxi, 14, 84

U

United Daughters of the Confederacy
    insignia, 330–334
Universal Negro Improvement
    Association, 318n.37
University of Chicago Law School, 17,
    43, 44
US Senate
    African Americans in, 14–15, 305
    election to, 259–267
    1993-1999 term in, 305–313,
        316–320, 330–334
US Senate campaign (1992). *See also*
    specific events and places
    advertising in, 90–93, 227–229,
        232, 251, 257
    criticism of organization of,
        142–143
    cronyism accusations in, 151–155
    domestic issues in, 149–150
    fatigue during, 160–162
    fundraising for, 85–89, 150–151,
        292
    impact of sexual harassment
        allegations on, 240–242
    media coverage of, 148–149, 258

opposition research in, 244–246
race as issue in, 154–160
"singleness" as issue in, 146
spending in, 251, 292
threats during, 108–110
US Senate campaign staff. *See also
specific individuals*
candidate's relationship with,
176–177
on the Carolvan, 175–176
at Democratic National
Convention, 135–136
on Election Day, 260–261
issues office of, 271–272
Kgosie Matthews's affair with
member of, 289–290
response to Medicaid fraud
scandal by, 188–190, 208–211
response to sexual harassment
allegations by, 242–244
tensions among, 225–227
warnings against complacency by,
167–168

V
Valleta, Diane, 150
Vedder, Price, Kaufman & Kammholz,
250, 275, 276, 278–279, 281.
See also Moran–Robinson
investigation
Vernon Park Church of God, 71
Vitullo, Lou, xxv, 194–195, 204, 205,
277–278
Volkmann, Roxanne, xxv, 208, 256,
279, 286, 287, 292, 296
Vonnegut, Kurt, 119
Voters for Choice rally, 140–141
Vrdolyak, Eddie, 156

W
Walsh, Bob, xxv, 37, 55–57
Washington, Harold, xxiii, xxv, xxvi,
18, 35, 37, 53, 54, 58, 73, 91–92,
107, 152–155, 223, 265, 308,
318
Washington Strategic Consulting
Group, Inc., 316
Washington-Williams, Essie Mae,
310n.35

Weber, Julie, 150
Weeks, Bill, 107
Wells, Ida B., 308
Wellstone, Paul, xix, 203
WGN (television station), 143–145
White, Jesse, 281
Wilkerson, Isabel, 148–150
Williamson, Richard, xxv, 38, 69, 79,
87, 90–93, 141, 145, 151–155,
157, 197, 206, 207, 227–229,
242, 244–246, 258, 259
Williamson–Moseley Braun debates,
218–227, 246–247
Wilson, Edith, 327
Wilson, Velma, xxvi, 40–41, 53,
58–60, 71–73, 75, 76, 78, 98,
243, 310, 322
WMAQ (television station), 184–186,
188
Wofford, Harris, 42
Women. *See also* Female politicians,
male vs.; Gender issues
on Clarence Thomas's
confirmation, 4–5
connection with, 60–61
Illinois Democratic Primary voting
by, 78
Kgosie Matthews's treatment of,
256
role of, in meetings, 87–89
sexual harassment as problem
for, 10
support for Ted Kennedy by,
141–142
in US Senate, 15, 305
Woods, Harriet, 20, 89
Woods, Jessica, 66
Wyatt, Addie, 71, 223, 306

Y
Yarrow, Peter, 147
Yeakel, Lynn, 252
"Year of the Woman," xv, 142

Z
Zwick, Jill, xxvi, 285, 292

About the Author

J EANNIE MORRIS began her career as a sports writer for *Chicago's American* and *Chicago Daily News*, and went on to create weekly sports features for Chicago NBC and CBS affiliates WMAQ-TV and WBBM-TV. During her almost three decades as a Chicago reporter, Jeannie earned 11 Emmys, numerous AP and UPI awards, and the Ring Lardner Award. She is the author of the bestselling book *Brian Piccolo: A Short Season*, which led to the beloved 1971 film Brian's Song.